STUDIES IN
MAJOR LITERARY AUTHORS

edited by

William E. Cain
Wellesley College

A ROUTLEDGE SERIES

STUDIES IN MAJOR LITERARY AUTHORS

WILLIAM E. CAIN, *General Editor*

FREDERICK DOUGLASS'S CURIOUS AUDIENCES

Ethos in the Age of the Consumable Subject

Terry Baxter

Routledge
Taylor & Francis Group

NEW YORK AND LONDON

Published in 2004 by
Routledge
711 Third Avenue
New York, NY 10017

Published in Great Britain by
Routledge
2 Park Square, Milton Park
Abingdon, Oxfordshire OX14 4RN

First issued in paperback 2014

Routledge is an imprint of the Taylor and Francis Group, an informa business

Copyright © 2004 by Taylor & Francis Books, Inc.

Library of Congress Cataloging-in-Publication Data

Baxter, Terry, 1970-
Frederick Douglass's curious audiences : ethos in the age of the
consumable subject / by Terry Baxter.
p. cm. — (Studies in major literary authors ; v. 35)
   Includes bibliographical references (p.) and index.
   ISBN: 0-415-97075-X (alk. paper)
1. Douglass, Frederick, 1818-1895—Oratory. 2. Douglass, Frederick,
1818-1895—Ethics. 3. Douglass, Frederick, 1818-1895—Public opinion.
4. Audiences—United States—History—19th century. 5. Rhetoric—Social
aspects—United States—History—19th century. 6. Oratory—Social
aspects—United States—History—19th century. 7. Ethics—United
States—History—19th century. 8. Public opinion—United
States—History—19th century. I. Title. II. Series.
E449.D75B39 2004
973.8'092—dc22
                                                        2003027568
ISBN 13: 978-0-415-97075-4 (hbk)
ISBN 13: 978-0-415-76268-7 (pbk)

This book is dedicated to Bruce Gronbeck,
who taught me a great deal about thinking and writing,
and to my wife who made the work worthwhile.

"Oh these touchy people! Principles! You're always standing on your principles as if they were stilts. You won't move on your own feet. If you ask me, if a man's all right — there's a principle for you. I don't need to know another thing. Zamiotov's a marvelous man."
"And he takes bribes."
"All right, so he takes bribes, so what do I care if he takes bribes!" Razumikhin was suddenly shouting in exasperation. "Do you think I praise him because he takes bribes! I just said that in his own way he was all right. If you insist on looking at everybody that way, how many good people will you find?"

— Fyodor Dostoyevsky, *Crime and Punishment*

CONTENTS

CHAPTER ONE

Introduction

In neat rows facing the platform, the curious and the committed file into their seats to hear a series of abolitionist speakers. The setting is a public hall, rented for the occasion, and the hall is indeed "public" in many senses. The feeling of publicness, the stifling atmosphere of social restrictions, dominates behavior. We can see the weight of social pressure even in this electric abolition atmosphere where speakers are known to overturn traditional norms about race, as well as gender and class.

Eagerly anticipating a most unconventional event — an eloquent speech from an imposing black man — the audience nevertheless allows its seating to be dictated by old-fashioned sensibilities. The black members of the audience sit a tasteful distance away from the nearest white person. On the streets leading to this New England anti-slavery meeting, just as on the plantation and in the national government, the races are kept separate. In every place the story is the same; everywhere, that is, except on the dais where speakers sit side by side, Frederick Douglass next to William Lloyd Garrison.

Since it is a Saturday afternoon, many of the audience members will attend a church tomorrow where the whites are allowed to take communion first. Only then will the pastor intone, "Come up, colored friends, come up! for you know God is no respecter of persons!"[1] If such displays happen in church, Douglass will inform the audience, they happen more frequently to him in secular circumstances, where he faces violent discrimination on trains and ships, and in employment lines.

Yet here he stands on the platform. Facing many people who would not ride in the same train car with him, some who would want to stone him if he dared to hold hands with a white woman in public, and some who just regard him with equal measures of interest and disdain, Frederick Douglass begins to lecture the crowd about the inhumanity of slavery and the converse humanity of black Americans.

INTRODUCTION TO THE PROBLEM

In this situation, the issue of rhetorical ethos is made painfully clear. Diaries written by his admirers and speech reviews from his skeptics reveal that Frederick Douglass was effective even in such difficult circumstances. At most abolitionist rallies in the 1830s, a speaker could be counted a rhetorical success just for placating the rowdies who were ready to throw rotten eggs. But Douglass went further, actually converting some of the hard-hearted to the abolitionist cause and generating sincere positive regard for African Americans. His presence also invigorated those with failing commitments and intimidated into silence many who wanted to contradict and humiliate him. Even those who denied his claims and despised his politics rarely launched a telling attack on Douglass as a person. In other words, he was a master at substantiating his arguments with rhetorical ethos.

It must be acknowledged, though, that Douglass lacked the classical markers of ethos. Just to take one famous formulation, he would have needed to establish a pattern of virtuous living, a facility for practical wisdom, and an abiding concern for the audience's best interests in order to be persuasive according to Aristotelian theory. Yet, in place of virtue, many in the audience viewed him as a subversive, and perhaps even as a thief, for "stealing" himself from his master. He lacked any kind of formal education, including the childhood religious instruction that was so necessary to the antebellum understanding of what forms a prudent individual. Finally, he boldly admitted that his primary concern was for the slave, not the best interests of whites in the audience; although he believed ending slavery would benefit both white and black, north and south, he would have demanded emancipation even if it cost his listeners their fortunes or lives in war. Regardless of such anti-Aristotelian stances, listeners were astounded by the ex-slave who displayed such eloquence.

We can think of similar cases in the late twentieth and early twenty-first centuries where American politicians have proved to be persuasive despite a lack of the classical markers of ethos. Presidents and representatives have been (re)elected by constituents who do not trust them. The highest profile examples are probably those of presidents Reagan and Clinton. For both, a series of criminal allegations backed with substantive evidence, and coinciding with widely known faults of character, wisdom, or discretion, proved to be only slight hindrances to their rhetorical success. Both presidents continued to be successful epideictic and deliberative speakers, even though their constituents (and sometimes the presidents themselves) acknowledged their failure to exhibit the highest character. Oddly, the appeal of a Reagan or Clinton has a great deal to do with how people perceive them — as likeable, attractive people. Like Douglass, they succeed where, say, Bush the elder or Dukakis fails in part because of the personality they convey in their rhetoric. Personality, though, hardly fits any classical formulation of the qualities of ethos. The questions raised by a study of Douglass's ethos, then, are still very much with us today.

In light of all the admonitions in rhetorical theory from Aristotle forward about establishing ethos, how is it that some speakers go into a speech with the traditional measures of ethos stacked against them, yet manage to reach audiences, persuade them, and create lasting change in real world circumstances? It is my argument in this dissertation that traditional standards of ethos — a set of qualities that will be discussed below, but which generally relate to elevated character, ability, and social standing — have lost much of their capacity to determine success for speakers in modern society. Therefore to explain the rhetorical success of many well-known orators of the last hundred and fifty years, we must look elsewhere to explain the power of their persons as a source of influence.

I will argue that a modern theory of ethos needs to begin with an examination of performances like Douglass's antebellum addresses. Douglass was a leader, along with other African American orators, in changing the ethos standards for public speakers.[2] He also stands as the epitome of the "new speaker," someone who represented the best of the classical virtues and the appeal of a modern celebrity. In the very early stages of mass media, when few people appreciated the importance of image control, Douglass controlled his public image so as to exhibit (in every sense of the term) the personal attributes antebellum audiences demanded from a public figure. For modern rhetorical theory to accommodate Douglass's praxis, as well as the kind of ethos he displayed such as celebrity, image control, and personality, the definition of ethos in the classical literature and recent communication scholarship needs to be reconsidered and revised.

In sum, the central question of this investigation is, in what ways did ethos expectations change in America in the middle of the nineteenth century, such that exalted morality was no longer the dominant factor in judging rhetors? Frederick Douglass's rhetoric is perfect site for studying those expectations. A subordinate task is the charting of the ethos expectations for rhetors — including black rhetors — prior to the period of change in mid-century (covered in chapters two and three). To know what changed we have to know what was prior and what was in the process of changing. Isolating trends in audience responses to rhetoric and their own commentaries on their expectations also allows us to see inside their "naive theories" of ethos. Those theories are essentially social forms for approaching and judging words according to the kind of person the source is inferred to be. Knowing audience expectations, the next move is to survey Douglass's rhetoric to see how he works within them, and stretches them (chapter four). Conclusions drawn from Douglass's praxis round out the study, by extending his insights to modern-day discourse practices, assessing the extent to which Douglass was unique in his approach to ethos (chapter five). That is, what do we gain by reevaluating the term *ethos* in light of Douglass's untraditional ethos proofs?

DEFINITION OF TERMS

For this study, the definition of the term ethos is by far the most crucial one. In a sense, this entire book is a project in the definition of ethos, so it would be repetitive to do much more here than introduce where and why my approach differs from standard sources. The rest of the dissertation is intended to detail a revised modern definition, one that flows from the special sense the concept of ethos takes on in the nineteenth century, partly in reaction to Douglass's speeches. Since Douglass's style of speech does not fit the classical models well, we will have to place a terminology and order on what we can see in his speeches and draw from audience responses to him, since he is both responsible and representative of the changing definition of ethos in his time. The standard approaches to studying ethos need to be broadened, but not entirely replaced, if we hope to account for the widespread appeal of an author who challenged prevailing moralities and the very definition of *human*.

Review of Literature on Definitions of Ethos

For an adequate definition of ethos, we have to go back quite a ways in the history of ethos theories, because the classical authorities are still the most frequently quoted. One *locus classicus* is Plato's dialogue, *Gorgias*, which depicts two distinct approaches to ethos. Socrates distinguishes between himself and Callicles by their different loves: Callicles loves the *demos* and so must follow it in all its whims, whereas Socrates's love is *sophia*, which "never changes."[3] The lesson about ethos is that a sophist or a demagogue, driven by his desire to please his beloved Athens, is bound to be fickle to himself and the Truth as he twists and turns to match Athenians' changing notions of the true and the good. He merely appears to be ethical without possessing true virtue. Socrates, on the other hand, demands of himself a submission to unalterable Truth in all his deeds and words. While Callicles and the famous sophist Gorgias are bound to have more popularity in the *polis* because they lead souls to comfortable beliefs and pleasure, the price for their rhetorical success is immoral speech.

One ethos — the popular, demogogic one — is based on pandering and telling audiences the "truth" they want to hear; the other incompatible kind of ethos comes when audiences see the fixed character and unwavering love of Truth of the philosopher-speaker. Plato's Socrates contends that popularity signals a lack of true ethos because the unswerving devotion to the True and the Good of a philosopher is rarely appreciated by the clouded minds of common audiences.

Plato's student, Aristotle, picks up the gauntlet thrown by his master and offers a counter-proposal. His system for analyzing the available proofs of persuasion is easily summarized into three qualities — ethos, logos, and pathos.[4] Aristotle's system places proper character as a concern of the rhetorical practitioner right alongside sound reasoning and inspiring the appropriate emotions. Against Plato, Aristotle asserts that one can be esteemed by an audience yet be ethical, just as one can seem logical to a popular audience without violating the Truth, and just as one can excite emotions without improperly inciting the crowd.

Besides making space for morals in even popular rhetoric, Aristotle contributes two crucial ideas that are still influential in discussions of ethos. First, Aristotle sanctions ethos as no less than one third of the art of rhetoric (and, "almost, so to speak, the controlling factor in persuasion"[5]). This, alongside his many statements linking the *Rhetoric* to his ethical treatises, legitimates personal character as a warrant for judgment (*krisis*). The warrant is not unqualified, though. Judgment must be tempered by logic and the right emotions. Audiences must also be aware that the rhetor may be "a person *seeming* to have all these qualities [of ethos]" and not a person whose character truly justifies faith in his words. Aristotle therefore sides with Callicles on the issue of whether a rhetor must actually *be* ethical.[6]

The difference between his position and Plato's is significant. For Aristotle, in situations where the Truth is impossible to know — that is, in rhetorical situations — a person's character should make his position more credible if, in the course of his speech, he responds in propriety to the reasonable (*phronesis*), moral (*arete*), and social (*eunoia*) demands of the moment, not just if he is in love with the Truth. Aristotle's definition of ethos thus uses a more inclusive notion of morality using a standard of responsiveness to the needs of one's situation.

The second great contribution of Aristotle to the theory of ethos is his separation of ethos into the three qualities of practical wisdom (*phronesis*), virtue (*arete*) and good will (*eunoia*). Scholars of communication have applied Aristotle's list-making method to their own studies of ethos, leading to numerous studies that argue for lists of orator qualities that are "keys" to success or failure.

These two trends have developed into two schools of thought in the study of ethos. One, based on the idea that audiences search for evidence of morality and propriety (proper logic and emotion), is reflected primarily in rhetorical criticism, and proceeds by locating the "ethical proofs" or evidences of good character used by an orator. Works in this mold cite a number of historical theorists as authorizing figures, but the names of Cicero, Quintilian, and especially Aristotle, emerge most often. They build upon the idea, codified by Quintilian, that the most successful speaker is a *vir bonus* or truly good man. The second approach seeks a complete list of persuasive personal characteristics in an attempt to quantify, measure and experiment with ethos. Experiments in this vein are labeled studies of "credibility" or "source characteristics" and generally try to correlate attributes of communicators (e.g., "trustworthiness," "dynamism," "expertise") with a particular effect such as increased persuasiveness or retention of the message.[7] This group too cites Aristotle as its founding practitioner.[8]

Writers pursuing both of these courses of study recognize that the characteristics Aristotle mentions are historically bound and prone to change in different social settings — a valuable insight.[9] But despite very different methods, both approaches exaggerate one version of Aristotelian theory and so neither can speak to the complexities of a speaker such as Douglass interacting with his curious and demanding audiences. For its part, the rhetorical model clings to the idea that ethos is exclusively the moral dimension of rhetoric. On the other hand, the quantitative model fails by removing ethos from its context of real speeches, audiences, and situations. These authors wind up studying person *perception* much more than the role of the Person in persuasion.

The Study of Ethical Proofs

The field of rhetorical theory contains numerous contributions to the Aristotle/ Plato debate from ancient times even into the very recent history of the field. Moved from a Greek to a Roman context, Quintilian and Cicero wrestle with the same issue. For Quintilian, following Plato, the *sine qua non* of the orator is that he be "the good man (*vir bonus*) speaking well." Quintilian's requirement competes with the more pragmatic Ciceronian guidance about the qualities the speaker wants to convey, including naturalness — so that you do not seem to be faking the qualities you are faking.[10]

Unfortunately, the terms of the debate have historically been set by Aristotle and Plato, and the irresolvable conflict between Appearance and Reality their formulae encouraged.[11] Either as a matter of seeming to be good or actually being Good, rhetorical critics have tended to assume that audiences are only influenced by (seemingly) virtuous rhetors, those who in some respect are not just higher or better than they are, but more renowned, wiser, and more honorable. The replacement of Neo-Platonism and Stoicism with Christianity after the appearance of Augustine's *De doctrina Christiana* did little to upset the debate other than laying out new standards of morality.[12] The idea that amoral or immoral personal qualities can be persuasive is more or less ignored by most classical theories, and so too by the rhetorical criticism based upon them.

Despite its faults, the classic works on ethos and speaker's ethics contributes an idea that is too easily overlooked. That is, ethos is first and foremost comprised of a relationship between the speaker's discourse and the way he has lived his life. Ethos is an effect of the rhetor relating to an audience by relating his life story. Ethos taps into cultural expectation about how a life can be (1) known by others (2) shared with others.

How can I know someone else's life and nature? For Aristotle, a life of character is developed over years of well-made choices. For him, humans are the "political animal." Thus, describing a series of social or political situations where he chose to be generous or courageous assured the audience that the orator was, indeed, a Generous or Courageous person because the pattern of one's life is proof on one's character. At various other times, the auspices under which a figure was born was thought to tell what type of person a speaker is, a phenomenon that ranges from falsified prophetic announcements at Alexander the Great's birth to biopic advertisements that tell voters that the candidate was born in a little town called Hope. Quite in contrast to Aristotelian philosophy, the Roman and American politician both used the eminence of events they had no control over to bolster their personal appeal. One great unexplored territory of ethos theory lies here in its dependence on philosophies of personhood as rhetors seek to establish in the course of speech the qualities that assure the audience that they are certain types of people.

How do I communicate in words and share my essential nature with others? This is what we might call the relationship of the rhetor to his or her speech. Understandably, this topic receives less attention that the rhetor-audience relationship because rhetoric is so clearly concerned with the social aspect of moving listeners to action. In very few contexts can a speaker establish ethos by merely asserting "I am a good person; listen to me." Listeners judge a speaker and *authorize* any attempt at proving-though-ethos according to prevalent societal standards. The rhetor-to-audience relationship (or, put another way, self-to-society relationship) is the vehicle through which ethos participates in and reveals social norms and standards: audiences heed those who exhibit some culturally valued attribute. But that social interaction relies on the first relationship of the speaker to his or her own discourse. Audiences are persuaded only when they perceive a real connection between the speaker's word and a valued quality he or she actually possesses.

This is why ethos *per se* does not influence us when we know the speaker is acting, lying or joking (i.e., despite Cicero's great stature, his audiences would not be moved to sympathy if he said "I just flew in from Gaul and, boy, are my arms tired."). Ethos persuades only when words have some connection to the agent as the subject of an autobiography, that is, when they connect to what is known or believed about the lived life of the rhetorical agent. Quintilian and Cicero, like Plato and Aristotle, disagree about whether that connection can be, in the final analysis, successful when it is falsified. However, all demand that some connection be established to the satisfaction of the audience.

In the Western tradition, the "apparent" ethos versus "real" ethos debate continued to be a topic of some concern, even for the English and Scottish writers who would have been most familiar to Douglass's audiences. Ever since Augustine, Catholic rhetoricians had worried about false religions and errant preachers who could lead multitudes astray with sham truths. In the eighteenth and nineteenth centuries, when the Catholic church's influence had waned, there was increasing support for creating "modern" rhetorics that took account of new epistemologies.[13] The idea that ethos equals morality was revisited and the old definitions of the person and the audience could, for the first time in centuries, be seriously challenged. Caught in the melee were such issues as whether humans all possessed certain innate ideas, and how individuals acquire the qualities — including the morality — that mark them. John Locke, for one, lent his voice to the debates by challenging the idea of original sin and the related notions of morality. Locke's more "scientific" approach holds that humans gather sense impressions to make sense of the world, and are motivated by pain and pleasure. They are not, therefore, motivated by innate ideas of Goodness and Truth supplied by God as they make their way through the world. It would follow that audiences might also be moved their senses, and by pain and pleasure, rather than by some innate sense of morality to find the Good Man.

But even with Locke's kind of scientific-philosophical investigation of the human mind and the growing appreciation of how knowledge and morality are acquired through interaction with the world (and were therefore fairly mutable, although the notion that reality itself was socially constructed was a long ways off), questions of ethos still hinged on whether the person needed to really be good to persuade. For George Campbell, Hugh Blair, Adam Smith, and others, there is a general consensus that being Good is preferable, but seeming good is acceptable for an orator.[14] Campbell's comments are representative:

> [I]t hath become a common topic with rhetoricians, that in order to be a successful orator, one must be a good man; for to be good is the only sure of way of being long esteemed good, and to be esteemed good is previously necessary to one's being heard with due attention and regard.[15]

At the same time, there are signs that a synthesis and new direction is emerging from the old dialectic. It is based on a sensitivity to demands for particular audiences, just as Aristotle would have it. Commenting on the previously quoted statement, Campbell demurs:

> No doubt the reputation of capacity, experience in affairs, and as much integrity as is thought attainable by those called men of the world, will add weight to the words of the senator; that of skill in his profession, and fidelity in his representations, will serve to recommend what is spoken by the lawyer at the bar; but if these characters in general remain unimpeached, the public will be sufficiently indulgent to both in every other respect. On the contrary, there is little or no indulgence, in regard to his own failings, to be expected by the man who is professedly a sort of authorized censor, who hath it in charge to mark, and reprehend the faults of others.[16]

We see here the rise to prominence of what are taken to be more or less amoral elements of ethos, such as skill in a profession and experience in affairs. Campbell intimates that politicians do not even need to seem good — they just need to be *good enough* — because their audiences know that "men of the world" are often called to compromise the strictest morality. With Campbell, then, the question of what the rhetor needs to be (or appear to be), expands beyond the terminology of morality.

Interestingly, though, he retains the *vir bonus* standard for the preacher (the moral "censor"), but adds to it the Aristotelian concern for appearances. The preacher must not only *be* a good man, he must also *appear* as such to his flock. Plato would have agreed with the first part, Aristotle more with the second, but Campbell combines them into a very stringent standard for the moralist. After describing the great demands on the moralizing orator as a set of balancing acts (He "must be grave without moroseness" and "firm in declaring the will of God... yet mild in his addresses to the people"), Campbell surmises, "From these few hints it plainly appears, that there is a certain delicacy in the character of a preacher, which he is never at liberty totally to overlook, and to which, if there appear any thing incongruous, either in his conduct or in his public performances, it will never fail to injure their effect."[17]

No doubt Frederick Douglass, a clear moralist and veritable Jeremiah-type in his rebukes of the antebellum North, would fall into Campbell's category of "censor" or preacher.[18] So, according to the dominant thinking in the nineteenth century, the highest ethical standards would have been required from Douglass the antislavery "evangelist." The room other orators had to negotiate ethos with professional skill, *savior faire* and other non-moral qualities, was denied to the preacher who deigned to lecture his audience on morality.

If rhetorical criticism had continued along the path laid out by Campbell, with the critic attempting to discern the ethos possibilities for each orator and setting, studies of ethos might have figured more prominently in communication and rhetorical studies and more would be at stake than reinterpretations of classical authors. Charles Taylor, for instance, in *Sources of the Self,* details some of the dimensions of the changing definitions of personhood since Plato's day.[19] The same dimensions could be extended as a study of ethos expectations across the ages.

Instead, there was, early in the formalization of communication studies in America, a return to the classical foundations of the discipline to ground the practice of rhetorical criticism in order to separate it from literary and historical inquiry.[20] Searching the classics and unable in good conscience to sit at the feet of Plato, rhetorical critics have generally followed in Aristotelian footsteps in criticizing speakers.[21] Their theorizing, therefore focused heavily on Aristotle's two poles: moral character issues, and lists of speaker attributes that prove persuasive.

As in theory, so in criticism where in the early days of speech communication as a discipline, neo-Aristotelian criticism dominated the practice of rhetorical analysis.

In such an approach, Aristotle's *Rhetorica* is extracted from his political and ethical works so that he seems to be concerned only with giving speaking tips, in the tradition of rhetorical handbooks. From this perspective, the speaker is a dominant figure, responding carefully and strategically to a problem using rhetoric that changes not only beliefs, but history itself.[22] The critic's only concern relating to ethos is discovering qualities that explain the effectiveness of the rhetor.

The underlying assumption of the neo-Aristotelian criticism of ethos is that the attributes of the righteous man can be communicated alongside his enthymematic arguments in a speech. They become an "appeal" akin to a logical proof, but in this case, the speaker's ethics provide an implied warrant. The idea is that, on balance, it is better to follow the advice of a good person in a tricky situation because their policies are less likely to be selfishly motivated or lead to great social harm.

The neo-Aristotelian generally divides criticism into three sections, focusing on logos (arguments), ethos (moral character), and pathos (emotions), in turn. As Stewart puts it, the neo-Aristotelian approach "unwittingly opened the door for continued 'cookie-cutter' studies in which the critic looks for a little emotional appeal, a little logic, a little ethos, a little style and did not recognize the interrelationships of these rhetorical principles."[23]

This would be bad enough, but of Aristotle's triumvir, ethos usually holds the place of least of importance for neoclassical critics. For this, there are good reasons: even while faithfully applying Aristotle's rubric to speeches, critics have recognized an incompatibility between his prescriptions and the rhetorical success of their subjects. The Aristotelian qualities of an ethical speaker have clearly not described certain modern demagogues, speakers whose ethos, like Douglass's, was effective while being noticeably immoral in certain respects. For example, several studies of pro-slavery Southern orators make brief mention of ethos, referring mostly to their good will towards their (white) audiences.[24] And while one might accept that as a kind of good will, an argument for the good morals or good sense of a slavery apologist is harder to defend.

We can also easily find critics who were forced to deny Aristotle's edict that ethos is "through the speech" and admit that preachers seldom resorted to overt "ethical proofs" in their oratory. Preachers have often relied instead on their reputation to impress audiences.[25]

Ethical Criticism of Douglass's Speeches

Although Aristotelian theory is easy to summarize and apply, its overly stringent application actually contributed to the devaluing of ethos. His approach to ethos consistently lacked explanatory power and failed to map to the situations critics were dissecting. Despite the limitations, there is still value in the published rhetorical criticism of Frederick Douglass. Much of it is neo-Aristotelian in flavor and has rightly celebrated his ability to win the audience's favor, but it has also manifested the several limitations of the practice of "ethical" criticism. One example is the master's thesis of Cornelius A. Ladner, under the direction of neo-Aristotelian A. Craig Baird.[26] Describing Douglass's 1846 speech at Finsbury Chapel in London, Ladner identifies "slavery is abominable" as the main logical claim (*logos*). The author notes that "[r]estatement, comparison, factual illustration, specific instance and testimony were the forms of support most commonly used." In the next section, he concludes that Douglass's emotional appeals (pathos) were targeted at the audience's values of liberty and religion, and he notes that Douglass made a special effort to elicit sympathy from the audience.[27] Aristotle's precepts function effectively in these sections to guide the critic to greater understanding of important contents of the speech.

Then, when he comes to the subject of ethos, the author makes the strange observation that Douglass expressed his appreciation for the opportunity to speak, while "[h]e denied at the same time his possession of any of the qualities of ethical character, because twenty-one years of his life had been spent in slavery. This had the effect of giving him an appearance of modesty."[28] The strange "ethical proof" described here by the Aristotelian critic denies all the standard ethical qualities to establish one personality trait, modesty. Ethics, as the general term for Douglass's self-presentation, is obviously stretched considerably by this description; modesty can only be an *ethical* appeal if pride, or confidence, is defined as unethical (not just unwise or ineffective). Moreover, sacrificing all other ethical traits for mere modesty hardly seems to be a winning strategy, especially inside an Aristotelian framework. By following Aristotle and not developing the Campbellian ideas regarding the extra-moral aspects of ethos, critics have little room to examine the complexities of ethos.

Nor is this the only time the Ladner faces a quandary in his criticism. Analyzing the same speech, he turns to Douglass's assertion of the Christian values towards marriage and chastity. According to Ladner, Douglass lauds these values as a way of establishing his morality with the audience.[29] While there is some truth in this, to fully appreciate the audience's opinion of Douglass we must also take into consideration his scathing criticisms of the Christian churches of America. Why would Douglass be most sharply criticized by his contemporaries following his attacks on the church if Christian morality were an unproblematic means of establishing his virtue and winning over the audience? Aligning himself with biblical commands about marriage and chastity might have established his character, but in the context of his condemnation of the churches promulgating those views, it is safe to speculate that something other than appealing to *doxa* and popular morality is at work.

This one piece of criticism is not singled out because it is bad criticism and particularly uncritical of its assumptions. In fact, I think the author has latched onto key elements of Douglass's ethos (albeit ones that need to be placed alongside their contraries to see how Douglass plays both sides, as I will discuss in the fifth chapter). The problem is with the terminology, not the analysis, and the problem is systemic. Ideas of "character" and "ethics" have clearly supplanted the more rhetorically sensitive term, ethos, with its much richer possibilities. Although the critic avers that he is seeking ethos, he is fixating on ideas of laudable character, that is, assertions of upstanding morality that make the rhetor the epitome of community norms.[30]

A more recent rhetorical analysis of Douglass also takes an Aristotelian approach to his rhetorical strategies. Chesebrough's *Frederick Douglass: Oratory from Slavery* recognizes the supreme importance of ethos to Douglass's rhetorical success and covers ethos as his first topic.[31] Chesebrough's analysis finds an essentially classical list of traits in Douglass speeches that establish *credibility*.[32] He proves his good sense, by establishing his subject matter expertise and by frequently quoting respected authors, particularly Shakespeare. He proves his good morals by telling stories of his integrity and faithfulness in tough circumstances. Finally, he proves his good will by opening many speeches with a message of deep appreciation for welcoming him and allowing him to speech.

Interestingly, in the midst of finding exactly what he was looking for (i.e. Aristotle's categories of ethos), Chesebrough realizes that one of Douglass's most common and powerful appeals is "endearing self-deprecation." Such a tactic must be seen as a dicey one if establishing credibility is the *sine qua non* of ethos, but according to Chesebrough, Douglass's purpose was to evoke the sympathy of the audience. Little more is made of the tension between pitying and honoring a speaker.

In a revisionist sort of way, analyzing Douglass's ethos exclusively in terms of character is a useful corrective to the years of his being ignored. But because Aristotle holds that ethos is supposed to be "the controlling element," the moral analysis of a successful orator easily crosses over from criticism to panegyric. As another of Douglass's critics declares: "No evidence of questionable character had been attributed to Douglass [in his career to that point]. In numerous instances, his character suggested that he was a virtuous man."[33] The accuracy of this assessment aside — for it is mostly based on apologists' and friends' assessments of Douglass[34] — it does indicate a problem. No one doubts that Douglass had a command of techniques for showing his virtue, or that he was eloquent in defense of himself when critics attacked his veracity or motives. Critics know that Douglass was and is respected by many people, and they are hesitant to portray him as unethical in any important sense.

Given that, what does the critic do with the criticisms that Douglass received from his contemporaries, that he was "uppity," self-righteous, and opportunistic in his political views? What about the more recent criticisms, that his rhetoric supported patriarchy in the United States, and that his compromises with whites in his later years — which hurt black Americans' chances for equality — resulted from callousness born of too much comfort?[35] These were not strategies to establish virtue (which the Neo-classical method trains us to seek out), but they were factors of his rhetoric. In the classical model that focuses only on character, they must remain as liminal, somewhere between anecdotal sour-grapes and background material showing the problematic nature of race and gender relations in the nineteenth century; they cannot be part of his complex ethos. The most problematic assumption the character-centered critic makes is to think that Douglass was not aware, and certainly was not in control of aspects of his self-presentation that made people uncomfortable. Of course, given Douglass's extreme self consciousness, there is every reason to suspect that he exhibited character "flaws" on cue, to make a point or excite a response. Probably it was quandaries like these that moved Hauser to proclaim:

> Quite apart from the ethics of person's views, there is always the question of whether the persuading agent is treating the audience with moral integrity. Thus we need to distinguish between *ethos* and *ethical appeals*. Questions of ethos focus on the perceptions of the speaker caused by his rhetoric. Questions of ethical appeals focus on the issues raised (or suppressed) and the quality of arguments addressed to them.[36]

In my view, the *ethos* criticism Hauser describes is precisely what is needed to make sense of Douglass's self descriptions. Questions of suppressed ethical lapses clearly apply to a "criminal" ex-slave lecturing whites on morality. But ethos criticism of the type Hauser calls for is rare today, partly because classicism has lost much of its cachet. Instead, in criticism that treats of the rhetor's person, the rhetorically rich history of the ethos concept is abandoned in favor of the single aspect of personal persuasiveness. Rhetorical critics accomplish a version of ethos criticism, albeit without acknowledging the subject, when they study a rhetor's "persona" or "voice."[37] This type of solution to the fallacious conflation of character and ethos will be discussed in the final section of the literature review below.

The Study of Source Characteristics

The second of the dominant approaches to ethos in contemporary literature is easier to summarize because it has had a shorter history. It extends the Aristotelian notion that qualities of the persuasive orator can be listed and studied, and so does not limit its purview to moral traits. Many articles cite the work of Hovland, Janis, and Kelly in 1953 as the beginning of the modern experimental study of source credibility.[38]

Procedures in this category of research can be as simple as crediting the same speech to a (presumed) high-credibility and low-credibility source and comparing the difference in persuasion.[39] More recently, researchers have tried to find some correlation between adjectival descriptions of orators and the auditor's reactions using factor analysis.[40] Because there is so much emphasis on how persons are perceived, rather than on the elements of an actual speech setting, many of the studies cited in communication journals as "ethos" research have been published in psychology or political science journals.

To say these various methodologies have been troublesome, especially for their practitioners in communication studies, is an understatement. There is a throng of articles that summarize past findings while trying to establish some coherence for the diverse works.[41] These usually include a call to change the methods and assumptions of the studies as well. In one early call, Whitehead asserts cautiously,

> Clearly, we can no longer regard ethos or source credibility as simply a three-factor structure composed of expertness, trustworthiness, and dynamism, [the 'source credibility' equivalents of Aristotle's triad] since more than three factors emerged [in his study]. These results suggest a needed extension in the credibility models presently being employed and further that additional testing with new scales, concepts, and subjects may be indicated.[42]

With the request for new "scales, concepts, and subjects," in other words, this author admits the need for a complete reappraisal of the credibility studies.

Most recently, Logue and Miller detail the various critiques of the source credibility researchers, especially their "neglect of the transactional, situational, and temporal character of communication." All this leads Logue and Miller to conclude that "it is not surprising that research based on 'the ethos or source credibility construct' waned as interaction models of communication replaced stimulus-response models."[43] Delia's comments are most telling when he condemns credibility studies based on their failure to "take into account the importance of context, to evaluate the person as communicator, and to view ethos in process terms."[44]

So in the end, most critics decided that the source credibility studies never really analyzed ethos at all, although the years of this type of study must have had some impact on how many scholars now conceive of rhetorical ethos. In the speech discipline, this program of research has apparently been abandoned. Of course, because the various methods in this school of thought were not intended to explain a particular individual, let alone a historical one, there have been no attempts to study Frederick Douglass as a "source." Nor was much of an effort made to consider race as a variable for either source or receiver. Research in this mold was primarily useful for suggesting the extreme variability of ethos because each study came up with new and different qualities that were "essential" to a speaker's ethos. Due to the repeated efforts to correct earlier studies and studies done by psychologists, the situation-boundedness of a communicator's ethos was brought to the forefront.

Alternative Approaches

Inspired by the confusion of this set of projects and reacting against the moralism and incompleteness of the other, several scholars have studied elements of ethos with little or no reference to the concept. These texts focus on how one "puts oneself into a text." After briefly summarizing the long history of the use of the ethos concept, Nan Johnson's study of recently published composition handbooks reveals:

> The concept of ethos rarely appears in current texts by name. Rather, it is discussed under such varied stylistic headings as 'tone,' 'writer's voice,' 'personal appeal,' 'attitude,' 'persona,' and 'credibility.' Often, these are presented as prepatory considerations in the process of composing under such titles as 'considering an audience,' 'convincing a reader,' and 'planning for aim and audience.'[45]

We see the hardiness of the neo-Aristotelian model here, because ethos is still being sought for its strategic value as part of a 'plan' for "convincing" an audience. Johnson does note that ethos can be a "prepatory" consideration for relating to an audience, but the terms *voice, attitude,* and *persona* signal for us how consumed recent scholarship is with the personal. As a result, audience preconceptions and responses to ethos (based on the idea that ethos might be *co-constructed*) are underemphasized in favor of examinations of the various ways authors express their inner natures in their texts. In practice, adjusting to an audience and find a means of self-expression exist in tension with each other. Solipsistic or narcissistic rhetoric that is only concerned about the self of the speaker, and expresses ideas in a way only that self can understand, is unlikely to find a sympathetic audience.

The concepts of voice and persona are valuable for exploring the autobiographical elements of speeches, but they rely on notions that wouldn't have occurred to classical critics. Putting something called a "self" into a text represents a relatively new way of thinking about invention that arose in the Renaissance.[46] It was bolstered by modernist philosophers, such as Descartes. His division of the self into two parts, the *cogito* and *sum*, suggests that anyone's awareness and point of view is something that can be placed in or expressed through physical reality or *being*.[47] The idea received sustained attention in rhetorical theory with the belletristic tradition when writing was systematically addressed for the first time. Many recent composition handbooks adopt the assumptions about self-expression that we find in the belletrists such as Hugh Blair. Many include some version of Blair's statement that "seldom or never will a man be eloquent but when he is in earnest and uttering his own sentiments."[48]

What we might classify as theories of "ethos as self-expression," build upon the idea that there exists an authentic self inside each person, and the writer or speaker's task is to find words to express it. This conflicts with one of the major findings of the "source credibility" studies, that ethos qualities are varied, among people, across situations, and even between two different moments in an individual's self-expression. And, insofar as self-expression becomes rhetorical, there must be some impact on an audience. A speaker's characteristics have to make some connection, by way of persuasion or identification, with a targeted "other." The qualities expressed in a diary never read cannot be called ethos, in other words. Self expression that fails to account for an audience and social situation is likely to be unsuccessful in supporting a conclusion or creating a bond of good will.

The idea that ethos is a "personal appeal" based on representing the self in one's discourse first appeared in belletristic handbooks on rhetoric published in the late eighteenth and early nineteenth century. This puts us solidly in Douglass's time frame. More importantly, we are getting closer to the ideas that would have currency for an antebellum audience, inasmuch as Blair and others who wrote handbooks on *belles lettres* were popular in antebellum America (although the emphasis on self expression over persuasion is a later development). As of Douglass's day, it would not have been widely accepted that an orator contributes little more to a speech than a self needing to be expressed.[49] Campbell's handbook, perhaps the most popular at the time, shows that social and moral considerations still dominated the appreciation of ethos even as theorists started to recognize that the classical list of character traits may need adjusting to match modern political realities. The increasing emphasis on self expression in the turn of the nineteenth century does suggest that audiences were increasingly curious about piercing beneath any veil a speaker might raise between himself and the audience. They wanted to know the true person giving the speech, in his own words, rather than the carefully crafted images that rhetors were more and more likely to hide behind. Speakers, in turn, had to choose words that at least seemed to have a real tie to their inner, hidden, and therefore somehow more "authentic" person

Literature Review: Conclusion

We can learn from all three of the major trends in the literature on ethos. I suggest that to build on the valuable past work we need to (1) accept the idea that in some cases people are persuaded by the speaker's moral character, but many times the good will or good morals of a speaker are unrelated to his or her ability to move an audience. We can certainly (2) look for a list of traits that successful speakers demonstrate, but we should historicize the audience and speaker under consideration, for time makes unique demands and forces particular constraints on the rhetor who is presenting him- or herself. Finally, we should (3) attend to the dual processes whereby ethos-proofs are related to the orator and co-constructed when the audience authorizes them. Ethos that is mere self-expression is stripped of much of its power to reach audiences, and leads critics to overlook the fact that the same "self" can be presented in a number of very different ways.

DEFINITION OF ETHOS

The challenge is to find a definition of ethos that applies all three lessons. Specifically, I have come to accept a definition very similar to James Baumlin's when he describes ethos as "the problematic identification of a speaker with/in his or her speech."[50] Baumlin's phrasing is wonderfully suggestive and properly evokes the crucial elements of a definition: Ethos affects discourse because of a reaction to the identity of the speaker; that identity is a part of his or her identification *by* and *with* the self and the audience; and all of this is accomplished with and in the speech.

More than Baumlin does, I would like to emphasize the role ethos plays in the reception of discourse, because any identification of a speaker has consequences. As it was for Aristotle, ethos is a means of persuasion. *Persuasion* has to be defined in a broad way here to refer to all the abilities humans have to influence each other through discourse. To persuade using ethos, rhetors discursively present their personal qualities, and, in certain settings, those of the opponent or client. Most often ethos is established indirectly through the types of arguments used or by narrating personal experiences which are intended to reveal the person's nature by the actions he or she chooses.

There are also non-discursive "elements" of ethos, such as physical characteristics (attractiveness, weight) and markers of status (being well-born, achieving a military rank). However, these too are often incorporated into the rhetor's discourse, so their contribution to persuasion is dependent on the rhetorical situation and the words of the rhetor. Military rank, for instance, is great for political stump speeches, but at an anti-war rally it can be a genuine liability — unless, that is, the speaker justifies himself properly. Non-discursive elements of ethos are always perceived through the lens of the speech itself, the words of the speaker refracting or occluding the audience's vision of the speaker's handsome visage or military ribbons.

This is why Aristotle remarks that persuasion through ethos "should result from the speech, not from a previous opinion that the speaker is a certain kind of person."[51] The instruction applies to the audience — who are admonished to look carefully at the logic and character exhibited in the speech as a way to judge the speaker — and to the speaker himself, who is warned not to rest on his laurels while looking for the "available means" of persuasion. As Aristotle recognized, nearly any impediment for ethos can be reconfigured in the course of the speech. Any flaw in the speaker's personal attributes or history can be explained away or turned to advantage.

Aristotle's insistence that ethos is built through the speech is an especially important reminder for a contemporary theory of ethos. Individual characteristics that would seem antithetical to ethos in one context can be powerfully moving to other audiences concerned about other topics. My explanation of Douglass's ethos hinges on the idea that the many elements of "bad" character that an Aristotle or

Augustine might scorn were often the very elements that attracted his audiences. And this is only possible because his oratory occurred in a context of changing norms about human nature and entertainment, and because Douglass portrays himself brilliantly with a mix of both "good" and "bad" qualities.

In any case, if the qualities the rhetor portrays suggest to the audience that he or she is worthy of attention and credence, we can say that person is persuading through ethos. Or to use the short-hand, we can say the person *has* ethos, much as we might say of a person using logical proofs that she *is* a logical person.

Ethos is not separate from the other elements of a rhetorical act but relies on them to a great degree. Aristotle was correct to note that the logic speakers exhibit and the emotions they evoke are indicative of their character and thus will establish or destroy their ethos. The different "modes" of proof (Aristotle: *pisteis*) are closely associated by nineteenth-century critics, more so than Aristotle would have wanted them. The blurring of the lines (which, of course, were merely analytical ones to begin with) is evident in the speech reviews and audience responses to Frederick Douglass's oratory. As spectators strive to make sense of their favorable impression of him, it is not uncommon for them to rely on two generic words — "eloquence" and "power." What each person means by these two terms varies greatly, such that they come to express all manner of qualities that critics of the past would separate under the categories of delivery, logic, style, pathetic appeals, and ethos. Logos and pathos are combined with ethos within an overall estimation of the speaker's ability. Critics, announcing the eloquence and power of Douglass, were finding an impressive speaker who combined logical arguments and controlled his audiences' emotions.

In the mid-nineteenth century, to say a speaker had "power" over an audience is the highest praise a critic can afford. Despite the fascination with powerful speakers, the exact means the speaker used to obtain power often remains unexplained (except to say, perhaps, that the person was eloquent). It is quite evident, though, that when popular audiences felt overcome, it was by virtue of some relationship they felt to the speaker himself (or, vary rarely, herself), not just a reaction to brilliant logic, or even to being affected by an emotion.[52] Qualities of the person himself were seen as indispensable elements of forcefulness.

The category *ethos*, then, as it is actualized in the nineteenth century forward, focuses our attention on the person of the speaker and on how audiences respond to the man or woman doing the speaking as represented in the words of the speech.

Ethos as Personality

Aristotle's pronouncements serve to introduce the various aspects of ethos as a proof, but we must leave him behind at a certain point. The limitation of Aristotelian theory is an overemphasis on the rhetor's stable character traits. Aristotle believed that morals were inculcated by habit and would therefore be stable. He also believed that since humans were political animals, the best morals served community rather than personal interests. In his framework, the measure of a person's character is how closely it aligns with the good of the community or *polis*. Additionally, because he believed that 'breeding will tell,' Aristotle advocated the view that we cannot judge a person adequately on one instance. We must instead look for a record of deeds, the better to see the person's habituated traits.

While contributing to a rhetor's ethos, the Aristotelian traits of character — good sense, good will, and good morals — need to be supplemented by another set of rhetorical possibilities from the rhetor's personality. There is a reason to believe rhetors whose public records proves them to be the ideal of wisdom, beneficence, and morality, because those traits support the greater good. But for real people (rather than characters in epic poems or spaghetti westerns) that moral makeup is revealed in a life context of idiosyncratic traits and unusual responses to complex situations which are often not aligned with moral norms.[53] Often, it is the social rebel who is most attractive to modern audiences.

The rhetor's unique set of interests, motives, and experiences that inform his or her actions are presented in a context. When rhetors present these elements of themselves, they are asking to be judged not as a morally ideal person whose stable traits always guide decisions, but as a complex person making decisions in situations with competing moral claims. Appeals to this kind of ethos can be labeled "personality appeals."

Together, an agent's character (stable and outwardly observable traits that aid the community) and personality (temporary or inconsistent psychological states that are generated by internal drives) are presented to an audience as an *identity*, a codified presentation of the self mobilized to do rhetorical work.

As Douglass's career shows, proper morals, and even Christian ethics, were not necessarily the compelling aspects of a rhetor in antebellum America. He was recognized by his antislavery coworkers as a powerful orator, even when they disdained one or more of his moral choices. As fellow lecturer Edmund Quincy wrote in a complaint to another abolitionist, "I am afraid we shall have trouble about Douglass's compensation [for his work as a touring speaker]. I suppose he thinks that his services are worth more than any one's else & sh'd [sic] be higher paid. This is probably true enough in a sense & yet to pay him more than others would set all the flax to flame — or, at least, all the *wool*"[54] The racist joke shows that Quincy's high evaluation of Douglass's abilities was not based on some blind devotion to black orators. Nor is he biased in favor of Douglass out of personal affection. He obviously prefers other black orators, such as William Wells Brown, who are of a "much higher cast of character" even though their eloquence and "intellectual power" are inferior.[55]

Quincy's letter is representative of many reactions to seeing Douglass on the platform. Despite the observers' prejudices and the orator's perceived character flaws,

Douglass's oratorical prowess is unquestioned. This is not to say that character, *per se*, was unimportant. It was, however, supplanted by or complementary to other elements of Douglass's persona. Based on evidence of this kind, this dissertation will work to resist the replacement of rhetorical ethos by classical, Christian, or other ethical systems.

The definition of ethos I have argued for encapsulates the contest between deeds motivated by moral consistency and actions resulting from perceptive responsiveness — the contest between *arete* and *kairos*, if you will. The image of the stable and moral individual that most rhetors want to portray, seems most vital and realistic to a modern audience when it is placed alongside the person's hidden traits and flaws, the ones tabloid readers greedily seek in order to make any hero "seem more human." Only in the nineteenth century do personality traits of this sort become a legitimate, publicly sanctioned part of appreciating a person and his or her ethos. Personality, though, has never been adequately theorized as part of ethos. This dissertation, with much help from secondary sources that provide crucial information on this period, will examine the shift in American culture from a neoclassical emphasis on virtuous character and external moral authority, to a regard for individual personality and the gratification of individual desires.[56]

Admittedly, I am not the first to assert that a study of ethos must include a study of personality, but to my knowledge, few authors have realized how much this diverges from the rhetorical tradition, and even fewer have justified using the term ethos in a non-Aristotelian (or, at least, non-classical) way. For example, Trevor Parry-Giles, obviously working with a different definition of *character* than mine or Aristotle's, writes about the "vulnerability and fluidity of human character" in his analysis of ethos in confirmation hearings. He notes, and yet essentially glosses over the idea that "much of American political identity is bound to constructions of individual character and personality in the public discourses circulating around the selection/election of our public officials."[57] I think he is correct to make personality coequal with character in his analysis, save that he never explains how the effects, importance, or construction of ethos changes when personality is considered. Furthermore, every author he cites on the study of ethos refers exclusively to its moral dimension and makes it synonymous with character.

Amazingly, this personality aspect of ethos was brought out by William M. Sattler in a 1947 article about "Conceptions of Ethos in Ancient Theory." He states explicitly, "The traits or qualities which make up *ethos* are of course approved and respected by the society in question, but such traits do not necessarily have the status of 'welfare principles' [i.e., traits that are supportive of community good]. That is to say, *ethos* refers to qualities other than those considered to have moral import."[58] Despite its excellent analysis, in discussions of ethos this article is never cited today.

Rather, the character traits sought by the neo-Aristotelians are normative. The orator, in their thinking, is meant to embody the highest of society's ideals.

In contrast, contemporary speakers, including the most well-known politicians and celebrities, are effective because their traits are desired by the audience — lusted after for their appeal to our baser nature — even though those traits may make the speaker socially undesirable. I believe it is necessary to develop the idea that ethos is a concept big enough to contain "desirable" human traits, even if those traits are destructive to community cohesion and welfare. Put simply, we are sometimes drawn to things that are bad for us. People with those qualities can be enticing and exciting. They are the rebels, the revolutionaries, and challengers of the *status quo*. As Douglass's audiences found out, such a person often wields a measure of power over us, especially when social norms are changing or losing their authority, as was the case in the first decades of the 1900s.

When there is a climate of opinion glorifying the individual over and against society, rhetorical practice is opened up to the possibilities of traits that do not support the community good. In some circumstances, such as Aristotle's Athenian *polis*, significant ideological pressure is maintained as a way of limiting the expression of individual desires and idiosyncrasies in oratory. That process has recently received much deserved attention.[59] The time and place in American history that personality received a rhetorical (and later, social) sanction on par with character in American rhetoric intersects with Douglass's rise to prominence. The social constraints and opportunities that made him a successful orator are, if anything stronger today, and so we have much to learn from his ethos strategies.

The literature on black identity and voice has already recognized that African American rhetoric has a special relationship to personhood and social standards in America. We understand a culture's approach to ethos when we answer the two questions, "Who is allowed to speak?" and "Whom are we inclined to believe?" The answers to both questions reveal the way personhood is defined and appreciated in a culture. Understanding an orator's ethos is necessary for fully understanding his or her speeches. Likewise, the standards of ethos of a given society reveal truths about its values and practices. Our ideals and prejudices are revealed by the personal qualities others must possess if they hope to persuade us and change society. At a deeper level, the search by an audience for orators with respectability and credibility suggests the level of skepticism of a culture and the degree to which they demand truth over probability. If we can define ethos expectations as Douglass emerges onto the national stage and explain why he was impressive because of or despite the audiences' demands, we can understand better the social forces in the years of his early career, 1840-1860.

That Douglass had to confront racism on the speaker's platform is no revelation. The underpinnings of slavery, and of American racism in general, have been analyzed at length and I will not pretend to add extensively to that literature. Instead, there is a need to address a different lacuna in the historical record. While we know well the attitudes about human nature that held Douglass and others like him on the plantation, the affect that Douglass's oratory, and his very presence on the stage, may have had on auditors' appreciation of the humanity and personhood of African Americans is still undeveloped. Finding an answer to that question is one of the overarching motivations of this study.

A closely related topic, also relatively unexplored, is the change in audiences' notions of ethos because of Douglass's rhetorical practices. Douglass managed his ethos appeals in a different way than his colleagues at the lectern who were white; he had to, for his challenges were much more severe. As audiences responded to him and other orators imitated him, he arguably became responsible in part for a shift in what audiences would sanction as ethos. His contribution needs to be examined, as does the durability of the shift to present-day rhetorical practice

This is not to say that the words and life of Douglass have not been studied. Far from it: Douglass has been the subject of a dozen major biographies, and his words, the subject of numerous studies.[60] Douglass himself demanded that attention to be paid to his person. He spoke autobiographically, always intermixing philosophical musings on humanity with his own testimony about the life of slaves and the experience of racism. By writing two pre-emancipation autobiographies, and another one several years after Lincoln's Proclamation when Douglass was a grand old statesman of American race politics, he invited his admirers to use his life as a lens through which to understand American slavery, abolition, and freedom. Many writers in many fields have responded to the invitation.

Insofar as Douglass is an important and perceptive recorder of events in his lifetime, using his autobiographical discourse to judge the culture is a sound practice. But whatever his ruminations reveal, they cannot be allowed to stand alone or to completely replace other sources. Douglass, too, had his biases, and memory is notoriously faulty. Even something as simple as accepting Douglass's often-claimed lack of training for a public speaking career can be extremely misleading when we try to understand Douglass's rhetorical choices about his ethos.[61] This claim was primarily a rhetorical ploy, the run of the mill humble *proemion* that orators have used since ancient times. Douglass's own writing shows that he had been giving speeches since he was quite young and that he was reared in debating societies. He was ordained as a lay minister in New Bedford and quite familiar with giving sermons after his escape North.[62] Yet the story of his raw natural talent shining through in his first halting speech at an abolitionist meeting has been retold uncritically in numerous articles. To correct the historical record other studies still need to be done.

We can appreciate one irony, though: In writing constantly about the Douglass who masters every detail of self-presentation to impress his antebellum audiences, some have forgotten to be skeptical of the Douglass who managed his self-image in order to persuade historians and critics. Following Douglass's own account of his life can hinder us from fully appreciating or even noticing his ethos proofs. Literary and rhetorical critics need to approach him skeptically in order to understand the layers of his self-image construction. Scholars in both fields have perpetuated myths started by Douglass himself, or by William Lloyd Garrison about his biography or his rhetoric.[63]

Appropriately, Douglass earns the modern critics' trust in roughly the same way he established ethos with any audience. He always seems to be merely speaking from his heart, detesting slavery in no small part because of his own hurtful experiences. He gives his immediate audience, and us as an extended audience, the strong impression that he is being entirely transparent. That this seeming lack of artifice was one of his strongest qualities of ethos is without a doubt (discussed in chapter five as a matter of *authenticity*). During many of the events where his emotional transparency lead to caustic comments that upset a particular audience, he was engaging in a rhetorical ploy. They (and we) tended to chalk this up to his great personal involvement. In other words, his feelings seem to show only because he is *too transparent*, not because acting them out is a rhetorical move calculated to elicit a sympathetic audience response. Telling the difference is a major challenge to the rhetorical critic.

The claims Douglass makes about his life and the rhetorical presentation of those claims also need to interrogated if for no other reason than to understand Douglass's changing sensibilities. He started his formal abolitionist career as a Garrisonian, but went into the Civil War years estranged from his mentor, convinced of the anti-slavery nature of the Constitution, and willing to advocate (or easily tolerate) violence as a solution to the slavery problem. Such turnabouts on important issues are almost commonplace in Douglass's life. Yet, too often, the authority of a particular autobiography or speech is taken for granted, as though Douglass's interpretation of past events would not change due to his altered circumstances.

Unwilling to make this assumption, the study of ethos should take as its subject the *presentation* of a person's life, anticipating that there may be important discrepancies between the public image and the historical individual. It does not suffice in this regard to side with the postmoderns who claim that the image is "more real" than the Real,[64] for the discrepancies between lived life and presented life are extremely revealing of the orator's rhetorical choices, conscious or otherwise. The details of a life that are left out reflect on the final picture the speaker creates. However, the image Douglass gives us is never to be regarded as a *mere* fiction. On the contrary, he may well have been discovering and even creating himself as he chained words together to relate his life's story.[65] All this makes ethos — the use of his self presentation for rhetorical effect — a complex interchange between history and discursivity. I am suggesting that Douglass should be studied differently, with his autobiographies approached as the subjects of research (i.e., as more instances of his rhetorical self-presentation) rather than the beginning points.

LIMITS OF THE STUDY

Because Douglass's life was long and he was extremely prolific (very few people write three autobiographies or participate in something called a "One Hundred Conventions" tour), the frame of my study has to be limited to one portion of his career, the pre-Civil War phase. The War and the Emancipation Proclamation mark monumental changes in his purpose and in the "rhetorical status" of blacks in society.[66] To address those dynamics of his ethos would take a much longer work.[67]

Attention here is fairly evenly split between speeches before and after 1847 or so. Before that date, we find him achieving astonishing success on the lecture circuit. After that date, he can rely more on his reputation to bring in audiences. Before he is famous, he speaks with the approval of a white-dominated organization. After he achieves celebrity status, he must struggle to touch white audiences who come to hear him *because* he is famous, but who have no intention of working towards emancipation. Put another way, I am taking the claims of Gerald Fulkerson seriously when he refers to Douglass's return to America from a British lecture tour as an "emergence" into a leadership role in the American abolition movement.[68] The lecture tour of the British Isles and Douglass's triumphant return mark a clear divide in ethos strategies for Douglass. Together, the two halves of his prewar career reveal how this least likely candidate crafted and exploited the ethos proofs that he would put to use throughout his career.

Another limitation of any study of oratory before the age of mechanical recording devices is the accuracy of transcripts. Douglass's gradual acquisition of a literate mentality enlivens his discourse,[69] but it also makes his early speech texts somewhat more reliable. He was less likely than, say, Wendell Phillips to correct a speech transcript for what he *should* have said but didn't.[70] In fact, Douglass never spoke from a manuscript until his abolitionist career was more than a decade old. The presence of gratuitous punctuation in the published versions of his speeches attest to the efforts of stenographers to record his speeches verbatim, with all of the run-on sentences and random asides intact. Thus, because the characteristics of oral consciousness helped him to stand out and improve the reliability of the versions of the speech that have come down to us, I have chosen to end my study in the period shortly after 1855. In those years his second autobiography was circulating with the title *My Bondage, My Freedom.* In many respects, the book is a retelling of his 1845 slave narrative, *Narrative of the Life of Frederick Douglass, an American Slave, Written by Himself,* with the clear marks of a literate consciousness and a conscious effort to cash in on his celebrity for the cause.[71]

Within my limited time frame — the period when Douglass was first making his reputation and then learning how to convert it to greater rhetorical success — it will be my goal to see how he worked within the confines of the standards of his time, which obviously favored white males and placed him at a disadvantage. I also hope to see how Douglass stretched the popular understanding of ethos through his rhetoric. Finally, I hope to draw some conclusions for present-day conceptions of ethos based on the trends evident in Douglass's praxis.

METHOD AND CHAPTER OUTLINE

The story of Douglass's success I want to tell will suggest that the personal persuasiveness of the ex-slave orators can be adequately explained neither by ancient rhetorical theories nor by the British treatises on rhetoric that exhibited such broad influence in the antebellum era. In regards to ethos, these theories, at most, set the boundaries for the black abolitionists to stretch and avenues of possible change for them to exploit. Frederick Douglass especially (although each African American orator played a part) took advantage of Enlightenment assumptions about human nature that were undercurrents in the eighteenth and nineteenth century texts and used them as a wedge to drive himself into the public arena.

It is important to begin with the understanding of ethos that Douglass's audiences would have had prior to hearing him speak so that his methods for broadening their conceptions become more apparent. Chapter two will explain why Douglass, the radical reformer, would face particular challenges because of the therapeutic mentality of antebellum audiences, and how he could use the desire of the audiences to be tickled with prurient displays to lure them into a serious discussion of social issues and the overturning of American slave-supported society.

The usual resources for understanding theories of ethos — rhetoric textbooks — were not the only venue, or even the primary one, through which audiences were prepared for impressive and thrilling black speakers like Douglass. Therefore, chapter three will cover the various opportunities people in Douglass's audience would have had to learn about ethos, focusing on three sources: edicts from rhetorical theories taught in the schools and in popular vocabulary, the examples of other well-liked speakers, and American practices of speech consumption (e.g., the way the lyceum movement and newspaper reviews of speeches shaped audience standards for oratory). I highlight these topics because it is my belief that audiences, even lower-class ones who never receive training in public speaking, learn about rhetoric in roughly the same way a professional orator does, through exposure to theory, imitation and practice. The set of influences detailed in chapter three are an attempt to show American audiences' exposure to bits of theory, the "imitation" of ethos from famous rhetors, and their own participation in rhetorical events.

Rather than reinforcing each other, these multiple experiences gave audiences a double-sided portrait of the ideal orator. The side of the portrait suitable for public viewing was based on classical notions of personhood and ethos. Audiences knew that they should be influenced by the *vir bonus* whose qualities proved his capacity for leadership, but who ultimately submitted his greatness to the will of the state to serve his fellows. Admittedly, this conception was subverted to a degree by the anti-aristocratic stream of American thought, when Davy Crockett and other "great" men became heroes of public life for "wrastlin' bears" or some comparable feat.

The other side of the portrait, the one everyone knew about but was slow to admit his or her taste for, revealed the attitude of subversion in all its glory. For, as we see in the example of Henry Clay abandoning the floor of the Senate to stump for his party's presidential candidate, eat off tiles around a campfire, and challenge to a fist-fight anyone who called him an aristocrat,[72] audiences of the Jacksonian era began to insist that their leaders *not appear to be* nobility. Never reflected adequately in the rhetorical theories of the time, Jacksonian era persuasion reveals that the "everyday" life of the common person who did no great deeds was increasingly valorized.[73]

As the example of Ralph Waldo Emerson further shows us, orators could also draw crowds without a public career or great deeds. Emerson represents the other counter-trend to the *vir bonus* standard, the fascination with the interior life of a person. People who were enthralled with Emerson, even if they did not understand his lectures, were drawn to his peculiar thoughts and his heartfelt expression of sentiments. There seemed to be something very deep inside him even that belied his sallow appearance and absence of public deeds.

Based on the way people in Douglass's audiences would have learned about ethos, we can begin to see the tension he used for his advantage. The audiences described in chapter three wanted someone who was a Good man yet proud of being as debased as they were. They were also beginning to allow as markers of ethos bits of the everyday life of orators and expressions of his or her deep interior states. With these allowances, audiences were primed for a display by a speaker like Douglass who spoke about his life, thoughts, and sentiments in defense of a cause.

It is easy to overestimate the egalitarian nature of the evolving definition of the self; Clay and Emerson were still white male property owners, of course. Chapter four, then, addresses the ethos expectations specifically related to black rhetors and for Douglass himself. New measures of ethos mentioned in chapters two and three — everyday life and interiority — provided opportunities for formerly shunned members of society to take to take center stage, but could not afford all the prerogatives of white men. Orators were still viewed by their race, first. All their attempts to establish ethos, through character or through personality, would be interpreted by their race. The black orator's constraints and the audience's expectations for them need to be explored alongside the ones that pertain to white orators.

When blacks exercised the opportunity to enter the public sphere using accounts of their lives and their feelings as their main ethos proofs, they faced many additional challenges. Primarily, their rhetoric reached audiences through autobiographical speaking and writing; autobiography, in its simplest form is little more than the combination of everyday life and interiority, and so was a readymade genre for establishing a measure of ethos with nineteenth-century audiences. Several blacks, both ex-slaves and freemen, made a career of retelling their experiences and reporting their (previously hidden) emotions and desires. Inasmuch as they were riding the subversive undercurrents of ethos expectations, though, black orators were forever limited to an outsider's or agitator's role and excluded from the mainstream. And, since they were appealing to the darker desires of audiences, desires to be entertained and hear racy stories, black orators were generally unable to turn the opportunity to be heard into an opportunity to radically challenge or change their audiences.

Since he was not the first African American or ex-slave orator and autobiographer on the scene, and was not even the best known abolitionist, there would have been expectations, based on his contemporaries, for what Douglass would accomplish on the lecture circuit and in his autobiographies. Despite the great eloquence of such luminaries as William Wells Brown and Henry Highland Garnet, Douglass more than any of his fellows became a celebrity, drawing whites and blacks to his speeches in great numbers. As I argue in chapter four, though, a rhetorical performance by Douglass needed to exceed the standards set by his immediate predecessors who were often ineffective in piercing their audience's racists expectations for black and ex-slave orators.

His rise to prominence, linked to events in his life and to the history of the abolition movement, shows that he did not just stick to telling his life story (as some of his mentors encouraged him to do[74]), nor did he aspire to exhibit the noble character of a Webster or a Lincoln. Instead, he synthesized a powerful identity by combining the subversive elements of the outsider's ethos with the socially sanctioned authority of the public servant. The contradictions he embodied allowed him to present himself as both a loyal American citizen who was nevertheless alienated and oppressed. Douglass's ethos, then, was itself a critique of American racism.

Chapter five provides the bulk of the textual analyses of Douglass's speeches, divided into the pre- and post-Britain parts of his antebellum career. Each section there focuses on qualities of ethos that Douglass's discourse exhibits. By beginning not with a theory, but with scenarios like the one I outlined above of a fugitive slave risked his life to convert hostile audiences, we arrive at a situation not altogether different from Aristotle's. Given a set of rhetorical performances, what characteristics does the orator evince and which of those are helpful in moving the audience? The first part of that answer relates to being flawed but authentic, the second part to authority and manliness.

SUMMARY

In sum, this work is an examination of modern notions of ethos that were formed in the rhetorical battles over personhood around 1850; I believe that most of these views are still with us today. Using newspaper reviews, contemporary rhetorical treatises, and close readings of Douglass's speeches and letters, we can situate the pre-Civil War rhetoric of Frederick Douglass in the society of the 1830s, 40s, and 50s along with the dominant expectations for rhetors in that period. I will show how he worked within those expectations to alter them.

The story of Douglass's success I want to tell relies heavily on a reconsideration of traditional notions of ethos. To lay the ground for the analysis to follow, I want to present as clear a summary of the nature of personality-based ethos as possible.

- Personality-based ethos forces a consideration of the inner-workings of the person, while character-based ethos is based on public actions.
- Personality is usually seen in the orator's everyday life, whereas character is best measured in outstanding public achievements and great deeds (standing firm against all odds, and so forth).
- Personality is "immanent in appearances" as a direct expression of the inner self, whereas character transcends appearances.[75] Therefore, we can make a good estimate of an orator's personality based on first impressions, but we need to see a person on several different occasions and in different contexts to understand his or her character.
- Personality is seen as a spontaneous expression of an internal state, and therefore tends to clash with social conventions simply because it requires conscious effort to conform oneself to society's demands.[76]
- Personality traits are presented in a context. Accordingly, others are asked to judge the person according to the demands of that moment, not by some overarching moral code or standard. Therefore, rhetors may use moral flaws as an appeal to personality.
- Personality traits (e.g., an orator's glamour) gratify the personal, selfish, and sometimes prurient desires of audience members, whereas character traits are beneficial to the community.
- Personality traits may be fleeting, while character is seen as the enduring nature of a person.
- Personality traits need not be consistent with each other; character traits, by definition, cannot conflict (someone's good sense cannot corrupt her good morals, for instance).

- Personality-based ethos assumes a rhetor who is, at most, temporarily better than an audience. In fact, the orator using personality as a proof may be morally *worse* than the audience, if this fact allows him or her to increase some other relationship based on personality, such as likeability or charisma.
- Personality traits are often desirable because they fall short of ethical standards. This increases the identification of speaker and audience because, in the modern age, Americans are prone to believe that everyone is flawed. Moreover, with an identification of orator and audience, a cathartic release may be experienced by an audience as they vicariously participate in breaking the chains of traditional morality.

CHAPTER TWO

Reformation and Resentment in Antebellum America

To appreciate how Douglass and his audiences were involved in a revolution in rhetorical ethos, we have to study the ethos expectations that preceded his transformative efforts. While ethos as a technical term would not have been familiar to many of those attending a lecture, every audience member would have had some notion of whose speeches were more apt to be believable and what type of person was worthy of their attention. Some would have gotten a smattering of rhetorical theory in school, because literature and rhetoric from the Greeks and Romans were the main objects of study in the American educational system.[1] The higher the education, the more familiarity the audience member would have had with the works of great speakers and technical rhetorical terms. But aside from those training for the pulpit or the bar, very few people would have read the sections of Aristotle or Cicero describing the necessary qualities of the eloquent speaker. How, then, did the Northerners filling the seats to hear Douglass speak acquire the standards they used to judge his efforts to persuade with ethos?

We must answer that question because "popular" audiences (in the sense connoting a lower class) would have had scarcely any experience with rhetorical training proper. The period of Douglass's rising popularity was the second quarter of the nineteenth century, commonly known as the "Era of the Common Man." At the time, popular audiences were the most prevalent kind. Douglass's audiences were less likely than most to contain the elite white men of his day. His audiences were an odd mixture of working class white rowdies, ex-slaves — the lowest class with the lowest level of education — and activist women who were the wives of middle- and upper-class men. Because of gender and racial restrictions on education, neither of the latter two groups would have been exposed to much formal rhetorical theory; few of them trained in colleges for legal or pastoral careers. So, in place of formal training, they constructed their own "naive theories" of rhetoric based on numerous exposures to rhetorical discourse and informal discussions of theory in popular media.[2]

Members of any audience, regardless of their background or education, as lay-theorists avail themselves of terms, ideas, and standards from experience and popular discourse.[3] Thus, to understand the expectations for Douglass on the matter of ethos, we have to consider his audiences' naive rhetorical theories and how they were formed.

CHAPTER PREVIEW: ANTEBELLUM RHETORICAL CULTURE

Ethos is a relational term: it captures the relationship between the speaker and the speaker's discourse on the one hand, and the relationship between the speaker and the audience on the other. As mentioned in the last chapter, modern-day rhetoricians who cross-applied Quintilian's or Aristotle's formulae for ethos had erred in not appreciating the cultural specificity of the ethos relationships. Aristotle's rhetorician, perhaps ideal for ancient Greece, cannot be set up as the standard for a speaker in New York circa 1850. The social scientific study of "source credibility" was no less mistaken when it took the study of person perception out of the context of actual speeches and audiences. On this count, Quintilian seems to be right: audiences are not just looking for the good person in a rhetor; they want the good person who *speaks well*. Understanding ethos in a time period is a matter of understanding the qualities of the rhetor and audience, and the relationship between them. The qualities that build up a speaker's ethos to an audience are not timeless lists or merely a matter of who holds the places of renown in society. Ethos expectations and practices are part and parcel of the culture of speechmaking, what has been called the "rhetorical culture."[4]

The idea of a rhetorical culture is meant to point us toward elements in communal life that influence the performance and reception of rhetoric. The rhetorical culture establishes many of the expectations, or constraints, for rhetors. For public speaking of the sort Douglass was famous for — speeches that target a large group of people or the general populace — part of the rhetorical culture is the people's attitude toward oratory as an element of public affairs. People attribute uses and values to speechmaking based on what needs it meets. In other words, rhetoric has what Marxists would call a *use value* in any social system. Like other commodities produced by human labor, it has the qualities Marx requires of a commodity, an "ability to satisfy some human want" whether this springs from "the stomach or from the fancy."[5] To say Frederick Douglass was a popular or effective speaker is to say that audiences attributed a use value to his rhetoric.

Although it is important, the use value of rhetoric in a social system is not the only part of rhetorical culture. Aside from the way rhetoric was commodified, we will have to consider other elements of rhetorical cultures, such as the rhetorical *theories* that become widely mentioned and influential in them, even if few people have read the words of the actual theorist. Rhetorical culture is also the result of numerous discussions and *criticism* of specific speakers' qualities by academics and popular authors, which are fed by the constant stream of rhetorical *acts*. These three, the rhetorical theory, criticism and practice that filter in to public awareness, are the occasions where ethos expectations are created in any rhetorical culture.

Finding the use value of rhetoric in the antebellum rhetorical culture is the focus of this chapter. A deeper investigation of the rhetorical theory and criticism of the day is the focus of the next.

In the broadest sense we can say the rhetorical culture changed markedly from the late eighteenth to the mid-nineteenth century because the need for rhetoric changed as the makeup of the audiences changed. As though anticipating Douglass's appearance on the scene, ever more room was made for entertaining speakers in the nineteenth century progressed through the Jacksonian era (1825–1844) and into the Civil War years when the trends changed once again. Speakers who contradicted the audiences of the "common man" learned quickly that the classical mode of rhetorical practice had been left behind. Speakers in the revolutionary era operated with the classical understanding, coming from Aristotle and holding through Quintilian, that speakers and audiences both came from the elite ranks and charted the course for the whole society. In antebellum society, however, the polity was receptive to many new types of speakers, not just the propertied elite, primarily due to the democratic mood and social reforms of the early 1800s that overturned many of the stratifications of the early American Republic. The upheaval leading in to the middle of the nineteenth century is important to realize since we can tell that Douglass took advantage of that peculiar moment in the evolution of ethos to inject himself into public consciousness. He did so by appealing to the desires of the democratic-minded audiences for heart-wrenching and sidesplitting oratory, an act that would have been impossible before the 1830s, when opinion leaders were all more or less staid aristocrats.

The peculiar moment of changing standards can be attributed to numerous social changes, but of all of them, the most portentous for rhetorical practice had to do with quantity. First, the sheer number of opportunities auditors had to hear and read speeches drastically increased. Second, multitudes of lower class Americans were attending public speeches for the first time in the nineteenth century. Together, these phenomena of abundance created a scene where many people heretofore unaccustomed to public life were presented with the opportunity to become active *citizens*. The Jacksonian era saw artisans, field hands, western settlers, immigrants, and upper-class women appropriating political voices for the first time.

But because of the newness of their status as public actors, these same people were faced with a quandary: How should they act in public? Putting on the airs of the aristocrats — the public men of previous generations — was out of the question for anyone from the rising classes in an America increasingly consumed with leveling and equality.[6] And too, women had few role models to teach them how to act in public. Women were still expected to act "feminine" in their public enterprises. So by what means did this diverse group participating in the *vita activa* for the first time decide what type of audience they would become?

The short answer is that they gravitated toward rhetoric with the proper use value, rhetoric that both affirmed their position as public actors and established an inherent behavioral standard for its democratic audiences. The most useful rhetoric established standards for audiences based on what had previously been acceptable behavior for lower classes and women in public and private — extreme emotionality. The new form of rhetoric sanctioned by the coalition of women and "common" men made it allowable to display emotions from boisterous joy to keening lamentation, but (and this is the key for ethos) *only as long as the speaker was given credit for producing the effect.* In the press coverage for the most celebrated orators of the day they are described, almost without fail, as speakers who had "power over" the audience to move them to emotional heights of laughing and weeping.

THE USE VALUE OF RHETORIC IN DOUGLASS'S AMERICA

People of every age make space in the governance of both the state and their personal lives for rhetoric. Exactly how they do it profoundly affects ethos expectations. If rhetoric is valued as a democratic practice that gives the citizenry the opportunity to participate in government (as was the case in democratic Athens), audiences will expect rhetors to prove themselves knowledgeable of political, historical and military matters as a justification for their policies. In a fascist nation, rhetoric is a tool for unifying the masses so audiences seek out their leader's discourse to know what practices and ideas are popular (or at least safe), so the backing of the state is the only necessary source of "credibility."[7]

Besides its particular role in the *agora*, though, rhetoric's ability to meet the private desires of the populace determines the societal value of oratory and sets demands for ethos. In Republican Rome, for instance, rhetorical training was sought most often as a means of advancing in law or politics to a high position in society.[8] Rhetoric had evolved out of its role in ancient Athens, and ethos was much more than a factor in judging the orator's policy or case; it was a gauge of how far one could advance in society.[9] Establishing ethos in rhetoric did not just make the orator believeable, it gave him the ability to acquire wealth and power. It could make you a "new man" or *novus homo*. Accordingly, ethos was not left to be established only in the moment of delivering the speech as Aristotle would have wanted. The Roman rules of rhetoric, as laid out by Cicero, state that ethos is largely determined by what an orator does in his life outside the speech. Roman audiences considered how much *dignitas* an orator had exhibited and how much *honore* he had earned.

In the flourishing of rhetorical activity in antebellum America, rhetoric served many purposes. In Douglass's particular case, he was attempting to build a career as an abolitionist spokesperson by tapping in to the widespread mood of reform. Messages of moral reform, given the influence of enlightenment thinking on American luminaries, were usually conflated with messages of political and social reform because personal improvement and education were seen as the route to improvement on a larger scale. In a sense, rhetoric of reform offered both a social use value — an improved society — and a personal use value — self-improvement — in the same package.

The major challenge for Douglass, and thousands of other speakers, was that the notion of reform was so widespread and so generally applied, that audiences had a surplus of opportunities to experience reform messages. The surplus is usually described as a "bright period" in American oratory, describing both the popularity and quality of the speeches. But for abolitionists, with their strident, uncompromising view of reform, there could hardly have been a worse environment.

As early as 1810, an editorial in the influential Monthly Anthology and Boston Review commented on the American mentality toward its oratory: "[n]otwithstanding the obstacles which the regular organization of parties, and the superior diffusion of intelligence, and a spirit of calculation among our people, oppose to its advancement," the editors assert, "we believe that greater effects may be produced by it among us than in any nation since the days of antiquity."[10] Many critics have agreed with this writer about the importance of oratory to American society in the early half of the century, what has been called the "golden age of American oratory."[11] The truly revealing part of the quotation, though, is the list of forces that were seen as "obstacles" to the genius of oratory — factionalism ("the regular organization of parties"), faith in the Enlightenment to raise everyone to a new consciousness (the ironically stated "superior diffusion of intelligence"), and a cost-benefit approach to life (the "spirit of calculation"). These very forces, still nascent in 1810, would grow in strength and shape how consumers of rhetoric chose their rhetorical outlets. Audiences were willing to abandon traditions and standards if they didn't measure up to the cost-benefit calculations. In addition, all oratory was compared to and influenced by the oratory of political theater that was bred from the extreme factionalism. Finally, audiences possessed an Enlightenment-inspired self-confidence that made the abolitionist brand of reform rhetoric seem unnecessarily strident.

The idea that prior to the Civil War, America was awash in a uniform kind of reform oratory, and that the method and message offered by Frederick Douglass and William Lloyd was essentially the same as that of the evangelistic preachers and reformers of every other stripe is simply wrong. Douglass and his allies demanded what amounted to a social revolution, a message that stood in stark contrast to the bulk of early nineteenth-century oratory.

The "Spirit of Calculation"

The first key to the antebellum valuation of rhetoric is found in the preponderance of oratorical acts that, in effect, saturated the marketplace of ideas and gave people a huge number of pastime choices. Audiences had to be calculating, carefully choosing which of the selections would best meet their needs and desires.

One of the first manifestations of the market revolution that would sweep America in the nineteenth century was on the speaker's platform. From the encomiastic Fourth of July orations to the most obscure informative lectures in lyceums around the country; from the halls of Congress where Webster, Hayne, Everett, Clay, and Calhoun set the course of the country with widely read addresses to the myriad pulpits where preachers (having refined their discourses according to the precepts of no less than Whately and Quintilian) commented on that course in their solemn sermons; from stump speakers who gloried in being base, common, and popular to the revivalist speakers urging the masses to answer a higher calling; and from textbooks and readers like Douglass's beloved *Columbian Orator* that cited the purple passages in celebrated speeches — from all these and more, most every American learned an appreciation and understanding of the power of rhetoric to move individuals, establish policy, and create community. And while rhetoric was important in people's lives, the surplus of oratory along with the ability of audiences to choose from multiple venues in the same short time and space, meant speech-making was one of the first American "industries" to be subject to the vagaries of the marketplace. This is a far cry from the early American experience where, as Clark and Halloran have described, political oratory was more or less dutifully attended and viewed as a process for building a properly elevated moral sensibility.[12]

Even slaves, who had a much more limited exposure to the public oratory of lyceum lecturers or congressional speeches, were immersed in oratory in their daily lives. Blassingame describes a slave community were slaves had ample opportunity to hear itinerant evangelists, and Genovese likewise explains that many slaves could hear church rhetoric on a weekly basis, both from white and black preachers.[13] Going even further, Asante maintains that because blacks brought to America "a fertile oral tradition augmented by the persuasiveness of *Nommo*, the generating and sustaining powers of the spoken word, the Africans' use of the word permeated every department of life."[14] In support of this view, Douglass himself tells how he listened critically to sermons to learn about oratory, and, while still a slave, he engaged in debating activities and even preached to fellow slaves.[15] Although his experience with such a full range of oratorical activities was not typical of all slaves, it does indicate the extent to which, in the nineteenth century, even oppressed people with little or no "free" time would seek out oratory for entertainment and enlightenment when not otherwise occupied.

The awareness of oratory for anyone who lived within a half day's ride of a town must have been something like the awareness of movies Americans have in the late twentieth century. If they weren't attending speeches in person, they were reading about them in popular magazines. The number of magazines increased from twelve in 1800 to almost 600 by 1850.[16] As Mott describes in his *History of American Magazines*, several different periodicals — especially those of the South — regularly published the entire texts of popular and political addresses as a way of disseminating the orator's message, but also as a way of exposing readers to the preeminent American art form.[17] Seemingly as frequent, a published collection of an orator's speeches would be reviewed by a magazine, providing an excuse for the writer to reflect on the state of American oratory. The death of a truly famous orator would bring forth eulogizes complete with appropriate comments on his character and the unique nature of his speechmaking for years to come. Years afterward, any given magazine might fill a dozen pages with a remembrance of Daniel Webster or John C. Calhoun and know that its readers would be interested. Oratory was a celebrated event and orators were celebrities in a way that is not terribly different from the way movie stars treated today. This was, after all, the era where image campaigns were invented, and American electoral politics first became concerned with mass appeals.[18]

Besides the abundant coverage in popular magazines, Americans were also exposed to oratory from newspapers and small-circulation periodicals. The year 1833 marked the beginnings of the "penny presses" in America, venues that relied heavily on local advertising dollars rather than subscriptions to keep them in business. These locally sensitive papers would carry news and reviews about local oratorical events so as to compete with larger circulation periodicals that carried national news.

From the 1830s through the 1850s, from both large and small presses, readers were treated to a steady stream of speeches and reviews. If a speech came from a famous figure or speculated on a topic that was a particular interest of the editor it was reviewed in the newspapers somewhat like a movie would be reviewed today. An oration received praise or scorn in print both for its message and the degree of artistry in its presentation. And, almost without fail, the response of the audience received comment — a loose parallel to the practice of reporting the top ten movies so as to recommend them *ad populem*.[19]

Orators were, by the nature of their industry, vying for audiences much as movie companies do today. Being built up as a celebrity lessened the challenged of gaining an audience somewhat. But most orators, even the ones with name recognition, recognized that the "customer is always right" motto was the best approach to acquiring and pleasing an audience. Pessen, for one, has commented that politicians became "sycophants, not statesman" at this time.[20] A more sensitive account is given by Tocqueville, who recognized that the orator's need to identify with the *interests* of the democratic audience did not necessarily mean they pursued the policies of their constituents. According to Tocqueville, this is why American political orators "include both an examination of all the great affairs of state and a catalog of all their [the constituents'] petty grievances" for it is "on these terms they promise to vote for him again."[21]

By pointing out the calculating mentality of antebellum consumers of oratory I am not trotting out another version of Plato's criticism of democratic oratory and sophistry.[22] Plato's concern was the demagogues' love affair with the *demos* (the people) and the resulting compulsion to offer the beloved whatever she wanted to hear. Against them Plato counterpoised his champion, the philosopher, a man in love with the Truth who would therefore speak truthfully even at the cost of his own popularity.

My depiction of rhetorical culture has little to do with the presence of Truth in nineteenth-century rhetoric, and everything to do with the commodification of speeches. In Athens, commodification was not a concern: there was no need to draw an audience to hear political speeches because the system assured a fairly static audience. Modern election campaigns attempting to win voters were unheard of, as were reform movements — those private collections of citizens banding together to raise public awareness about a social issue. Most importantly, there was not a series of "lyceums" in Athens, but one. Boston's rhetorical culture was therefore very different from Athens's and dominated by the need to acquire audiences. As the *New York Review and Antheneum* suggested in 1825, the "readiness with which an audience is obtained" in all these lyceums for "every species and variety of popular discourse" was "at once proof of their interest and utility" for Americans who had a felt free to attend any of the dazzling variety of oratorical offerings.[23]

Does Plato's critique of Athenian demagogues apply at all? He was not concerned with the way orators piqued the interests of possible audiences, nor with the actual utility of lyceum lectures in people's private lives (*per se*). In the nineteenth century both were factors that drew people to a lecture and away from other entertainment venues; interest and utility were the reasons people followed oratorical events so closely in their newspapers when they could not attend in person. For one example, starting in 1834, politicians were competing for audiences with events such as circuses, whose bandwagons were much more fascinating and exotic, and whose large, illustrated advertisements were meant to "excite the curiosity of the people."[24] In such a context, orators had to pay close attention to their star appeal.

In contrast, Plato's complaint about the *demos* wanting to see its every whim mouthed by the sophist assumed a citizenry that was already dutifully attending political assemblies in order to decide public policy. The obligation Athenians felt to participate in the government was much more like Clark and Halloran's description of the early American republic, where the participation of elites in oratorical events was part of *noblesse oblige.* Antebellum audiences were not *obligated,* they were *courted* by public figures, and the audiences, in turn, sought out celebrities who, they felt, would assure them of a good show. In a society where entertainment goods were industrialized, celebrities were like brand names that the consumer trusts to delivery quality. There were, as the *New York Review* exulted in praise of Edward Everett, "men whose gifts and acquirements entitle them to attention."[25] The press accounts of orators, like the movie reviews of today, helped people to make good "calculations" about the spending of precious free time.

The "Regular Organization of Parties"

The comparison to late-twentieth-century movie culture brings to the fore the place of oratory as an entertainment medium and individual speeches as productions vying for audiences. The comparison does fail at certain points, however. Much more so than today's movie culture, nineteenth-century oratorical culture was acutely partisan in its politics. Mott writes that "The violent political contests of the times are, in general, mirrored in the magazines."[26] Partisanship played several important roles in the commodification of oratory: (1) it subtly altered the nature of oratorical contests by emphasizing repeated, almost predictable or "staged" factional disputes; (2) oratory was therefore treated as a medium of entertainment, almost as though it were a sport, sought for its pleasing qualities and competing with plays and circuses for audiences; and (3) middling and lower class audiences, aware of the similarities in entertainment media, carried over their raucous, emotionally charged responses to other low-brow forms of entertainment to their newfound pastime of oratory.

Speeches were indeed given a great deal of coverage in American periodicals, but for speakers who advanced policies contrary to the editorial stance of the paper, or — a worse offense in the hyper-partisan Jacksonian era — if speakers were members of an opposing party, they could rarely receive a positive response from that press. Although many magazines and some newspapers were ostensibly non-partisan, in the ones that were not, writers were averse neither to presenting counter-arguments in the course of reviewing a speech, nor to impugning the character of the orator. One of Webster's democratic critics, for instance, writes "No, Mr. Webster, this is one of the tritest of falsehoods. The 'great interests of society,' so far from being 'harmonious and united' are discordant and separated.... Will any sane or sagacious man pretend that any two of the leading classes of society, have common interests?"[27]

Rather than convincing the public that every politician was a liar, a fool, or a crook (or that the media had a concealed liberal or conservative bias), these antagonisms seem to have served to raise prurient interest in political oratory as a form of contest, especially for middle-class voters who suddenly found themselves the audience for much of this speech criticism.[28] This "constant necessity and consequent love of argument and discussion"[29] as one critic called it, was particularly acute if an oration could be placed in the context of a debate, such as the ones between Webster and Haynes, Brownlow and Pryne, or the minor ones in debating societies throughout the country.[30] This means democratic-minded audiences enjoyed a certain type of moral rhetoric — the kind found in stylized contests between two clearly defined sides.

Audiences at the turn of the twenty-first century tune in to shows such as *Crossfire* where representatives of the right and left argue with each other. Just as the entertainment value and not the moral lessons inherent in the clashing of perspectives is the primary drawing card for those shows, so antebellum audiences attributed to many of the debates they heard roughly the same degree of significance they might give to a melodrama or a cock-fight. Because it presented stories of good and evil in an appealing package, oratory was just another pastime for many Americans, with little to distinguish it from the theater and the Wild West shows. And, just as they worried about other lower-class endeavors, the upper classes fussed about the moral degradation resulting from the morality of the popular culture that was as flimsy and palatable as a circus confection. They worried about how people would act in these public performances, if social order and divisions could be maintained. They were also concerned that real morality went unrepresented.

The criticism of popular oratory in the early stages of the Jacksonian period sounds very much like the criticism heaped on other popular amusements such as the theater. This is one of the best proofs of the rarity of revolutionary rhetoric that rebuked the masses for their moral failings. A comparison to the arguments over melodramatic theater reveals how upper class reformers and their foils, the popular audiences, esteemed oratory and other forms of public entertainment. The connection is not as tenuous as it might at first seem because orators were not infrequently compared to actors, and their platforms to stages.[31] Prior to 1885, many students in secondary schools participated in extracurricular programs in oratory with "musical exercises interspersed." These exhibitions "were often criticized for their 'theatrical cast' which at the time did not seem quite moral enough for the public"[32] according to the elite critics.

Antebellum theater critics complained that melodramas, with their simplistic warfare between good and evil, were "'vulgar,' tasteless, perhaps even violations of moral decorum."[33] The most vehement critics worried about theater's propensity to present spectacles with little moral substance merely to draw a large audience. In this they drew on the ideas of the belletristic rhetoricians who saw taste as a faculty that needed to be cultivated and refined. Worse, the elites worried that without exposure to better art the surly crowds would be overwhelmed by their unruly passions.[34] Summarizing the concerns of many critics, Grimstead notes that drama "had to attract all segments of the community and to appeal instantaneously without alienating any significant portion of the its audience; plays [as one antebellum critic put it] 'had to be addressed to the people immediately' and arouse in them 'an ardent sympathy.'"[35]

Critics were expressing similar concerns about all forms of popular culture by arguing that a work of art could not lead people to make good moral choices if it refused to take any strong moral stance or deal with any serious issue. They saw that if topics of social concern such as temperance and abolition were ever broached on stage, they "were put in a form that could be resolved by a moral platitude."[36] As much as the lack of artistic depth caused by the need to appeal to all factions in the audience, these critics show that arousal of "ardent" emotions was an equal cause for concern by men and women of standing. The theater was disconcerting to those who knew how to be reserved and dignified in public because of the coarse spectacles were arousing undue emotional and vocal responses. Women especially, whose natures were more delicate, were in double danger: they could be at the mercy of a man in the audience who was overwhelmed by his sensuous nature, or their own innate higher virtue might be subverted by the spectacle before them.[37] The lower-class theater audience, just like the lecture audience, was perceived as one step short of constituting a mob.[38] The difference is that an outpouring of emotion during a play constitutes merely a breach of decorum, but if citizens are consumed by emotion while participating in governance, the results could be disastrous for the country.

However accurate the critics' analyses may have been about the prurient nature of popular pastimes, it is clear that the audiences were unmoved by the reformers beseeching them to pursue more redeeming pastimes. There is little in the way of direct evidence of popular responses to aristocratic complaints, but the people were showing their lack of response by their continued presence in the theaters. In the second quarter of the century they were flocking to playhouses in droves to spend their off-work hours in an hour or two of diversion. Once there, to the reformers' dismay, they were often treated to moral dilemmas that were shams, because the complications were smoothed over and the problems too easily solved, all because the producers wanted to keep the entertainment value high.

For their part, audiences felt entitled to relaxation and diversion after working long hours in the repetitive jobs that they were offered in the dawn of the industrial revolution. Relaxation could be found in the melodramas, or by spectating at oratorical contests through actual attendance or, as all good fans do of their sports events, by reading coverage in print sources. Miller, describing the diversionary implications of political debates puts it well when he writes, "For a citizen of the second quarter of the nineteenth century, the closely printed columns of the *Globe*, or, more likely, of his own local penny paper reprinting long congressional speeches, were a more potent equivalent of today's C-Span.... Politics was your baseball and maybe your situation comedy as well."[39]

Even women, not yet entering the work force in great numbers, felt justified in capitalizing on diversionary pursuits. This helps explain the (often guilty or reluctant) presence of women at theaters and popular lectures, inasmuch as advice books were commenting on the stresses of antebellum life, which were a special strain on women's delicate natures. Ladies' advice books were even recommending that they needed the relaxation afforded by such entertainment venues.[40]

In sum, both men and women demanded the right to be audiences for any kind of diversion they chose, a miscellaneous list that included competing "carnivals, parades, executions, ship launchings and other free fare... hosts of low-priced exhibitions in museums (including theatrical performances)" as well as "concerts, lectures, and other kinds of presentations."[41] And so, antebellum orators were faced with another form of consumerism — the need to compete not only against other orators for the attention of audiences, but against other forms of public entertainment that were little more than spectacles. Ironically, orators encouraged some of this competition by taking their performing cues from actors in the elocutionist school of rhetoric (such as Thomas Sheridan's *A Course of Lectures on Elocution*) and by delivering their speeches so (melo)dramatically that many observers had trouble distinguishing orators from thespians.

By the mid-nineteenth century, melodramatic qualities infiltrated most oratorical practice. Audiences were content to let the simple morality plays work themselves out on various rostrums in the form of debates and orations, as reformers championed labor reform, utopian visions, tract societies, or what have you. At the same time, they were becoming increasingly unwilling to *participate* in the moral dilemmas themselves. Banner's analysis is probably accurate:

> one suspects that restless Americans, enthused by their ministers' nationalist and millennial rhetoric to expect rapid social improvement in their country free from the vices of Europe, would not long remain satisfied with the obvious inability of Bible and tract distribution [among other reforms] to accomplish the revolutionary social effects their promoters claimed for these charities.[42]

Some of the lower and middle class Americans would meander from movement to movement. The majority, though, simply became jaded and learned to scorn any strong reform rhetoric.

Of all the lectures and presentations, the abolitionist variety of rhetoric was particularly prone to being advertised and promoted as a diversion or showpiece. As one opponent snidely remarks in a New York *Times* review of an abolitionist gathering, he expected to see more "Negress speakers" in the future merely because they would draw curious onlookers. He even attributes the bulk of the audience to curiosity rather than commitment, saying: "I leave it to New-York auditories to say that, after eliminating all who go from curiosity, and all who go as I do, to spy out the nakedness of the language, the remaining portion of elect zealots is very small, very heterogeneous, and very feeble."[43]

As much as they might scorn such comments, the abolitionists tended to bring them on themselves. Garrison, for example, clearly took some cues from the busker tradition in building Douglass's reputation. In the biggest speech of Douglass's young career as an abolitionist speaker, Garrison introduced him with all the dignity of a carnival announcer: "It is recorded in holy writ that a beast once spoke," he declares, then announces, "A greater miracle is here tonight. A chattel becomes a man."[44] Additionally, the call-response style in the oratory of ex-slaves, a hold-over from the oral cultures in Africa and the plantation,[45] gave to abolitionist rallies a boisterous mood that other oratorical events could not offer. The slaves became the oppressed heroes rallying the crowd to be on their side in the fight against evil overlords. And, as in the case of the melodramas, many "refined" critics only needed to see these elements — the strong emotional audience response to a good-versus-evil morality play — to condemn abolitionist rhetoric as low class boosterism, an immoral way of arousing undue "ardent sympathy."

It was rarely admitted that even the most proper congressional oratory was consumed by audiences in much the same way. In fact, the floor of the Senate chamber had its share of public spectacles. On the occasion of Webster's reply to Hayne over states' rights, "The very stairways were dark with men who hung to one another like bees in a swarm" so crowded was the place with politicians and "men and women of fashion and influence." In Webster's famous speech that day he assumed the moral high ground and interjected a comment about the "morbid sort of fervor" the topic of nullification had aroused in all quarters,[46] as if he were not the culprit ultimately responsible for fanning the flames of a nullification "crisis."

The Therapeutic Value of Oratory

In terms of consumption practices of audiences, then, antebellum reform oratory, even some delivered in the halls of Congress, needs to be considered alongside the less laudable diversions of prizefights and melodramas as *spectacles of confrontation* staged for the viewing pleasure for audiences, male and female alike. Audiences of all backgrounds, but especially the newly publicly active categories of women and middle-class men who were raising their social status by virtue of long and draining workdays, derived a use value out of diversion and entertainment. Despite the qualms of moralistic reformers and intellectual critics, this "emergent public" refused to repress their desire for lowbrow entertainment from their politics. They sought out the staged controversies and even engaged themselves in the conflicts through cathartic expressions of emotion. Serving its functions of satisfying desires and providing catharsis, the antebellum rhetorical culture was constituted as a thoroughly *therapeutic* one inasmuch as its primary purpose to make people feel better and adjust to the pressures on their lives.

Thus, in the 1830s and 1840s, many audiences were not only resistant to messages by reformers, but they were downright fed up with oratory that castigated them for sins or demanded their response to social ills. Because they were showing a growing consumer consciousness, the people making up the audiences began to act more like consumers even in choosing which rhetorical performances to attend or "consume." They were led by a therapeutic mentality, as Philip Rieff describes it in *The Triumph of the Therapeutic*, where entertainment is the highest good and boredom the most common evil. Therapeutic goods are sought for no other reason than their ability to manipulate ones' sense of well-being.[47]

T. J. Jackson-Lears has also persuasively argued in *The Culture of Consumption*[48] that consumer culture was attended by a "therapeutic" mentality: the nineteenth century American public began to seek out goods in hopes of making themselves feel better. Drawing on magazine advertisers from the 1870s through early 1900s, the author shows how advertisers played upon the emotional needs of audiences to sell products. Before the heyday of advertising, though, during Douglass's ascent in the early decades of the century, vaunting and hucksterism happened live and "in person" as organizers and promoters attempted to draw people to attend their production that evening. Although Jackson-Lears may be right that American society as a whole would not be driven by the therapeutic ethic until the turn of the twentieth century, the rhetorical culture saw the effects of consumerism much earlier first because public oratory was the means that citizens had always used to secure their identities. Only later did the market become the focus and determinant of people's identities.

The elements of the therapeutic culture that Rieff and Jackson-Lears lament all appear in the rhetorical culture of Douglass's day. For instance, Douglass details in one of his later biographies how, in his early days as an unknown speaker, he would have to walk through the town of his evening's lectures, banging a pot and announcing "Frederick Douglass, abolitionist lecturer to speak tonight!" in order to literally drum up his own audience.[49] Orators were forced to work this way — in effect, to sell themselves — to convince people that their speeches offered something that people needed and wanted, even if it meant parading oneself down the street as a curiosity.

Jackson-Lears explains that "[i]n earlier times and other places, the quest for [mental and physical] health had occurred within larger communal, ethical, or religious frameworks of meaning." What happened to make the nineteenth century different is that "those frameworks were eroding [and] the quest for health was becoming an entirely secular and self-referential project, rooted in peculiarly modern emotional needs — above all the need to renew a sense of selfhood that had grown fragmented, diffuse, and somehow 'unreal.'"[50]

Jackson-Lears attributes people's quest to "find themselves" to a lack of contact with harsh realities and sobering commitments. This certainly applies to the 1870s and later, but it also applies to the citizens of the emergent public who faced a similar surreal political terrain from the abundant possibilities for asserting themselves socially, and the simultaneous remission of restraints and social stratifications. They certainly didn't want property restrictions for voting, and every American wanted to be called a "gentleman" or "lady,"[51] but when the much-scoffed-at social barriers were actually removed it resulted in a sense of *ennui*. Instead of being known by their trade and organizing their whole lives around an apprenticeship, local shop, and regular clientele, many workers became wage laborers in a factory process. Sharing the same hours, work and pay with dozens of others left them with a weak sense of self, and less knowledge of how they should act in public with their newfound "equality."

Thanks to printing presses and less than scrupulous printing houses, a surge of self-help tracts was available to those seeking control and stability in their lives.[52] Like the first robin signals the coming spring, self-help literature is a clear indication of a therapeutic mentality. People read them to learn how to act, or to feel better about the way they were already acting in public. In a world of shifting standards, the self-help tracts and magazine articles promised to provide internal control over the external chaos.

For the lower classes, oratory provided an especially useful therapeutic salve because it had already been sanctioned as a respectable pursuit for the most elite members of American society. However, the new audiences chose to attend oratory that roused strong emotions. Strong emotion perhaps provided a sense of reality and broke through their *ennui*, but it also gave code of behavior for public action since it was "caused" by a great orator.

Examples of audience submission to orators abound, but reports of Henry Clay's popularity are perhaps most revealing. After hearing one of his speeches, an audience member declared it would stand as an "epoch in our lives" such that they would date events according to whether they happened before or after seeing Clay.[53] Men hugged each other and women routinely fainted from the extreme emotion Clay inspired. If someone in the aristocracy of American oratory made them feel and act that way, though, they felt it must be acceptable.

Members of the emergent public found a similar use value for public messages that emphasized the inherent goodness and improvability of audience members, such as Emerson's lectures on self improvement. Equally useful was entertaining rhetoric, which may not have improved the listener's life in a substantial way, but provided an escape from the pressures of a self-nullifying or alienating job situation. The orator who either brought people to tears or peals of laughter, or who made people feel ennobled swiftly received the designation "eloquent." Orators who stroked the egos of their audiences could become popular figures, quite aside from any depth or vitality of their words. The powerful orator helped replace the lost sense of order and selfhood in the lower and middle class by lording it over them by invoking emotions, thereby making his hearers a certain type of person, people who felt and thought a certain way.[54] Orators who failed to incorporate these elements in their speaking, who only made people feel humiliated, could not fare well with the therapy-seeking public that was filling the auditoriums.

The upper classes did not, of course, immediately give their approval to the new forms of therapeutic oratory. Elite critics had been spouting the dangers of demagoguery for years in hopes of shaping the emergent public in the classical mold. In one speech, the 1809 version of the annual address to Harvard Phi Bea Kappas, the speaker gave a charge to the distinguished "men of letters" about the consequences of wasting one's leisure on the "profligate productions" of morally suspect speakers. The danger was having one's "passions disturbed" and one's mind "dissipated."[55] In other words, men of status were not to act like their emotional, irrational inferiors. By 1831, it was only the few remaining Federalist-leaning magazines that continued to criticize public displays of emotion by rhetors or audiences: "Let us leave to our western savages... the moral sublimity of an adverse doctrine, and endeavor to fortify the outworks of our social dominions against the fury of uncivilized sallies and licentious encroachments."[56]

The condemnation of emotional outbursts by the moralistic elites in the early phases of the democratic reforms was eventually replaced by an uneasy acceptance of the practice. By the 1850s the therapeutic use value of oratory was so ingrained in American life, the specter of "licentious encroachment" had become a symbol of the power of the orator. Even Whig critics were admitting that "Human nature itself... was made to be moved, excited, [and] impelled."[57] They concerned themselves with what the audience was impelled toward, in terms of policies or morality. The Democrats, though more egalitarian in their politics, were equally unconcerned in their criticism about audiences being overpowered by words, and could even be seen in print praising the Whiggish orator who inspired audiences and exhibited his "power."[58]

An entire school of rhetorical theory evolved to praise the values of "elocution" whereby a common speaker could cover his rough origins with formulaic gestures and delivery cues. One of the cornerposts of this theory was that orators must express their own emotions in order to excite the emotions of the audience. American critics were inspired by these in vogue theories, and gave high praise to the orator who clearly expressed his own emotions.[59] E. L. Magoon, who wrote two volumes on American orators (in 1848 and 1849 respectively), is representative of the trend where orators are fairly worshipped by commentators. For Magoon, though, power and eloquence only seem to come through the expression of strong emotion. "Magoon is a devotee of the oratory of bursts and flashes," Barnet Baskerville notes, "[h]e thinks of the noblest oratory as a collection of high emotional moments, spontaneous outbursts of powerful feeling which fascinate and enthrall the audience."[60]

Critics had the additional motivation of justifying to the world the American contribution to world literature. Many critics perpetuated the cult of the "powerful" orator, who was a "force irresistible"[61] and could play on the heart strings of an audience with a virtuoso's skill. They applied the same logic that warranted outbursts in the lower classes, namely, that such behavior was acceptable if it was caused by a "great man." This attitude is exhibited by the editors of the *American Quarterly Review* when they write:

> Great eloquence is impossible, unless it thus strip those to whom it is addressed of their independence, invest them with its own life, make them obedient to a strange nature, divest them of their peculiar qualities and affections and turn a multitude into one man....[62]

Desperate to bolster the American reputation for intellectual achievement, they allowed that the greatest "literature" might arouse more than moderate emotions.[63]

So although Rieff and Jackson-Lears both write about the heyday of the therapeutic mentality which occurred after the 1870s, its American roots reach down to Douglass's early career in the 1830s, 40s, and 50s, when the foundations were laid for the therapeutic mentality in the equalitarian reforms of the early nineteenth century. The "triumph" of the therapeutic mentality was established first in public life before moving into private life by way of magazine advertising of household products. In the period when therapeutic consumption was still public, political orators, even the aristocratic and powerful ones, found themselves catering to democratic-minded audiences. Unlike Plato's demagogues, the antebellum orators were not primarily concerned with advocating popular policies to curry favor. They were giving the people spectacles of entertainment, exciting their emotions, and presenting moral problematics that were easily solvable.

Therapeutic Rhetoric: Ramifications for Ethos

The outstanding consideration determining the use value of most rhetoric, including "reform" rhetoric, was therapeutic benefit. The antebellum rhetorical culture and its incipient consumerism offered success to an orator who had an ability to entertain, but only if he or she could avoid what was perceived as undue stridency and only if critiquing and rebuking the audience were avoided at all costs.

The tension between the power of an orator and the demands of audiences to be coddled gave rise to a social contradiction. If rhetoric was sought by popular audiences to help them adjust to pressures in their life or to make them feel better about their public actions as lower class actors, how could orators and leaders continue to be society's elites? How can the silver spoon crowd continually praise their "inferiors" and their inherent greatness without implicitly, and even explicitly, criticizing themselves?

In fact, they could not, and this meant orators had to change their ethos — the way they were identified in their speeches. Orators of the Jacksonian era were famous for attempting to be as common as their audiences. The most direct method to identify with the audience was by expressing extreme emotion in public. This phenomenon is most familiar to students of the political oratory of this era. Brogan comments about the political campaigns of the 1820s and 1830s, that "[i]t became ever more necessary for orators to flatter the sovereign people."[64] In the midst of the famous "log cabin" campaigns where politicians were stumbling over themselves to be more common and have more humble beginnings than their opponents, appearing morally superior and flaunting it were serious blunders (so much for Aristotelian ethos!). If an orator could not point to some kind of humble beginnings, log dwelling or otherwise, he could at least do as Webster did and publicly opine his privileged upbringing.

The abolitionists could hardly accept these limitations and remain principled in their demand that slavery be abolished starting immediately, regardless of the personal and financial cost to listeners. Unafraid to critique the noncommittal as vehemently as they attacked their ideological opponents, the abolitionists alienated many in their audience. The antebellum emergent speech-goers were accustomed to using participation in public life to shore up their identities. Orators were routinely identifying with them, lauding their wisdom and essentially moral natures. Abolitionists were therefore among the first to feel the backlash from capitalist consumers of rhetoric who preferred the patronizing appeals of General Jackson or the more conciliatory words of a less confrontational abolitionist such as Lyman Beecher or Henry B. Stanton to the stinging rebukes of an uncompromising Garrisonian orator.[65]

The antebellum rhetorical culture forced the abolitionists to come to grips with a new therapeutic mentality. The news was not all bad for reformers such as Douglass and Garrison. On the one hand, their stirring invocations of ideals of freedom and equality so reminiscent of the Revolutionary period and their sympathetic appeals using exquisite details of the physical and moral abuses of slaves made for good theater. Entertainment value was an important commodity and drew many people to abolitionist rallies that otherwise would have had no use for them. On the other hand, the moral mission of the rallies was vilified by many critics for requiring too much of its listeners. It led the country toward disunion, some said, while for others it was an attempt to circumvent the sanctifying power of God in society. Still others simply found abolitionist rhetoric too moralistic for their tastes — however much they agreed with its basic premises.[66]

The Garrisonians were aware of the political realities brought on by years of pandering rhetoric. If anything, the slave system was growing more firmly rooted after the first twenty years of the abolitionists' work while middling class voters were choosing the politicians and policies. Douglass and his allies had to break the cardinal rule of antebellum rhetorical culture: they condemned the audience for their public actions, their votes, and their complicity with racist laws and bigoted social norms. This meant they could not create a simple relationship of praising the audience and trying to identify with them as a social equal.

THE "SUPERIOR DIFFUSION OF INTELLIGENCE"

So far I have argued that a major goal of antebellum audiences in attending public lectures was therapy, the effort to manipulate their sense of well-being and ultimately confirm their prurient and "baser" desires. But there seems to be a counter-factual nature to this claim because of the type of oratory that the American landscape was famous for in the afterglow of the Second Great Awakening that led to what historian Henry Steele Commager has called "The Era of Reform."[67] Common opinion holds that the churches, buttressed by numerous traveling evangelists, temperance advocates, and educational reformers, drew people with a kind of oratory that challenged them to put aside their own needs and desires for a higher purpose. Realizing that this was not the case puts Douglass and his colleagues in the correct light, as part of the relatively tiny minority of speakers not offering easy, pleasing speeches. Douglass's effort to awaken listeners to the evils of slavery was, by all indicators, doomed to be ignored by audiences seeking to have their ears tickled by pretty speeches because those speeches were much more available and more suited to the "calculating spirit." The mistaken preconception that the early nineteenth century was awash in the rhetoric of rebuke and castigation needs to be addressed to fully appreciate the challenge faced by a fiery reformer of Douglass's caliber. In fact, rebuke rhetoric was rare in the pre-Civil War years because the key to social happiness for many antebellum preachers and reformers was the enlightened individual, not collective action or governmental proclamations.

For a better analysis, we need to make a distinction between what philosophers Austin and Searle have called "speech acts."[68] Speech act theory suggests that to understand the force of utterances, we need to look at more than just the locution of a speaker (the words used). We must attend to the illocutionary or social-performative aspects of someone's speech, and the perlocutionary aspect that creates social affects. Promising, apologizing, or warning someone are all examples of actions performed in speech.

By looking at the words and the relationship of speaker to listener, we can see a distinction between the speech acts used by Frederick Douglass and his cohorts and those of most other reformers of his day. One act is *scapegoating*, when the speaker places the blame for social and economic upheaval on a minority group.[69] Many politicians both then and now have tapped into the power of this act. The act of *exhorting* requires not only different words, but a different relationship between speaker and audience. Exhortation does not focus on blame for a wrong action. Rather, it calls the target to a better action or higher good. Neither blame nor condemnation is a necessary part of the act and therefore the speaker usually does not need to stand in a socially superior position to the audience. Finally, there is an act that Douglass, Garrison, and a few others were famous for. This is the act of *rebuking*. Rebuke rhetoric demands a change from the target. It also blames the very people targeted by the act for some problem as a result of their actions.

In the antebellum rhetorical culture, rebuke rhetoric was used to call the audience (and America generally) to account for their actions and urge them to do whatever was necessary to change their blameworthy behavior, including sacrificing their goods or, in extreme cases, their lives. The ethos of the speaker who rebukes an audience is built upon the ability to adopt a morally superior stance. The speaker's opportunities to identify with the audience are clearly limited by this speech act.

Categorized this way, we can see that rebuke rhetoric was a relative rarity in antebellum America, in both north and south, especially in the height of Jacksonian politics prior to the 1840s. The few speakers who made use of this act often aroused virulent reactions. So rare and unexpected was rebuke in the rhetorical culture, Garrison felt is was necessary to confront others' reform efforts in his famous statement in the first issue of his *Liberator*: "I will be as harsh as truth and as uncompromising as justice.... I will not retreat a single inch — and I will be heard."[70]

It is no surprise, then, that many of the responses to abolitionist rhetoric remark on their "holier-than-thou" attitude. Even in churches, where one might expect to hear stern messages of rebuke, parishioners were more likely to hear finely crafted speeches about the unlimited potential of regular people than to hear they were "sinners in the hands of an angry God." The role of the church in establishing public morality was forever altered by the Enlightenment "superior diffusion of intelligence." The Puritan era was fading and along with it the jeremiad form of speech that Sacvan Bercovitch has described, where the speaker stands as a prophet calling the people to repentance.[71] For such an appeal to be acceptable, the audience has to see salvation as an eternal and personal matter, not a means of humanitarian reform or a step towards a utopian society.

Church sermons gave the largest portion of Americans their first and most frequent exposure to speech making. Although sermons may have had primarily a hortatory motivation on the speaker's part, there is evidence that many attendees applied the same consumer logic to them that they did other forms of entertainment. By the 1820s, as Hocmuth and Murphy write, "Sermons had clearly become 'literary efforts' and were thought of as artistic productions, quite as much as were the essays in the *Monthly Anthology* or the *North American Review*."[72] This claim is supported by the great modern rhetorics that addressed themselves to the poor quality of pulpit oratory, from Hugh Blair's[73] and Richard Whately's[74] to the numerous homiletic handbooks published in the nineteenth century, which appropriated more advice from classical rhetoric than biblical texts for their advice to preachers. The homiletic handbooks became more popular as the nineteenth century unfolded. The small entertainment value (lamented as a "lack of eloquence") of pulpit oratory was even a topic of mention in literary magazines, which would find fault in a preacher if he had a tendency to travel "far into the recesses of doctrine" or used "a technical phraseology," or, really, allowed anything into his sermons that would reduce his appeal as an orator *qua* orator.[75]

The performance pressures on their religious counterparts were so famous, even secular rhetors were aware of them and felt moved to comment (and, usually, approve). Emerson, in his discourse on "Eloquence," tells a humorous story about a Harvard divine who "so disliked the 'sensation' preaching of his time, that he had once prayed that 'he might never be eloquent;' and, it appears, his prayer was granted."[76] More pointedly, Angelina Grimké Weld expressed the resentment of the abolitionist leadership when she told a Philadelphia gathering in 1838 that

> the great men of this country will not do this work [of abolition]; the church will never do it. A desire to please the world, to keep the favor of all parties and of all conditions, makes them dumb on this and every other unpopular subject. They have become worldly-wise, and therefore God, in his wisdom, employs them not to carry on his plans of reformation and salvation. He hath chosen the foolish things of the world to confound the wise, and the weak to overthrow the mighty.[77]

Because of all the emphasis on beautiful speech, for a large portion of the church-going public, a Sunday service may have been in part — or little more than — an opportunity to hear a rousing good talk. And if the topic was some tantalizing sin or if the sermon text was drawn from an absorbing epic from the Old Testament, the speech could be that much more entertaining.

Ironically, as the growing turmoil over American slavery in mid-century, as well as lesser dilemmas over immigration, Western expansion, and wage labor provided every person with at least some motivation to seek moral direction over difficult public issues, sermons increasingly lost the message of personal culpability that was one of the hallmarks of evangelical sermonizing from the late 1700s and the earliest years of the 1800s. In fact, as the century progressed, clergy showed a reluctance to make strident demands of parishioners for social action. Evangelists were taught by their famous predecessor Charles Finney to become more "theatrical," and to address the "animal feelings" of the listener.[78] Explaining how the nineteenth-century sermon served as public discourse, Hirst describes a

> theory shared by the majority of Northern, and by many Southern conservative clergymen in the nineteenth century, and its principles were made particularly clear in debates over social reform, especially concerning slavery. Fundamentally, the theory was that *individual* moral/spiritual and intellectual transformation, initiated and then aided by the right kind of preaching, was the key to social happiness; from the fountain of regenerated individual character would spring the right, enforced, and lasting response to every kind of social ill. Direct confrontation of social problems though rhetoric that attempted to incite mass movements only bred division and (usually) violence, and the changes it effected could only be partial, even when it was directed against real evils such as slavery.[79]

Why engage in the rhetoric of rebuke when it served only to create violence or resentment, especially if individual intelligence was a far better solution? Many divines, swayed by this conviction, engaged in a non-rebuke, entertaining style of "reform" rhetoric that flattered their flock and enticed them to rise above social ills, rather than condemning them for their culpable participation in the system.

With so much riding on the improvement of the individual, we can see why vituperative rhetoric assailing social ills was more rare than one might first expect from the era of abolition, temperance reforms, and the Second Great Awakening: appeals to improvement would, according to theory Hirst describes, have to addressed to the individual, not targeted to any group such as slaveholders or white Americans. It is one thing to launch into a jeremiad and confront an entire nation or community with its sin. But rebuke is a different task if both the source of problems and their solution lie within the individual, because it requires the orator to single out individuals publicly and call them to repentance with a list of particular sins.[80] More often than not, reform rhetoric in the "era of reform" consisted of encouragement toward personal improvement — a more acceptable mode of personal address to the calculating crowds, and a clear sign that individuality and faith in self-improvement had fought a battle against Puritan ideas of predestination and won.[81] Or, as both Perry Miller and Lois Banner argue, the revivalists held no hopes of controlling the crowds through their calls to repentance; they were desperately adjusting to social and economic conditions by giving the people the theology their optimism demanded.[82]

The faith in the common person to improve him- or herself was not exclusive to the pastorate. As Smith and Windes contend, the same self-improving spirit that inspired the Second Great Awakening led people to the popular belief that the forces of modernization and enlightenment would eventually get rid of slavery without direct confrontation.[83] Douglass himself was not averse to arguing a similar case, as we see in his famous Fourth of July speech: he predicts that modern travel is "shrinking" the world to such an extent that global pressure will eventually force the backward Americans to relinquish slavery. Like Douglass, many social reformers caught up in the excitement of millenarianism, preached a coming better age, thoroughly motivated by their faith in the perfectibility of human society. For them, there was little reason to rail against the people for slavery and other ills when all such problems would soon pass away as the ignorance that caused them was eliminated. What for Douglass was a calculated message in an address scripted to appeal to broad audiences, was an unshakeable tenet of most reform speeches. However, most of Douglass's and other Garrisonians' speeches were far from promoting a faith in a distant, progressive solution to slavery from an enlightened populace.

The waning of rebuke rhetoric is apparent in the way political topics where handled from the pulpit. Citizens newly active in the political arena were understandably upset with a clergyman or reformer who railed against one of the tenets of their first political party. The only truly safe "reform" rhetoric in the majority of Protestant churches was a strategy of scapegoating, blaming the "banking power" or the competition from Catholic immigrants for the economic woes of the common man.[84] Those speeches called for aggressive action against an Other, and so did not call for people to blame themselves, repent, or sacrifice anything substantial in response to recessionary woes. As Kenneth Burke recognized in his analysis of Nazi rhetoric, there is a socially curative — that is, therapeutic — function to the scapegoating speech act.[85]

As in politics, so in preaching, where it was easier for a speaker to assuage the flock with its mixture of party allegiances and middle-class parishioners who expected to be flattered by not giving sermons advocating personal blame and self sacrifice. The one safe "reform" topic for the preacher — the evils of drinking — was still fair game as a social issue. Why? None of the various political parties had established pro-drunkenness as one if its tenets. But in most other instances, the fire and brimstone that might have energized Christian reform rhetoric from the pulpit were supplanted by attention to oratorical excellence and audience delight.

Hatch in *The Democratization of American Christianity* and Hirst in "The Sermon as Public Discourse," explain that by the third decade of the nineteenth century many seminarians also had another tendency that led them away from rebuking parishioners, namely, a decidedly populist bent.[86] These populist preachers decried the traditions of pastoral education and claimed divine inspiration for themselves. As anti-aristocrats, they scoffed at the educational program that more traditional theologians advocated as a way of realizing the *vir bonus* standard, and according to their critics at least, were often guilty of building followings as a cult of personality, especially through ecstatic, highly emotional preaching.[87] Thus, in the 1840s can be found the beginnings of the Charismatic strand of American Christianity, which relies on charismatic orators.

If he wasn't building a following based on personal magnetism, the populist preacher was frequently a careerist who treated preaching as a respected means of social advancement and thought of pastoring as a profession, rather than a calling. His church was a business, with parishioners for clients. The populist preachers strove more than anything to please the masses. Audiences needed not even be devout to join their flocks, as long as they were devout in their attendance and giving. For populist preachers, as for politicians, reform rhetoric aimed at spurring large segments of the population to repudiate slaveholding or racial hatred was not a serious consideration. They did not want to infuriate their parishioners, that is, their customers.

THE RESENTFUL REACTION TO STRONG REFORM RHETORIC

Despite the constraints, the abolition and colonization movements picked up steam in the 1830s and 1840s. As the movement added converts, and increased their speaking itineraries and newspaper subscriptions, there was a growing sentiment, in the South especially but also in the North, resenting moral reformers of all stripes.

The reaction to an abolitionist lecture from the Geneva (IL) *Advocate* in 1846 is fairly typical. After attending a local abolitionist meeting, the writer proclaims of the speakers and their followers: "There's not a holier set of individuals in the world (in their own estimation) than this same fraction of the 'Great Heart (one idea) fraternity.' — and the language of their looks as well as their tongues is — stand aside, I am holier than thou!"[88]

Abolitionist rhetoric challenged the therapeutic benefits popular audiences received from other messages. It criticized their voting practices and inaction on slavery. It called them to sacrifice and work hard to bring about a social system that seemed to disadvantage them by creating still more competition for scarce jobs. It also called upon listeners to admit a certain level of equality with blacks.

The last call was most damaging to the newly active polity's sense of identity. Middle class whites were accepted into the franchise by being recognized as worthy of the vote. To further expand the franchise, they would have had to admit that their license to act for the public benefit was no more valid than that of women and minorities. In Condit and Lucaites's terms, this would be admitting their "social equality" with women and blacks.[89] The emergent public was ascribed a capacity for acting in public predicated on being equal in reasoning and morality to the aristocrats who had always assumed the place of political leadership. In their hierarchical imaginations, they could not adjust to the idea of being equal to their "inferiors" (non-whites and women) while maintaining their equality with their "superiors" (the aristocrats). If anything, the anti-therapeutic nature of Garrisonian rhetoric entrenched the popular audiences against abolitionists because their newfound sense of well-being was being challenged before it was cemented. To have it affirmed, they could simply choose different oratory to enjoy.

Many histories of abolition have missed the connection between the therapeutic impulse and the resentment of the antislavery movement in the 1830s. Merton L. Dillon in his book *The Abolitionists: Growth of a Dissenting Minority* perhaps comes closest when he observes:

> Neither the antislavery arguments abolitionists used nor the measures they employed in the early 1830s differed fundamentally from those of previous years. If Southerners reacted more shrilly and with greater degree of unanimity against Garrison's *Liberator* than they had reacted against [earlier abolitionist] Lundy's *Genius*, it was not because Garrison had hit upon more effective argument or because he employed more vivid and persuasive language than his predecessors had used; it was simply because the growing ease of communication in the 1830s and the increasing number of newspapers willing to take note of Garrison's writings gave his words wider circulation than had previously been possible.[90]

Dillon here recognizes that reaction to abolition rhetoric had to do with quantity, not quality, of the arguments.[91] Yet, he assumes that the dissemination of Garrisonian rhetoric increased the threat to slaveholding interests, and so the strident counterattacks he suffered were acts of defensiveness by those who relied on the slave economy. This does not explain, though, why many Northerners were as hostile to Garrison's message as people who actually owned slaves, especially if, as Dillon remarks, there were no major differences between the content and form of Garrison's rhetoric and that of his predecessors.

Another explanation for the revolt against Douglass's stinging rebuke rhetoric comes from Richards, who explains the most violent reactions — mob attacks on antislavery rhetors in the 1830s and 1840s — as an attempt by "gentlemen of property and standing" to maintain their elite status in society.[92] The upper crust of northern society, he asserts, were already reeling from Jacksonian social transformations and saw the abolitionists as advocates of miscegenation. This was the ultimate threat to the superiority of aristocratic whites, because it uncompromisingly declared the equality of all men even in social and economic relationships. Accordingly, it deserved the deepest antipathy and even justified violence. The leaders of Northern anti-abolitionist mobs saw themselves as protecting their way of life from an insulting intrusion by blacks, men who wanted to bed their women and take their jobs.

This explanation may account for the Northern loathing of the antislavery appeal after the 1830s, but does not explain the lack of violent reactions in previous decades. Nor does it apply to the physically non-violent but still angry responses of those who hated the abolitionist for being "holier than thou"; if anything, according to Richards, they should have found the abolitionists morally despicable miscegenationists. For these pieces of the puzzle, Richards implicates mass communication, as Dillon does:

> [T]he Garrisonians were weak and ineffectual; they had neither the means nor the power to disrupt the established order. With the revolution in communications and the creation of mass media, however, organized antislavery suddenly appeared to be a major "conspiracy" against the status quo.... Their exaggerated vision of a relentless, powerful [antislavery] "combination" terrified anti-abolitionists.[93]

By this explanation, mass communication lengthened the shadow of the movement, making it seem larger and more threatening. It is unclear why Dillon thinks this would concern those who were curious or noncommittal about the slavery issue yet who became furious over the rhetoric of *uppity* blacks and their allies. Such people, based merely on the appearance of widespread power, would have been more terrified of the powerful "combination" of pro-slavery interests. The strength of the "slave power" and the South in general in Northern politics would have been a much greater concern to most Northerners and a much more apparent one given the publicity lavished on Southern coups like the Fugitive Slave Law and Bleeding Kansas. If the simple formula of "expanding message = stronger reaction" were true, the antimasonic and nativist movement would have inspired its share of mob responses, and pro-slavery rhetors even more so because of the very real ability of the slavery power to influence the economics and politics of the North made them a truly ominous combination. Instead, widespread acknowledgment of the threat of southern domination was slow in coming and did not coalesce until just before the war in the very late 1850s (and then, only with Republican rhetoric directly inciting public fears).

So, while the increased opportunities for diffusing their message were indeed a great boon to Garrisonians, Dillon and Richards do not carry their cause/effect arguments to their logical completion. Neither considers the results of having vast numbers of arguments on *every* topic carried by mass media to new audiences. Abolitionists hardly had a monopoly on the media. Colonization advocates also had their allies in the news industry — more than the abolitionists, to be sure. But more importantly, arguments about tariffs, Western expansion, war with Mexico, accusations of Mason conspiracies, calls for increased missionaries to the Orient, and innumerable other topics were filling column after column of newsprint at the same time as the mere preponderance of abolitionist speeches was supposedly worrying opponents. Add to this the already-mentioned popularity of lyceums, the tradition of commemorative speeches on the Fourth and other days, and the sermons that, across the nation, were being treated as simply one more occasion to hear a speech, and you get a better sense of how antebellum audiences might have felt: the "tidal wave" of abolitionist speeches that modern critics see flooding public discussion in the 1830s and 40s would have been viewed merely as one of so many streams that fed into a tidal wave of public debate.

The ability to communicate abolition messages across distances was still an important change in the rhetorical culture, but not nearly so portentous in scaring opponents as it was in positively frustrating those who were uncommitted on the slavery issue. The comparative superabundance of all types and topics of rhetoric in an age of growing consumerism allowed people to opt for therapeutic discourses over the reformer's message of sacrifice and economic upheaval. In the midst of so much more pleasing rhetoric, abolitionist oratory created instant antipathy. It seemed, and in part was, the opposite of all the entertaining speeches that told audiences how enlightened they were.

Rhetoric as Therapy: Repercussions for the Ethos of Reformers

In light of the transformation of the sermon from a tool of religious exhortation to an artistic production, we need to review the stringent standards for clergy ethos that George Campbell laid out in his *Philosophy of Rhetoric*. This ordained Presbyterian minister, assumes that a religious leader has to balance carefully between extremes of temperament — he must be "grave without moroseness" and "firm in declaring the will of God" yet "mild in his addresses to the people" because auditors tend not to accept didactic messages from a person who rankles them, depresses or abuses them. At the same time, because the minister of the gospel is offering the Truth on matters of eternal importance, his attitude must also convey that seriousness, and "firmness" in response to the word of God.

When sermons are treated as oratorical events (an eventuality that both the apostle Paul and Augustine worried about because audiences would move their focus away from the content of the message[94]), the ethos demands for a preacher sway pendulously toward the "mild" end of the scale. Oratorical virtuosos put flourishes into their sermons that do not concern the strict moralist. The preacher/artist's words are judged for their beauty, elegance, and symmetry, as in other ceremonial speeches.[95] Of course, ceremonial speeches, what Aristotle called the "epideictic" speech genre, traditionally do not call for the audience to make a judgment. They are called merely to witness the orator's efforts and certainly don't expect to be called to any great action outside the church building.

SUMMARY

Antebellum rhetorical culture created a tendency to resent caustic or revolutionary reform rhetoric, first because oratory was quite prevalent — so prevalent, in fact, that
as discretionary income became a reality for Northern workers, speakers found themselves subject to the forces of consumerism and competing for audiences. Oratory was
often reported by the press and treated by the public as a spectator sport. We can draw
parallels between it and other entertainment institutions, in part because oratory
competed with theaters and sports as entertainment commodities vying for audiences
and their money. Commodified status had a deleterious effect on the ability of
oratory to be productive of major reforms. Competition and electioneering further
discouraged reform messages, at least ones that accused the audience of complicity,
because audiences could "silence" uncomfortable rhetoric by giving their attention
elsewhere. Lectures blaming social ills on immigrants or bankers were more pleasing
to the ear. Moreover, riding the tides of anti-aristocratic fever, orators had to appeal
to the interests of audiences, not merely rely on their social standing to impress
listeners. The appeal, in the aftermath of Jacksonian politics and democratic reforms,
tended to involve flattery of the "common" people in the audience (for little else than
simply being common) rather than admonitions to put moral reform ahead of their
personal desires. Sermons escaped neither the forces of consumerism, nor the pressure
to avoid criticism. The ideologies of individualism and enlightenment convinced
many preachers that criticizing the laity was less useful than exalting them. These
preachers were seeking, above all, to build big constituencies based on being likeable
and eloquent.

CHAPTER THREE

Antebellum Rhetorical Culture in Theory, Criticism, and Practice

The purpose of the last chapter was to present an argument about the value placed on reform rhetoric in the era when Frederick Douglass would have been engaged in public speaking. It argued that most Americans in the 1820s through the 1850s had little use for strong reform rhetoric, or what can be termed the *rhetoric of rebuke*. Entertaining rhetoric, though, along with extreme emotionality and a combative stance all had uses as therapy; the middling classes sought them out as ways of cementing their place in the public sphere and to make them feel good about their participation in public affairs. Partly due to the limited use of rebuke rhetoric, and partly because of the great surplus of oratory in the American "Golden Age," the abolitionists' favored mode — rebuke rhetoric — inspired strong, sometimes violent, responses.

In further describing the ethos expectations in antebellum rhetorical culture, this chapter builds on the foundation laid in the last one. There I discussed how people, especially from the lower classes, situated rhetoric in their daily lives, giving it social significance as a factor in ethos. Here I want to continue the "bottom-up" reconstruction of the rhetorical culture by addressing three major influences on the layperson's theory of ethos: rhetorical theory, criticism, and practice. All three prepared audiences, especially the white members of popular Northern audiences, have negative expectations of, but a positive response to, Douglass as a rhetor.

First, rhetorical theory can be seen to gradually abandon the *vir bonus* standard. Late-period theorists such as Whately begin to address personality appeals, and other rhetoricians show an increasing (and increasingly leery) recognition of the democratic audience. Second, a study of antebellum rhetorical criticism reveals a rift between writers who drew from literature for their critiques and those who approached oral events with an oral mindset. Many critics were upholding the ideals of character-based ethos, but were doing so on the basis of elite, literate audiences who took a more distanced and analytical approach to oratory. Other critics, those who didn't substitute a literate audience for the actual oral-minded audiences that were flooding to lyceums, show an appreciation for personality appeals. Third, the evidence from the rhetorical practice of the most celebrated orators suggests that many of them were beginning to see the power and necessity of using personality to reach potential voters. These three areas all indicate that a new kind of ethos was beginning to take the stage in the antebellum rhetorical culture that is comprehensible if we apply the idea of a character and personality distinction.

RHETORICAL THEORY MADE PUBLIC KNOWLEDGE

Of the major influences on ethos expectations, the impact of formal rhetorical theory is perhaps the most removed from popular audiences. However, the theories that orators learned in their school training, including the lessons on ethos, would have been apparent, in varying degrees, in the practice of the orators. Just like an orator who learned his craft from an elocutionist would have certain inflectional patterns and gestures, each orator would exhibit different personal qualities in an attempt to identify himself according to the theories that influenced him. Furthermore, there is evidence that even uneducated audience members would have been exposed to rhetorical theory, particularly through the magazines and newspapers they scoured for news of debates and speeches. Because of the unusual amount of attention to oratory in the first half of the nineteenth century, university-taught rhetorical theory is a legitimate source for understanding even the perspectives of popular audiences.

Rhetorical Theory in the Training of Orators in the Late Eighteenth Century

Some of the orators who found themselves adjusting to the mass audiences of the Jacksonian era were trained in the earliest days of the Republic. According to Guthrie's survey articles, "The Development of Rhetorical Theory in America,"[1] the late 1700s were consciously Republican and Roman in orientation. Cicero's *De Oratore* was very popular as was Quintilian's *Institutio Oratoria*, to a lesser degree.

Although the latter is more strictly moralistic than community minded, both of these Roman rhetorics promote an essentially civic approach to ethos. They demand that the orator establish himself as an urbane gentleman, one who comports himself with proper decorum and whose passion is for the social welfare. The so-called Port Royal rhetoric, a popular French text on rhetoric that made an effort to account for the modern distaste for topical systems, was a sensation in colonial America, but even it drew most of its advice on ethos from Cicero. The Port Royalists advised readers, "it is of importance that an Auditory has an esteem for the person who speaks.... Wherefore in an Orator these four Qualities are especially requisite, Probity, Prudence, Civility, and Modesty."[2] Ciceronian ideals can be seen in the distribution of the virtues: the personal moral quality of probity is supplemented, or balanced, by *three* virtues required of a proper public servant — *savoir faire*, and the social niceties of civility and humility.

Aside from the Port Royal textbook and the Roman texts, Guthrie cites the influence of Ward's *Systems of Oratory* as one of the most powerful influences in the late 1700s. Many college students relied on Ward's synthesis of the classical ideas and never read the originals. From his text, they obtained only one lecture on ethos out of fifty-four, or, the same amount of attention given to topics such as confutation and speech conclusions. And, if Ward's slight attention suggested that ethos was of little importance for the modern orator, his approach to the topic reinforced the idea. He recommends a "propriety of manners" to cover the orator's natural deficiencies.[3] He also specifically commends to the reader four qualities quite circumscribed in their scope: they amount to wisdom, honesty, kindness, and modesty. According to Ward, these four attributes are to be pursued, not because a thorough personal and civic goodness is necessary, but because the orator wishes "to please the palate" of his listeners. The emphasis from Ward's rhetoric is placed on the cultivation of a public persona and maintaining a good relationship with the audience, not on establishing an enduring, personal, moral code. Yet, morality and character were still at the heart of the image, however much a sham the image may be.

With the emphasis on appearances and public image in all these sources, orators schooled in the last years of the eighteenth century, if Henry Clay is a good example, seem to have received the message that "private" morality was less important to one's rhetorical effectiveness than a record of public deeds. Clay was part of that tradition of charming Southern politicians (still with us today) who are dogged by allegations of adultery and political corruption throughout their careers. He responded to the moral challenge by stressing his civic values, "by referring to his length of service, his legislative accomplishments, and his wisdom and experience" and by repeatedly making mention of "the sacrifices he had made or was willing to make for his country."[4]

Perhaps teachers of rhetoric in the late 1700s felt that Christian morality was sufficiently upheld by the church institutions so that the mention of private morality would be redundant. They might also have felt confident that public figures would come only from the best breed. Teachers would probably have held the chivalrous idea (one that persisted in the South well into the 1800s) that the nobility has an obligation to serve and protect its country and its lessers. Such men needed little advice about decorum from their rhetoric teachers. Both they and their equally aristocratic audiences had been trained in it since boyhood. As John Calhoun was purported to have said to Josiah Quincy, "I think you will see that the interests of *gentlemen* of the North and those of the South are identical." Quincy interpreted this as Calhoun's belief that "*Gentlemen* were the natural rulers of America."[5] Whatever their disagreements, their identification as part of the elite class tied these speakers together in a largely unspoken code of ethics. In the good ol' boys network that constituted the pools of speakers and audiences in the eighteenth and early nineteenth centuries, one's personal life was a secondary issue to one's public deeds.

Given a chance to see a performance from a follower of the Ciceronian school of Republican rhetoric (which included Ward and Quintilian), audiences would have seen them carefully displaying their refined mannerisms. The orators would have evinced a benign concern for the State and their constituents, and gone about the business of making policy. Responding to charges of moral lapse by political opponents, they would have defended themselves by pointing to their spotless record of public service.

Rhetorical Theory in the Training of Orators in the Early Nineteenth Century

The emphasis shifted in the nineteenth century away from classical authors, to modern authors who were adjusting their theories to account for mass audiences, the increased diffusion of education, and the latest philosophical and psychological developments. While Ward and the classics still found a place in the colleges as an authority on the rhetorical tradition,[6] George Campbell and Hugh Blair quickly became the reigning figures in nineteenth-century colleges. Their guidelines for ethos would have been held in high regard up through the Civil War years.

Campbell's and Blair's assertions about ethos are most indebted to Quintilian: they teach that a man must truly be good for ethos to support his argument, but each alters the classical formula a bit. Of the two Scots, Campbell's treatment of ethos was the most responsive to the needs of nineteenth-century orators in the States. He encourages them to develop a "sympathy" component in their ethos. This is a link established with the orator when an audience acknowledges the speaker's character. Sympathy, the "common tie of human souls," is the much like the "good will" construct of Aristotle and Cicero, but with a slight epistemological twist. Sympathy must first be established before the orator can rouse the emotions, and rousing the emotions is preliminary to achieving persuasion through the will. It is therefore an essential step in touching all the faculties recognized by Campbell's modernist psychology.[7]

The real significance of Campbell's formula, however, is not in the "chain of faculties" notion. Sympathy is Campbell's effort to respond to the modern person's sense that he or she is alienated from others and anonymous to them. Something must bridge the gap between orator and audience during the speech if the orator is going to share himself and help listeners feel and believe as he does. Endorsing sympathy as the key to rhetoric is only a step away from recommending that the orator "identify" with a popular audience by showing off his rough qualities. Indeed, Campbell fails to discuss how a refined orator can create sympathy with a provincial and earthy audience without being "immoral" even though he must have realized that his theory entailed just such a posture.

Balanced by his other writings on ethos, though, it would be a mistake to see Campbell as an advocate of sycophancy. As a result of the democratic reforms that swept England before America, Campbell vents his frustration at "party spirit" that can ruin the sympathy, or good will, the orator would establish. "Violent party men," he admits with clear distaste, "not only lose all sympathy with those of the opposite side, but contract an antipathy to them. This, on some occasions, even the divinest eloquence will not surmount."[8]

His criticism becomes more pointed when he remarks that the "gross" are most susceptible to prejudices. While the "men of sense and education" consider what is spoken, the "rabble" are more enamored with the speaker than with the speech, "From a consciousness, it would seem, of their own incapacity to guide themselves."[9] But in this last count, Campbell is wrong, as the last chapter showed. Audiences knew, and got from orators, precisely what they wanted to meet their needs. It is therefore not accurate when Campbell writes that democratic audiences

> are ever prone blindly to submit to the guidance of some popular orator, who hath had the address first, either to gain their approbation by his real or pretended virtues, or, which is the easier way, to recommend himself to their esteem by a flaming zeal for their favourite distinction, and afterwards by his eloquence to work upon their passions.[10]

It is worthwhile to carefully address the correlation of Campbell's words to the historical evidence. In the first place, audience approval was hardly blind; they kept a sharp eye out for those who confirmed their identity as public actors. In the second place, virtue, whether real or pretended, had little to do with the consumers' choices. Campbell's third point is more true than not: orators did ingratiate themselves with popular audiences by taking advantage of their zeal for "distinctions." On this count, though, Campbell can be faulted for assuming that the audience would blindly support the policies of an orator who had earned their approval. The logic of consumption dictates that orators would not be safe for long with this kind of appeal: the audiences would continually return for more, or they would gladly switch to another product (orator) that showed more promise.[11] (Campbell himself argues in the same section "to be good is the only sure way of being *long* esteemed good"[12] as partial recognition that ethos judgments are ongoing processes and the orator must prove himself anew each day.) Fourth and finally, in the passage above Campbell errs by interpreting the working up of passions as a way for the demagogue to move the relatively stupid commoner. In fact, emotional rhetoric was desired by and politically useful for the lower class audience much more than it was a tool for manipulation by the upper class orator. In seeking therapy through emotional rhetoric, the common audience was at its most calculating, not its least.

Despite his miscalculations in attempting it, Campbell's kind of rhetorical theorizing is closely involved with the concerns of the day and the dangers inherent in the democratic audience. It is at least possible that some American college men, reading their copies of *The Philosophy of Rhetoric* and the author's distress over party spirit and easily aroused crowds, read between the lines. Putting aside his reprimands, they could have decided that, to be popular, they needed to cultivate charisma rather than character. When more democratic rhetorical situations unfolded in America, these students would have been aware of the possibilities for power democracy afforded the orator.

Hugh Blair and the Moral Imperative of Sincerity

Despite the harbingers of change in Campbell's work, most theories in the early nineteenth century were still trumpeting the venerable *vir bonus* standard. What changed was the justification for the standard, a reflection of the changing definition of "good." An example of this is Blair's *Lectures on Rhetoric and Belles Lettres*, which was the "most widely used textbook" in American colleges, at least for advanced coursework.[13] Although he does not talk at great length about "ethos," his entire text could be read as a meditation on related topics. Since he couldn't presume that either orators or audiences would be from the ranks of the genteel, he links virtue (the traditional territory of ethos) with both taste and reason. The *vir bonus*, according to Blair's definition, is necessarily cultured and reasonable. More than an ethical framework, moral sensibility is a measure of aesthetic and intellectual acumen and represents the type of speaker that Blair hoped all the common and popular speakers would strive to become. Blair even ascribes an inherent aesthetic value to morality. The implication is that speakers should be good because they will benefit from the superficial attractiveness of an ethical life.

The belletristic qualities of the refined speaker's ethos are surprisingly close to other non-belletristic rhetorics. Blair mentions "probity, disinterestedness, candour and other good moral qualities of the person" as the things that "give weight and force to everything" one utters and even "add a beauty to it." The list is classical in its orientation, down to the recommendation of the *vir bonus* standard. In this case, though, the orator is encouraged to be a good man in large part so he can improve his own reason and taste and thus be a more discerning judge of the affairs and letters he might be asked to judge.

Above all the items on the list Blair holds a special place for "sincerity." Sincerity and vehemence, although moral qualities because they spring from "honesty," are necessary for being a speaker to be "natural." Blair does admit that craftiness in presenting a false image of oneself "may entertain and amuse." The problem with presenting oneself disingenuously is that audiences view the speaker's ethos "as artifice, as trick, as the play only of speech; and viewed in this light, whom can it persuade?" Only in the sincere expression of "noble sentiments" about "great subjects" can true eloquence be found.

The aptness of Blair's advice in this matter is hard to judge. Ethos must be connected to the speaker as the subject of an autobiography to work as ethos. However, it seems unnecessary to dismiss the power of being entertaining and amusing as Blair would prefer. The emerging public was drawn to entertaining speakers and was also clearly moved by them. Douglass's case is most applicable here, since he was certainly able to build his ethos using both resources. He was always an entertaining speaker, and humor, especially self-deprecating humor, was an important part of his appeal with white audiences. His wit, though, had clear resonances with the truth and was always based on his own experiences; the struggle on the plantation later provided a way to mock the slaveholder, and various relationships with pretentious white preachers helped him to subvert northern racism.

It is rather natural for the oppressed to assume the mantle of trickster or ironist, as Gates has argued.[14] It would be downright unnatural for them not to adopt a mode of relating to the dominant culture that does not challenge its negating authority. Hugh Blair, writing as he does for the most elite members of society in the effort to bring them up even higher, has no reason to familiarize himself with the type of person who can be mocking, crafty, and even duplicitous in self-presentation, yet still be absolutely true to his life experiences.

Richard Whately and the Particularity of Ethos

After Blair, the final important modern rhetoric is Richard Whately's book, *Elements of Rhetoric*. Written later than either Blair's or Campbell's, it also trailed them in popularity with American colleges.[15] As democratic reforms were increasingly solidified, so one of the most notable features in Whately's discussion of ethos is his lengthy treatment of party biases. Continuing the trend of recognizing the unique demands of the democratic audience, it is the most extensive analysis of factionalism yet seen in rhetorical theory. Whately even includes a clever analysis of *ethopoeia*, an underappreciated part of rhetorical theory that concerns the shaping of an other's ethos in your speech — quite a necessary tool in the popular political orator's repertoire and a tactic against which wise listeners defend themselves to keep themselves from falling blindly into party spirit.

With democratic reforms clearly in mind, he alleges that the importance of ethos increases in proportion as any country enjoys a free government because only ethos tells us whom we can trust when people other than the educated elite enter the public sphere. Whately is quick to point out, however, that merely conforming to the demands of hearers leads to popularity but also a reputation for eloquence that is undeserved. And, he admonishes the speaker not to seek applause, but to show good morals.[16] For, he notes, (as Aristotle says in the *Politics*) only upright men know how to sacrifice their own interests and short term gratification for the public good.[17]

Aside from the increased attention to democratic politics, one other major distinction separates Whately from his predecessors: the situatedness of rhetoric is always before his mind. He contends that, just as there is no eloquence in the abstract but only speeches skillfully adapted to audiences, we cannot discuss ethos without a consideration of a specific audience.[18] His comments are probably inspired (if not based) on an astute reading of Aristotle's instructions (in Book III of the *Rhetoric*) for arousing various emotions in different types of people, so his ideas are not without precedent. But wherever the ideas come from, Whately's remarks show he is keenly aware of the many different kinds of situations and speakers — the surplus of oratory — pervading the landscape in the nineteenth century. He even tries to limit the importance given to experience as a marker of ethos, because he feels that each situation calls for a particular type of experience. A merchant who knows corn may not know wheat; a Minister of State in Persia would be at a loss in European government, and so forth. In this way, he demolishes all but the most particular and situational ethos qualifications. Remarkably, the casualties include the *vir bonus*, which Whately reserves only for preachers who alone must be good in every way to meet audience expectations of them.

His situational sensitivity will not allow him to offer anything beyond a few passing remarks when it comes to specific recommendations or qualities for ethos. There are, for instance, different rules for the barrister than the man of the cloth, because the barrister only needs to be successful with a particular audience once. Just when it seems Whately is going to give the reader some firm ground on which to ethos proofs, he offers his most emphatic declaration on the subject: "to enumerate the various kinds of impressions favorable and unfavorable that hearers may have would be tedious and superfluous."[19] Unfortunately, he explains neither of these charges. Tediousness we can almost be sure of given his predilection for individual cases. Whately even goes so far as to advise his readers that changing with circumstances is often laudable, advice many classical authors could never have written since they so closely associated ethos with ingrained habits of character. But, after noting as he does the importance of ethos in democratic societies and in cases where scientific proof is unavailable, the only justification for calling a list of favorable impressions (along with the means for inducing them) "superfluous" seems to be an Aristotelian belief that the truth always has the stronger case. Then, the orator can trust that audiences will form their most favorable impression of an orator who is truly most qualified to assess the situation. With Whately's Aristotelian leanings, he feels safe in summarizing the topic of ethos with the advice, "set forth the truth as strongly as possible."

Rhetorical Theory in the Training of Orators: Conclusions

Whately's text marks something of an end for the classical tradition in America. Throughout that tradition, the key relationship for ethos, for both the classical and modern British rhetoricians, was *moral and social elevation*. The Republican rhetorical tradition of the Revolutionary years required the orator and audiences to be elevated in terms of wealth and class. Decorum was self-enforced inside the exclusive club, and prudence or practical wisdom in affairs of state had to be exhibited as a license to continue holding the wheel of the ship of state. These demands were modified, but only slightly, by Campbell and Blair in the later tradition because they were more familiar with the phenomenon of lower class persons acting in the public sphere. Accordingly, their doctrines do not assume an elite company of rhetors speaking to elite audiences or presume that true morals are the only means to oratorical success. They do, however, contain plenty of appeals for the orator to exhibit and actually strive for excellent character. In Campbell's case, the appeal is based on pragmatics: being a good man is the only way to assure public esteem in the long run. For Blair's brand of elitism, the *vir bonus* can be anyone who puts on the appropriate airs and works to improve his aesthetic and intellectual sense.

From all of these rhetorical theories, orators in training would have learned that being on the upper levels of the social stratification was essential to ethos, if not beneficial to society. The close tie between ethos and social welfare, as I mentioned in the first chapter, is one of the hallmarks of theories that associate ethos only with character.

The call for moral and social elevation is still presented, but also fundamentally challenged by Whately's late rhetoric. Although he would clearly prefer a nation of virtuous and dignified orators, he is cognizant of democratic audiences and their varying demands. He worries that the only way for an orator of one party to establish good ethos with listeners of another is to betray the party allegiance and play the sycophant. Moreover, he admits that consistency of position is not always beneficial to one's ethos — a direct criticism of the idea that ethos comes from ingrained (and moral) habits of character.

Yet Whately — who was a Bishop in Dublin — remains true to his Christian heritage in urging the orator always to be truthful. How can a Christian orator, who must be truthful and moral, reach a less scrupulous audience without identifying with them? His solution to this thorny problem concludes his discussion of ethos. Whately relates two techniques that allow the orator to *divert* the prejudices and passions of the democratic masses. While still being true to himself, the orator may arouse some "contrary" emotion to the one that works against his ethos. Or, he may give the listener's passion a new direction, a new object to center upon.

As the last chapter showed, antebellum rhetorical practice bore out this advice. American reform oratory was indeed characterized by the arousal of strong emotions.

Often this served to ingratiate the orator to the audience by replacing any anger or resentment they may have felt at the rebukes of the orator with terror, pity, or delight. The contradicting emotion was yet one more part of the "power" the orator was allowed to assert over his audiences. The diversionary tactic was used hand-in-hand with a scapegoating strategy. Since audiences would not suffer themselves to be blamed for social ills, yet demanded answers and action, antebellum orators could maintain his popularity by fanning the flames of anger, but directing the inferno to an object other than himself (e.g. "the banking power"). He could do all this without sacrificing his integrity and nobility and without giving in to party spirit.

ETHOS IN SPEECH CRITICISM

Even if no orators actually practiced the theories they read about in these textbooks, Douglass audiences would probably have been exposed to them in other ways. Many more people read about rhetorical theory in literary magazines, newspaper reviews, and grammar school readers than studied them formally in universities. For Americans who could not read, or had little interest in doing so, the magazines and newspapers will still topics of conversation, and their articles filtered into even non-literate parts of society. The literary culture surrounding oratory contributed to rhetorical expectations in diverse ways. Readers could learn about Cicero's ideas through an article entirely dedicated to summarizing his life and works, or they might be exposed to a specific claim from his theory as a passing comment in a review of an orator's performance. The question is, what sorts of things were the second-hand readers of oratory theory learning about ethos that would have guided their expectations for black abolitionists?

The Response to Belletrism Dominates Popular Criticism of Oratory

Perhaps the most widespread notions about rhetoric had to do with its definition and scope. In 1785, Warren Guthrie observes, "American rhetoric was closely allied with oratory, but gradually moved more and more into the realm of composition and criticism — *belles lettres*."[20] Or, as Borchers and Wagner put it, "in keeping with the general movement toward belles lettres" there was in the colleges a "tendency more and more evident toward the half-century mark" to treat oral communication as "elocution" while reserving the title "rhetoric" for written composition and criticism.[21]

If anything, the institutions of higher learning lagged behind the rest of the educated sectors of the country in making the switch to a writing-centered view of rhetoric. Many speech critics in magazines and newspapers — including a Boylston chair of rhetoric, Edward Channing, who was also the editor of the *North American*

Review — were first and foremost men of letters and distressed about the deficiency of the American contribution to literature. Channing was so heavily focused on the written kind of rhetoric that teachers of elocution had to be appointed during his tenure to supplement the student's knowledge of oratory.[22] It was a signal of things to come when, in 1840, one critic referred to eloquence for the first time as "a department of literature."[23]

Although the repercussions of this move were far-reaching, the ramifications for ethos of the "literizing" of rhetorical theory have not been sufficiently explored. For his part, Channing felt that ethos and the individual rhetor were increasingly unimportant as societies become more sophisticated. According to his own rhetoric text, audiences of the 1800s (he was Chair of Rhetoric from 1819 to 1851) were more interested in the subject matter of the speech than the speaker. This excused him for giving the qualities of a successful speaker a few scant pages of his text.

Channing, though, seems to have based his analyses of audiences on readerships, not public attendance, which is a crucial flaw in his formulations. Out of the presence of the person of the orator, ethos becomes less important and less immediate; the power of the orator that audiences and critics were lauding across America is more difficult to achieve. The belletrists' critical pronouncements map poorly onto the world of oratory because they are the result of what Walter Ong would call a "literate mind" speaking about an "oral society."

Despite all the great pamphlets from Revolutionary days and the rising prominence of newspapers and magazines, the antebellum rhetorical culture can still fairly be described as an "oral" culture. This is especially true of the lower class society. Popular audiences had a passion for oratory and the daily lives of industrial workers placed little relative importance on "craft literacy."[24] For the electorate, literacy, like public education, was only slowly implemented in schools starting in the 1800s. So according to the historical record, only the youngest and wealthiest audience members in the pre-Civil War era were more likely than not to be literate.[25] Even then, according to Ong's theory, the fully literate mindset and culture would have lagged years behind the acquisition of basic literacy.

How would an oral person's analysis of antebellum oratory have differed from Channing's? On the topic of the oral versus literate mindset, Father Ong suggests that "Writing fosters abstractions that disengage knowledge from the arena where human beings struggle with one another." Since they are always in the midst of the struggle, oral people tend to have very antagonistic cultures. Oral cultures also favor and celebrate boisterous physical behavior while the literizing of a society "eventually pulls the focus of action more and more to interior crises and away from purely exterior crises."[26]

Ong also helps explain another important response of the popular audiences that troubled elite (literate) observers. Oral cultures, he contends, are "empathic and participatory."[27] Audiences get personally involved with an oral performance, and tend to identify very closely with the performer. No surprise, then, that the therapeutic audiences were prone to strong emotion as they became engaged — not so much with the sympathetic story — but with the emotions of the orator himself. The identity of the speaker and the relationship between speaker and audience are central issues for any good critic's judgment of the speech. Edward Channing, the magazine editor and critic, can only have missed this by ignoring the importance of the immediate audience in favor of the secondary audiences reading the speech transcripts.

Using readerships — and properly refined ones at that — rather than live audiences as his standard, Channing saw American audiences as people who only want to see the "light of truth" in a speech. Ethos was a consideration only insofar as the orator proved he had the right kind of character, the kind that compels one to tell only the truth.[28]

Critics who spent more time among the oral cultures of the lower classes were more sensitive to the different dynamics of interaction between speaker and audience, even though the critics themselves may not have possessed an oral consciousness. Seeing the sort of bias Channing and many belletrists exemplified by characterizing rhetoric as a literary art, critics of oratory were forced to ignore popular theories in order to accurately capture the kinds of things they observed. The emphasis in oratorical criticism therefore shifted toward all the things that an orator can do to move and impress an audience that a writer cannot. As elocution became a subject matter separated from "rhetoric" and writing in the universities, speech criticism in the public realm quickly and subtly adopted its own set of elocutionary or at least speech-centered standards. Critics justified their fixation with powerful delivery by comparing oratory to unfulfilling print versions of speeches and written rhetoric. "Who can print the electric language of the human eye, the expressive tones of the human voice?" asks one by way of comparison, "Who can convey to the reader not only the sentence and paragraphs of a discourse, but the glance and gesture, which enforced them?"[29] The elements elocutionist critics praise necessarily elevate oral rhetoric above its written counterpart. The "electric" eye, expressive voice, and forceful glance and gesture are also, and not coincidentally, features that make an orator powerful over an audience.

The "one matter upon which the majority of commentators agree," writes Baskerville, "is the high emotional content of eloquence (or oratory)." He adds, "A common way of assessing this quality is by its effect on the hearer."[30] The arguments over abolition bear out Baskerville's statement since both sides in the slavery debates used this logic regularly to praise or condemn speakers. For example, after one pro-slavery speaker addressed a hostile audience, a sympathetic reviewer offered simultaneous praise of the speaker and an insult to the supposedly cowed audience:

"[The audience] squirmed, shook their heads, whiggled in their seats, scratched their heads, and once or twice interrupted the speaker — but it was all in vain — Mr. Mitchell stood forth like a man, a Whig and a Christian.... He spoke like an American, a patriot, and a minister of the Gospel."[31]

Critics like this one were astute in making an assessment of eloquence based on audience effects. Many did not have the guide of rhetorical theory urging them to find the most emotional and antagonistic crowds as a measure of the best orator. In fact, the weight of theory was decidedly against approving of the audience of "rabble" and their tendencies.

To our more literate minds, their panegyric heaped upon powerful orators seems overwrought. Surveying the critics and their habit of "apotheosizing" orators, Baskerville's opinion about the tendency to tell tales of the orator's great power and presence is clear:

> [In the nineteenth century] a tradition was built up, based on these and similar stories, a tradition of the orator as a superman, a Godlike creature whose superior powers gave him dominion over other men. The remarkable thing is the complete credulity with which these tales were accepted. Now and then someone expresses wonder that such marvelous effects should have been wrought by speeches which, when read, seem so commonplace, but the explanation that the speaker's physical presence made the difference is sufficient.[32]

Underappreciated they might be as critics. But the late-century author who defined eloquence as a mixture of Truth and Art, with "Personality" knew his subject well.[33]

Audiences were being moved by personalities, they capitulated to the orator's power, and they were in awe of his very presence. Whatever the collegiate class of critics might have asserted, these qualities were essential for ethos. So on one count, at least, Channing was accurate. *Character* as a quality of ethos was indeed downplayed by audiences. If they saw truth in the speech, truth that could be established by the content itself if it referred to empirical observations and the scientific method, they still looked to the speaker's ethos, now centered on his personality, for confirmation. Personality was conveyed by the artistry of an emphatic, emotional delivery: thus, Truth, Art, and Personality were indeed at the heart of nineteenth-century notions of eloquence. We can even give a specific date to the decline of character if we accept Lewis Perry's testimony: "By the time that Andrew Jackson defeated John Quincy Adams in 1828, the idea that virtuous character was the criterion for office holding was nearly as discredited as the idea of hereditary privilege."[34]

Ethos Characteristics Important to Speech Critics

Character may not have been emphasized, but the idea of elevation did not entirely disappear from accounts of ethos in the press. There will always be a sense that the prospective leaders who stand before us must have some qualification that makes them deserving of our trust and attention. For example, "love of country" is still frequently cited by antebellum commentators as a quality of a good orator. This is in line with classical thinking and is easily fit under Aristotle's traditional category of "good will." In a similar vein, a commonplace of antebellum rhetorical criticism is commentary on the subject's orthodoxy and Christian faith. This fits under the heading of Aristotle's "good morals" since Christianity was not just a belief but a set of behaviors and a moral code.

Critics also looked for less traditional qualities as well, notably the orator's "commitment" and "sincerity." They wanted the best orators to show more commitment and sincerity than the average person — again, a kind of elevation. Critics could find support for this doctrine in both the belletristic and elocutionary rhetorical texts where fervency was discussed as a way for the orator to meet the all-important requirement of *naturalness*. Simply allowing one's heartfelt beliefs to express themselves was the best was to assure eloquence. Nothing so turned audiences against speakers as the appearance of artifice.

How could the elocutionary texts, teaching a standardized system of gestures and tones, believe they were destroying artifice in the students' speeches? The answer is provided by Richard Sennett in *The Fall of Public Man*.

Naturalness as a Cure for Anonymity

Sennnett notes that the "rise of the bourgeoisie" is more than just a hackneyed phrase. "The appearance of a new class" such as was seen in America can "create a milieu of strangers in which many people are increasingly like each other but don't know it."[35] He then raises a connection that has become familiar to us, the close parallels between the stage and the platform: "The audience problem of a milieu of strangers has been identified with the problem of audience in the theater: how to arouse belief among those who do not know you."

Sennett argues that in the early days of industrialization and urbanization in England, codes were invented for public action in the eighteenth century to allow members of the public to know each other. Through the codes, the actor — and soon the orator after actors began writing elocutionary books on rhetoric — could "represent" emotions without having to "express" them. The answer to anonymity was to present one's feelings according to a recognized norm of expression. The feelings were then "authorized" by others who acknowledged the form of expression so that, in a way, the emotion had no reality until it was socially sanctioned. At least, an unusual expression of emotion was destined to be ineffectual in making the audience feel what the performer felt. The elocutionists' drive to find "natural" expressions of emotion was really an effort to find the universal symbols that would allow anonymous people to communicate and arouse emotions in each other.

In speech reviews as the nineteenth century progresses, elocutionary style is increasingly derided in favor of unique expressions of ideas and emotions. The ability to express deep emotion comes to be interpreted as the ability to *feel* deep emotion, to be a person of gravity and sentiment, and it doesn't make sense that such a person could have merely learned the universal gestures and facial expressions for "dismay" or "surprise." The emphasis on exhibiting emotion remained, but the reliance on normalized codes faded as people sought out the individual more than the universal. The elocutionary theories fell out of favor at the same time. The definition of the "natural" had changed in a way that favored another pole of expression, the individual and idiosyncratic. It was the belletrists who addressed this need by insisting that an orator cultivate his own personal "style." The idea that natural expression was a matter of presenting universal signs of emotion was replaced in the nineteenth century by a firm belief that every individual *personality* had to be expressed differently.

Material forces also played a significant role in the shift in emphasis toward personality. With industrialization, rows of miscellaneous, mass-produced goods and clothing were billed as purchases that reflected the buyer's uniqueness. Following the logic of commodity fetishism, this was an effort to stimulate the buyer into investing an object with personal meaning far beyond its use value.[36] Sennett suggests that a lost sense of being-in-the-world that industrialization produced was also partly to blame:

> As the gods fled, immediacy of sensation and perception grew more important; phenomena came to seem real in and of themselves as immediate experience. People in turn were disposed to make more and more of differences in the immediate impressions they made upon each other, to see these differences, indeed, as the very basis of social existence. These immediate impressions different people produced were taken to be their 'personalities.'[37]

In terms of how rhetors can shape their identities to receive a sanction from their audience, character has the advantage of stability. An orator can benefit from being a "known commodity." That very predictability was also a detriment in front of nineteenth-century audiences. Because the symbol structure, whereby one could show character, had been thoroughly standardized in the late eighteenth century, it was also easy to depict one's morality fraudulently. In an age where great crowds were pressing in all around in burgeoning urban centers, when democratic reforms were giving more control to every Tom, Dick and Harry in determining the future, the anonymity of strangers was profoundly disturbing. In tiny Athens with a small number of citizens who were all constantly in the public eye, each person's habits of character were well known. Without a personal knowledge of the candidate, and recognizing the questionableness of the "natural" codes of expression, the American voter in Douglass's America found himself asking, "How can I know whether to trust this politician?"

Speech critics responded to this challenge by looking for personality, the spontaneous expression of interior mental states and intimate, even unseemly emotions and thoughts. Though they were not looking for character, they were still seeking an elevated person to follow, someone better than average in some respect. Expressions of profound though or deep emotion suggested to listeners that the orator was, deep down, thoughtful and possessed of great emotion. Emerson, who frequently baffled even educated audiences with his metaphysical pronouncements, garnered his ethos through this process. Neither he nor his audiences felt it was his ethical duty, contra Cicero, to teach his audience.[38] His ethos was based on evincing an ability for serious thought and profound emotion that impressed all listeners with his sincerity. He confused them, but did so out of a sincere desire to express his ideas. Impressed by a commitment that was so great it led to a "bad speech," audiences flocked to hear him and were impressed that he had presented his true self.

Although measuring orators by the excesses of their personalities was a major rhetorical change, the practice largely went unrecognized, especially in formal theory. Many of the terms critics had always used were still operative even though the meanings had changed. This allowed critics to think they were practicing and judging rhetoric in roughly the same ways their predecessors had. The key element of all ethos, the *elevation* of the orator, had remained. Likewise, the individual expressions of emotion, in an age of increasing individuality, were redefined as "natural expression," natural *to the person*, that is, not natural insofar as they are common to all people and likely to help audiences make decisions on shared communal values.

RHETORICAL PRACTICE PRIOR TO DOUGLASS'S APPEARANCE

Rhetorical theory does not always translate into rhetorical practice, of course. For this reason, we need to look beyond the theories to what we can learn from the actual rhetorical practice of famous and successful orators of the early 1800s to see what speakers themselves were indicating to antebellum audiences about ethos.

Along these lines, Antczak presents a critical observation on nineteenth-century orators and their ethos:

> For all the diversity among lecturers and messages, there was one constant among them; on the circuit of public speech the rhetoric of democratic education was a rhetoric of identification. The speaker had to be a sort of representative figure — representative in the sense of being one with, one *of* the democratic audience.... The promise, the draw, the *lift* of this democratic rhetoric was that in identifying

with the speaker's character and thought, the listeners could become more themselves.[39]

Here we have the second major element of the ethos of the public orator. It was first, elevated, but it was also, to a certain degree, invitational. The orator's ethos showed him to be essentially alike the audience, yet superior in some way, a way the audience was asked to join.

This is the first American twist on the rhetoric of moral and social elevation that it learned from the classical and British theories. Americans tended to view themselves both as chosen and as created equal. They also were a nation of people wanting an equal opportunity in their desperate struggle to get ahead and be better and more successful than everyone else. Because of both impulses — egalitarian and self-aggrandizing — they responded well to the image of an orator who was better than them, yet gave them hope that they could be better as well. Their faith that they could be as good as the person speaking was unquestioned.

In this kind of ethos, as opposed to traditional ethos based entirely on moral elevation, there is ultimately no superiority. The orator is *for the moment* better than the audience, but not because of a life filled with carefully calculated choices and the denial of passing pleasures in favor of things that are truly Good, the kind of life long work that teaches one to make wise decisions based on the what is True and Good not what seems true and feels good. The popular orator Antczak describes achieves a heightened status through the application of some knack. If the audience learns the same technique, and applies effort, they can reach the same lofty position. The promise behind the American fascination with the "self-made man" is found here: if people can remake themselves in the mold of success, there is no important difference between the audience members and either a speaker who identifies himself as a man of deep moral conviction or one who has ascribed status due to wealth or family background.

INDICATIONS FROM SPECIFIC ORATORS ABOUT ETHOS

If Daniel Webster was the most highly regarded of the major orators during the American "Golden Age," he was also the most traditional in terms of his ethos. According to Robert Oliver, the notable qualities of Daniel Webster included sincerity and honesty: "He did not indulge in the common political practice of trying to blacken the reputation of his opponents in order to lessen respect for their views."[40] His character was so highly regarded, one of his most famous opponents, Robert Hayne, admitted "he never heard him [Webster] utter a word in a careless or vulgar style" and Webster "seemed never to forget his own dignity or be unmindful of the character and feelings of others."[41]

Being the very picture of moral elevation was a conscious choice on Webster's part. He recommended that political campaigners, despite democratic audiences, "Show ourselves uniform and just, by acting according to our principles...."[42] According to his personal correspondence, he placed a high value on moral excellence, telling a friend that one personal quality he found necessary "especially in lawyers and public men, [was] respectability or 'excellent private character.'"[43]

Putting aside for the moment the veneration this stance earned him with colleagues and with much of the public, it is important to remember that Webster never achieved his desire of being president. Part of the reason can be found in the complex political wrangling in the antebellum era when the major parties were changing drastically. Nevertheless, in the log cabin campaigns when Jacksonian-style politics ruled the nation, Webster never ascended to the highest office. This is at least some indication that his public image, much like that of another popular orator, Henry Clay, did not resonate sufficiently with the popular voters candidates desperately needed to impress in order to reach the White House. In a time when personality was beginning to dominate, Webster's excellent character was insufficient to win him a majority of the votes.

Webster represents the highest measure of the classical standard, but not all orators followed his example. Henry Clay, already mentioned for his moral difficulties (and opposing social graces), was a man of notable ethos in a way quite different from Webster. According to Gunderson's article, "The Magnanimous Mr. Clay," Henry Clay was a "glamorous political personality."[44] Burgchardt calls his personality "magnetic," his smile "engaging," and adds "his power as an orator cannot be gauged accurately from reading his speeches. Audiences reacted warmly to his physical presence."[45]

These critics' terminology reflects the changing nature of ethos. Clay infused his identity as an orator with elements of dynamism, celebrity, and likeability; it surely was not his morality that his devotees found magnetic or glamorous. He was also one of the most renowned of the log cabin orators. He identified himself with the interests of his constituency rather than expecting them to identify with him as their superior moral and intellectual representative. On both counts — personal magnetism and constituent identification — Clay was actually too successful for his own political good. He, like his fellow Southerner John Calhoun, was so beloved by voters in his own state and so identified with them his hopes of being considered a representative for the entire nation were hopelessly marred.[46] Campbell's and Whately's worries about party spirit were painful realities both of the men.

Clay, at least, had the added advantage of a warm personality. Wonderfully successful for influencing individuals, his likeability helped him move policies like the famous Compromise of 1850 through a divided Congress since he had the opportunity to personally charm his target audience. But before the television age, his magnanimity and his magnetism were translated poorly in the speech transcripts that were used to reach national audiences.

John Calhoun, the third member of the famous triumvirate, was nearly the opposite of Clay. In fact, Clay construed his counterpart as "tall, careworn, with furrowed brow, haggard and intensely gazing, looking as if he were dissecting the last abstraction which [had] sprung from his metaphysician's brain...."[47] Another congressional observer fancied him a "college professor demonstrating to his class."[48] His oratory was, as rhetorical biographies have concluded, nearly devoid of humor.[49]

As I mentioned in the first chapter, it is rather hard to find a recent assessment of Calhoun that comments on his ethos, probably because of his nefarious defense of slavery as a "positive good." Many of the traditional markers of ethos fail at that point.

An additional problem in evaluating his ethos is an amazing inconsistency in his own actions and the judgments of others about their merits. Besides the slavery issue, many of the other policies he advocated during his career were inconsistent with each other. The antebellum journalist Nathan Sargent judged that "his principles were not very firmly fixed [or] at least they were easily abandoned for others."[50] This made him seem like a political opportunist to many observers. At the same time, he took difficult and politically unpopular stands on slavery, on denying abolition petitions, and on nullification. His resignation from the vice presidency was followed by a threat from Andrew Jackson to hang him for treason, a threat that hardly seemed to faze him.[51] Another piece of the Calhoun puzzle: however fickle his political postures were, even those who had no particular fondness for the Great Nullifier or his policies highly regarded his personal morality and religious commitment.[52] In sum, he was a man whose variability was even inconsistent.

Yet, as odd as it sounds, the strength of Calhoun's ethos came in the form of "sincerity." Sargent depicts him as a man who spoke philosophically and proposed intricately reasoned plans, but "spoke with a warmth, earnestness, and enthusiasm which indicated that his whole soul was in 'the system' he had projected."[53] "Warmth" here should not be mistaken for personal charm. It indicates the heat and passion with which the man filled his presentation. Whatever his program at the time, while speaking about it his body poured forth signs that embraced it to the depths of his being, from the brow "charged with thunder" to his practice of "walking rapidly from side to side of his cage."[54] As a measure of character, which must remain consistent across circumstances, his behavior is obviously inadequate; the vigorous defense of a policy *du jour* is actually more despicable than if he had offered them only lukewarm support. As a measure of personality, though, Calhoun was deemed an oratorical master and a man of the highest caliber by the many people who were seeking a reason to follow the Southern senator and found it in his sincerity.

In another of the many contradictions about Calhoun, his use of rebuke rhetoric undercut any broad appeal he could have earned by his sincerity. In this respect, he appears almost as the counterpart to William Lloyd Garrison; each man was a prophet speaking to half the nation. They stand as two of the few antebellum rhetoricians to engage in the rhetoric of rebuke. Calhoun's congressional speeches are positively laced with stinging attacks on the diabolic nature of the antislavery forces. His targets included fellow politicians who, though planning to table the motions immediately, would dare to even accept antislavery petitions on the floor of the Senate.

As the speech act of rebuke requires, Calhoun had to adopt a morally superior stance toward his audience. His elaborate defense of slavery as a positive good was necessary to this part of his public identity. Rebukes cannot be made from the moral low ground. But because of his clear superiority and authority, he could not promise the uplift Antczak remarked as typical of the most effective orators. The jeremiad promises blessing or forgiveness to those who repent, but repentance cannot turn one into a prophet. There is no leveling after a rebuke just as there are no self-made prophets (or at least *true* prophets always are authorized by a higher power).[55]

Ultimately, Calhoun, like Garrison, was only really appealing to his disciples. His rebukes were aimed at anyone who was not as rabidly proslavery as he was, which meant his sincerity could give but a small group a reason to assent to his leadership. Most others tended to find him distasteful, especially those who found themselves the special targets of his rebukes. Some of those same people, notably the abolitionist Wendell Phillips, had a "grudging admiration" for Calhoun.[56] However, this came not from his principles, but from his staunch defense of them.

ETHOS EXPECTATIONS IN THE ERA OF THE PERSONALITY SHIFT

As Webster, Clay, and Calhoun, the old guard orators, were leaving the scene they left openings for orators who weren't statesmen and saintly Christians. The changes began slowly at first, with critics sensing the importance of personality but describing their reactions in terminologies compatible with the older ideals of character-based ethos that they had been trained to accept. Bishop Whately's rhetoric challenged some long-accepted notions and added impetus to the change by showing that the situational aspects of rhetoric overrode universal pronouncements about pure moral and class-based elevation. In the final analysis, though, it was the American people themselves, Campbell's "rabble" and Sennett's audience of "strangers," that would lead the charge into a new era of identity-based ethos, where both personality and character would be measured in an orator.

We are firmly in that era now, even if we haven't recognized it. For modern critics, for example, the term *personality* is the preferred term for analyzing Clay's oratorical identity. The term has slipped into common usage in contemporary authorship on ethos, but without much critical attention from rhetorical scholars.

There are, however, two groups of scholars consciously using the terminology. The contributions of these authors are necessary to complete the story of the evolution in ethos expectations that allowed Douglass, an uneducated African American ex-slave, to dominate the rhetorical scene in a way that would not have been possible even in the late 1700s.

THEORETICAL JUSTIFICATION FOR THE CHARACTER/PERSONALITY DISTINCTION

The complementarity of the terms Character and Personality is examined by two very different groups, American cultural historians and classicists. Sharing as they do the interest in cultural understandings of selfhood, the writings of the American historians and the classicists on this distinction are both relevant to our study of rhetorical theory. Although one applies directly to the situation in Douglass's America, and one affords us the perspective of 2500 years, they both help explain how an audience's notion of personhood can change the possibilities for persuasion through ethos. However, they each evolved from particular definitions of the term "character."

Character/Personality in Socio-historical Studies

The way cultural historians have described the character/personality split directly relates to the antebellum revolution in ethos. In their analyses, character refers to an ideal of "moral constitution" that has been in decline from the nineteenth century to the present. From this perspective, Warren Susman presents a set of specific assertions about the turn of the century in American society. It is his conviction that in the nineteenth century *character* was both a "significant cultural form" and a "key word in the vocabulary of Englishmen and Americans."[57] The standard of improving character was carried across many philosophical discussions, handbooks of popular morality, and especially into texts on child rearing. Susman draws upon Rieff's critique of the current therapeutic culture in arguing that character usefully served the society of that age in two prominent ways: it was an ethical ideal for self development, and it guided how people presented themselves to society. It thereby constrained personal morality and social relations in the nineteenth century.

Then, as that century drew to a close, say Susman and Rieff, a shift happened that is crucial for understanding contemporary society: America became a culture more interested in personality than in character. The key social formation fomenting this change was the increasing importance of the private individual, inspired by the intense inward scrutiny of Freudian psychology, Romanticism, democratization of teaching practices and the availability of printed material. The closely examined life that resulted, while presumably worth living, was disassociated from collective society by becoming so highly individuated. In previously unimagined proportions, the legitimation and naturalization of individual differences resulted. And as a consequence, in the twentieth century we have the culmination of the therapeutic society or "culture of the individual," which concentrates economic and social energy on maintaining a safe place for the satisfaction and justification of peculiar desires. In fact, in our age of entertainment and capitalism which always demands more and more products, being unusual often gives *entrée* to a rhetorical platform as the next in a line of consumables.

Obviously much of this scholarship has found its way into the previous sections. My story conflicts with most of these authorities, however. By studying the actions and reactions of popular audiences to public oratory in the nineteenth century, I have been making the case that the shift to the therapeutic culture of the individual happened much earlier than most historians suppose. At least, the antebellum rhetorical culture was thoroughly therapeutic and individualized.

Character/Personality in Classical Studies

Examples of personality-based criticism are provided by the second group of scholars searching for bifurcations of character and personality. This group is led by Christopher Gill to look at classical texts, especially the moral lessons implicit in the lives of ancient Greek tragic characters.[58] Gill associates dramas with a label of personality or character based on how the people in the play are presented. Do we see their innermost thoughts? Are their actions explained by some individual trait rather than some external norm? If so, we have a work that is concerned with personality. Revealing personality is a way for the playwright to respond to his characters empathetically, not on strictly moral grounds. In such works, the author gives the audience standards for appraising the person that arise from inside the character, not from external social norms.[59] This implies that if we could only "walk a mile in their shoes" we would know why they acted a certain way.

By contrast, literature associated with character treats its figures primarily as moral agents, and as responsible for their own actions before society. It places them in an ethical framework suitable for judging them.[60] Another way of putting it would be that figures in a play associated with character are treated more like Types or ideals than like everyday people who have situation-based reasons for failing to measure up.

Alongside Gill, other classicists have developed this study by showing the connections to ancient practices of biography. The personality/character distinction is evident in the way the life of people is portrayed in a work that is meant to reveal people to the public. Here, the important question is: from a myriad of possible events and deeds, on which ones does the author place his focus? Since this is the genre of biography, a modern audience would expect an emphasis on personality; that is, we want biographies that give us inside information on famous figures that might not comport with their public facades. Yet in most classical biography, each incident that finds its way into the text is there to prove a consistent pattern in the speaker's life.[61] A similar trend is found in classical oratory where we rarely see an inward view of the speaker's psyche. We get instead a socially acceptable image of outward compliance with conventional morality. The result is that a classical biography is rarely different from an oratorical encomium in its moralizing view and two-dimensional presentation of characters. The speaker is most often presented as an ethical prototype, unambiguously good, while the opposition (say, in a courtroom speech) is equally and oppositely bad. This is an emphasis on character, according to Gill's use of the distinction.

Character/Personality in Rhetorical Studies

Despite the fact that speakers were exhibiting personality-based ethos, and even though the terminology was in use by other fields that would make sense of such appeals, the notion of ethos remains wedded to character in nearly all rhetorical studies literature. It is directly prescribed by Aristotle — the first time he prescribes anything in the *Rhetoric* — where he recommends that "one should take coincidences and chance happenings as due to deliberate purpose; for if many similar examples are cited, they will seem to be a sign of virtue and purpose."[62] Of course, the exact opposite can be true in different societies and legal systems, something Aristotle must have been aware of. If, for example, the courts make allowances for justifiable homicide or temporary insanity, it can be a winning tactic to present the context of situation as though it dictated the defendant's action over and against her good character. Likewise in deliberative rhetoric, a moment of vulnerability can have a powerful effect. A fine example that probably would not have escaped Aristotle's notice is Demosthenes's Third Philippic, where some of the most powerful moments come when he expresses puzzlement and weariness that cause him to search for words.[63] The impression that he has momentarily let down his guard and has stopped playing the part of the morally certain rhetorician suggests the sincerity of his rhetoric.

Personality appeals of this sort have received short shrift in rhetorical theorizing because orators and audiences prior to the nineteenth century were presumed to be elites. Their kind of elevation is based on moral and intellectual superiority to the rest of the population. And because their needs are met, they can put aside selfish interest and make policies with the social welfare in mind. The elite are a sort of "talented tenth" of the population expected, by themselves and others, to protect and guide those less qualified to lead. With democratic reforms and liberal individualism, this myth could not be maintained for long.

The myth was challenged in the antebellum rhetorical culture before it moved on to the rest of society because rhetorical situations, in the Golden Age of Oratory, were the first places non-literate audiences went to perform and verify their public identities. Rhetorical situations, therefore, were also the first to challenge the identities that popular audiences were trying to construct, as reflected in the elitist comments by theater critics and old school orators.

Trained in the art of audience assessment and adaptation, rhetors were also quick to respond to the new demands of their audiences. No longer was it acceptable to be the *Übermensch* rhetor, lording over the audience an almost superhuman morality, intellect, and patriotism. Popular audiences, interpolated to accept their inferiority to upper-crust elites, permitted rhetoric that either lauded them for their lower status and standing (e.g. "coonskin democracy" and log-cabin campaigns) or that promised to uplift them to a higher level. With the commodification of oratory, audiences also had an unprecedented level of choice and the consumer mindset to use it in selecting oratory that met their demands.

Ethos was therefore taken out of the realm of strictly social norms and the ability of a rhetor to perform public service. It began to move in the direction of individual qualities, especially those that offered a clear window into the soul of the orator. Morality, they knew, was too easy to fake between strangers. For further evidence, they need only look to all those men "converted" by the evangelists who, after publicly establishing their morality, came back to the privacy of their homes and continued beating their wives and their slaves. Insight into the individual quirkiness of the orator was the surest way for audiences of strangers to be sure they were getting a true impression of their leader. The other possibility was to rely on celebrity status because such people were known quantities, sure to award attendance with entertainment, emotion, or antagonism. From all this, the resulting rhetorical culture was therapeutic and individualistic to a degree that the broader society wouldn't reach until decades later.

It is worth repeating that a rhetorical presentation of character — especially to an audience which values personality — has a way of alienating one from a community, both in Douglass's America and in the present day. Because a politician (e.g. Daniel Webster or Bob Dole) is depicted as such an exemplar of national ideals, he or she is therefore above us and unlike us. Therefore, persuasion through character could actually have a negative outcome for the speaker's identification with the audience, even if the audience believes the rhetor is virtuous. For, in a therapeutic culture where numerous vices are excused and even used for mass entertainment, audiences believe that *everyone* fails to live up to community ideals from time to time.

It is also important to note that there are some close affinities between the historians' and the classicists' formulations of the character/personality distinction that are relevant for a rhetorical analysis of ethos. Both formulations revolve around the amount of self-consciousness, self-interest, and individuality people expose in their discourse. The revealed sense of self is an indicator of the way one relates to society. Audiences seeking for character allow people a voice only if they meet certain standards. Spokespersons are viewed through a moral lens with a mentality of judgment (and those that pass are more persuasive). Audiences accustomed to judging personality allow people a voice primarily for entertainment. The audience's goal is to find interesting personal revelations. Those they can empathize and identify with tend to be more persuasive. Put together, the two formulations suggest that the range of acceptable sanctions for a rhetor's actions will differ substantially depending on whether an audience is predisposed to look for character or personality.

CHAPTER FOUR

The Construction of Blackness and the Constraint of Ethos

Reacting to social changes and material conditions, ethos expectations were changing. The antebellum rhetorical culture offered a unique opportunity for orators who weren't from the elite ranks of society to lure and dominate audiences and have their messages read by voters in a dozen states. In terms of ethos expectations, the radical departure represented by the democratization of public action is hard to conceive fully.

In the first place, orators could now draw fully on two sets of resources for establishing ethos — their personality and their character. And, for perhaps the first time since Classical Athens, public audiences were willing, at least in theory, to ascribe anyone on the speaker's platform (or stump) the necessary qualities to persuade them with ethos. Given the therapeutic proclivities of the audiences, it can even be argued that rich aristocrats had a more burdensome initial ethos to overcome than a lower class yarn-spinner such as Davy Crockett.

At the same time the fortunes of blacks were, in some ways at least, especially good because the changing notion of the self led people to give serious consideration to internal states — no matter how deep or how fleeting — and to their ordinary lives as important determiners of their identities.[1] This evolution of definition was reinforced by the conditions of the nineteenth-century public sphere. The standardized codes that established class, morality, and status had become passé or were easily counterfeited, so the public needed new measures for their public figures. Instead of the timeworn codes of public emotional expression, people looked for a sincere expression of deeply held feelings. The deepest emotions and the most overwrought expressions were believed to be impossible to fake. There was also a corresponding desire of audiences to peek into the daily lives of their representatives. All of this was based on their sense that a person's public acts, even heroic and noble ones, were not really representative of his or her worth. Nor was a record of public deeds necessary to prove merit. The omnipresent influence of Reformation Christianity had accustomed Americans to consider their day to day activities as valuable and morally significant.

In these areas — the expression of interior states and the recounting of everyday events to establish one's nature — slaves were on equal ground with white males. In their autobiographical rhetoric, they could prove that they too had heartfelt sentiments to express (strong ones about slavery), and could talk at length about interesting events in their daily lives (few of which put slavery in a good light). Moreover, with the sanctioning of personality appeals, merely giving eloquent voice to these elements of their lives established ethos where it would not have done so fifty years before. As the ex-slave shared both his feelings and the working out of God's grace in the course of a difficult, work-filled life, the audience heard words they could appreciate. They were words even white audiences wanted to hear, especially considering how exotic the slave's life seemed and because blacks were known for their strong emotions. Thus the reputations of black people actually raised expectations for their oratory as a good show.

These factors go a long way toward explaining Douglass's opportunity for success and popularity. The changes in the rhetorical culture allowed him to draw an audience that would at least be willing to hear him. However, to assume that Douglass and other black orators merely had to relate their autobiographies to reach the hearts of eager audiences would be to overlook the monumental constraints on their efforts to establish ethos. The distinction between character and personality appeals becomes crucial for explaining why. While black orators could not be denied the appeal of their personality, a central tenet of the dominant antebellum ideology held blacks to be incapable of acquiring the qualities of character, and that ideology was perpetuated with rhetoric.

With a constant stream of speeches and articles, the proslavery forces hoped to set in audiences' minds a series of negative expectations for black orators. They wanted to construct a "common sense" image of black men as so reprehensible and prone to lie that respectable folks would not even attend a lecture, let alone assent to their arguments. Or, failing that, they wanted to provide a naturalized way for audiences to interpret the ethos-related statements of black orators: a black speaking to whites as an equal would be construed as "uppityness," for instance.

The effort to control expectations, to keep blacks "in their place" by any means was an attempt to constrain the audiences for black rhetoric and limit those audiences' appreciation for the speaker. The competition for the right to define the nature and character of blacks made race the issue of the day. Being of African descent marked the orator as Other and was the first matter he would have to address to have any hope of building a serviceable ethos with white audiences. If the previous two chapters shed light on the ethos possibilities for an antebellum black *orator*, the purpose of this chapter is to examine audience preconceptions facing Douglass as a *black* orator. How would predominantly white audiences have approached any orator with a dark skin? For those willing to listen, what standards would be used to label an orator like Douglass eloquent or powerful, while other ex-slaves such as Henry "Box" Brown were merely "earnest?" This is the interaction between race and the expectations for the orator's performance.

To address the issue of racial constraints on ethos this chapter is divided into three sections. The first looks at the way black personhood was constructed by analyzing some of the major public and political pronouncements about race in the early nineteenth century. Essentially, it was publicly proclaimed and widely believed that blacks inherently lacked Aristotle's three characteristics of character-based ethos, good sense (*phronesis*), good morals (*areté*) and good will (*eunoia*). This discourse created an "ideology of inferiority" that constrained black attempts to establish ethos by securing the widespread acceptance of the inherent ignorance, corruptness, and selfishness of blacks. The second section shows that the ideology of inferiority was so strong that even the best efforts of black rhetors to rehabilitate their reputations and establish character were reinterpreted as further evidence of their inferiority. In other words, in addition to creating a set of negative expectations to overcome, the racist discourse limited the possible methods for (re)establishing ethos. The third section reveals the routes that most black orators followed in the face of the two constraints — on expectations and on redemptive efforts. Some denied the ability of whites to judge their character and refused to defend themselves from the charges (or, like Martin Delaney and Charles Lenox Remond, their response included the claim of inherent black superiority). Others, rightly assessing the enormity of the obstacles to their ability to establish character, attempted to base their entire appeal on personality characteristics.

THE IDEOLOGY OF BLACK INFERIORITY AS A CONSTRAINT ON ETHOS

Despite the increasingly inclusive nature of the rhetorical culture, character and public deeds had not been removed from citizens' considerations. They were still compelling factors for audiences in their assessments of a public actor. True, personality gave some people from the margins *entrée* into the public sphere, but it did not fully legitimize their political or social equality. In fact, the expansion of the franchise and public sphere put added pressure on white American men of all classes to limit the expansion and justify the exclusion of others and to legitimize their identity as public actors. Both audiences and orators had to be qualified for the privilege of charting the course of the ship of state. They found that standards of character could be used as a barrier to keep undesirable groups away from the real avenues of power in government and society. This was accomplished by asserting white male preeminence in ability and worth over black men, first, but also over women.

The bifurcations, by sex and by race, allowed the men of the 1840s and 1850s to adopt the same mantle of leadership that had worked for previous generations of society's leaders — innate superiority. Orators from the two groups of Others had negative ethos expectations to overcome. Although able to draw audiences and even move them, these orators still found that the classical qualities of character such as wisdom, morality, and good will were quite appealing for the voters (and still are today, although to a lesser degree). Those same qualities were also an absolute prerequisite for anyone who wanted to make major political or social changes as the abolitionists did.

The gendered constraints on ethos would take decades to change, in part because antebellum women's rights activists consciously put their agendas on the back burner in favor of agitation for emancipation. They judged slavery to be a greater injustice and its remedy a more pressing need. They also had an advantage blacks didn't: women could claim an innate virtue thanks to the "cult of domesticity" that glorified their ethical and genteel natures. A certain power came from this construction of femininity that made their lots more tolerable.

Dark-skinned orators were not so lucky. Defaming them was the ultimate therapeutic remedy for the ennui of the democratic public. It provided a natural hierarchy that solidified the white male's right to participate in civic affairs. Better still, the hierarchy was not subject to interpretation or guesswork for, like women, blacks' differences from white males were clearly signified in their physical characteristics. At least part of the racism in judging orators on the color of their skin rather than the content of their characters should be seen as an attempt to clarify and simplify the social structure. In an age where audiences were constantly asked to judge the worth of anonymous strangers, making a "skin-ocracy" (to adopt a phrase Douglass himself used) allowed people to make immediate distinctions between haves and have-nots based on unchanging and obvious traits. In this environment, for blacks to seek equality with white males was to contest the latter's status as public actors and throw the whole hierarchy and social order into disarray. This helps explain the resistance to expanding the "blessings of liberty" to anyone else as more than just racism and sexism.

But cooperation from whites aside, the real front lines of the rhetorical battle involved the voices and bodies of black orators presenting their own petitions to northern audiences. More than the agenda — which southerners regarded as pernicious but most northerners viewed as merely misguided — the very presence of these Others on the platform, some of whom, like Douglass, spoke as though they already were equal to the whites, angered people by *performing* their challenge to white supremacy. Typically, claims (logos) can be refuted and logic can serve either side, as Calhoun proved in his philosophical defenses of slavery. Emotions (pathos), though extremely powerful, were more like geysers in the lyceums and assemblies; they erupted fiercely but quickly cooled down as they met audiences' cathartic needs. In comparison, the power of ethos once established was nearly impossible to counter. Claim blacks were ignorant, and Douglass's brilliant, often extemporaneous speeches could present a unique rebuttal. Claim they were barbaric, and Douglass's stature and composure while delivering "a most gentleman like speech" turned the claim into a lie.

THE STANDARD STORY ABOUT DOUGLASS'S CHARACTER

Based on this logic, many authors have offered what I would label the "standard story" of Douglass's effectiveness as an antislavery orator. The origins of the story probably reach back to a standard introduction Garrison gave to Douglass's speeches: Garrison had a habit of "observing that [Douglass] was one who, by the laws of the South, had been *a chattel* but who was now, by his own intrepid spirit and the laws of God, *a man*."[2] In his newspaper and on lecture tours, Garrison perpetuated the idea that the character Douglass revealed in his speeches forced opponents to acknowledge that manhood, and moreover, that it overwhelmed all biases or resistance. As he states in his preface to Douglass's first autobiography, his protégé "has borne himself with gentleness and meekness, yet with true manliness of character. As a public speaker, he excels in pathos, wit, comparison, imitation, strength of reasoning, and fluency of language." Therefore, he concludes,

> Let the calumniators of the colored race despise themselves for their baseness and illiberality of spirit, and henceforth cease to talk of the natural inferiority of those who require nothing but time and opportunity to attain to the highest point of human excellence.[3]

According to Garrison, Douglass's speech, more than winning praise from audiences, is primarily useful for silencing the revilers. So, after a speech from Douglass, Garrison would frequently follow him to the platform and address the audience to ask "if they deemed [Douglass] a man, and capable of taking care of himself." Most often, with friendly audiences, he elicited shouts of approval from the audience.[4] This step completed the performance. The audience felt as though they had witnessed a drama where a beast had become a man before their eyes. To anyone sitting on the fence about the slavery issue, the claim that visual, experiential proof had been given of the slave's humanity probably had a quite a strong influence.

Because this is the story that the abolition movements' chief propagandist wanted to communicate, it has gained a wide currency to this day. Another example comes from Francis Grimké, one of Douglass's friends when she praised him in a eulogy thus:

> Morally, what a splendid specimen of a man he was — lofty in sentiment, pure in thought, exalted in character.... For more than fifty years, he was before the public eye: Not infrequently during that time he was the object of the bitterest hatred, and yet during all those years, in the face of the strongest opposition, with the worst passions arrayed against him, no one dared even to whisper anything derogatory of him, or in any way reflecting upon the purity of his life, or upon the honesty and integrity of his character.[5]

But there are also more recent purveyors of the standard story, such as a 1972 dissertation on Douglass's rhetoric. Having come to an analysis of Douglass's ethos, the author declares "whether it was determined by his reputation or whether it resulted from the content and manner of his speaking, Douglass's stature as a man representative of his own arguments and proof was overwhelming."[6] The qualities mentioned here — strength of reasoning, purity, moral excellence and stature — all have to do with character. The standard story casts Douglass as the *vir bonus* and his audiences as witnesses to his ascension to his proper station in society.

The Response to the Standard Story

Now, there is no doubt Douglass's claim to be fully and equally human is "overwhelming" to readers today. His speeches are moving and brilliant. Indeed, righteous indignation is my most frequent response to reading his speeches. He fares especially well in comparison to the bigots who would have kept him in bondage. But this does not do away with the fact that Douglass himself despaired of his effectiveness, that it took a war to end slavery, and that a Jim Crow environment lasted long past the war's end. *On occasion* Douglass was truly overwhelming to his audiences. To the curious and uncommitted the Garrison-enforced interpretation of his performance aided by the call/response elements all had to be stirring. As I will argue, though, Douglass's ethos could not have been solely or even primarily based on the traditional appeal of good morals, good sense, and good will.

Ethos determines the people we listen to and are inclined to believe. It is co-constructed between the speaker and audience. Recognizing this we can see the flaws of the standard story. White audiences would never have listened to him on the basis of his character. Few white men would have assented to the noble and great character he was known for or granted that he had character in the first place. The historical evidence shows that even some people in Douglass's own camp questioned his character; they charged him with egotism and with a selfishness that impaired his decision making. All this is to say that ethos cannot be forced upon an unwilling audience, as Douglass's apologists (and the speech critics obsessed with describing the orator's "power") would have us believe.

In reality, the culture imposed stringent limits on black rhetors that could only partially overcome with traditional appeals. The proslavery forces held most of the cards in the effort of Douglass to establish ethos, simply because orators are not completely free to identify themselves as they choose. An identity cannot be completely fabricated in the heat of the moment since no one is completely anonymous to an audience. Even if their information is incomplete, inferred from the nature of the event (e.g. an environmental rally attracts certain kinds of speakers), the speaker's clothing, or what have you, the audience has some impression of the speaker as he or she strides to the lectern. Ethos is built *in* relationship to an audience and is built *on* what it is given in terms of expectations. Borrowing from McCroskey, we might call the expectations for any individual orator *initial* ethos.[7] During the speech, how Frederick Douglass handles audience expectations during the process of identifying himself determines his *derived* ethos (the topic of the next chapter). Just because Douglass is an exemplary *vir bonus* in relationship to a reader today, does not mean his moral supremacy was so clear to his first audiences most of whom had wholly different expectations. In the end, the process was more complicated than exhibiting a true greatness of character and waiting for people to acknowledge it.

THE RHETORICAL CONSTRUCTION OF BLACK PERSONHOOD BY WHITE ANTAGONISTS

The history of the standing of African Americans in this country is a well-covered topic, so I have no intention of retelling that story. The way race relations affect ethos is another matter, one largely unexplored. For the antebellum period, few scholars have made the connection between social standing, naive theories of personhood, and rhetorical ethos,[8] although African Americans' efforts at discursively constructing identities have received wide attention. One limitation of many studies on identity is that they focus on written discourse, particularly the slave narratives. In non-oral rhetoric, the interaction with the audience is less immediate; the element of participation in communal emotional expression is missing, as are several physical elements of ethos that were crucial to nineteenth-century audiences such as the "fiery eye" and the forceful gestures that signaled to audiences the depth of the orator's feelings.

This is not to say the slave narratives weren't crucial for setting expectations for orators. They were. Many people drawn to the movement and first introduced the idea that a black person could have interesting things to say through the popular slave narratives. President Lincoln is even famous for crediting *Uncle Tom's Cabin* with starting the Civil War. From time to time, the antislavery press wondered publicly if abolitionists should de-emphasize lecture tours in favor of publication, based on reasoning akin to the "standard story" of Douglass's natural appeal:

> This fugitive slave literature is destined to be a powerful lever.... We see in it the easy and infallible means of abolitionizing the free states. Argument provokes argument, reason is met by sophistry; but narratives of slaves go right to the heart of men.... Stir up honest men's souls with such a book and they won't set much by *disclaimers*; they won't be squeamish how radically they vote against a system which surpasses any hell which theology has ever been able to conjure up.[9]

However, just as the panegyrics about Douglass's impact on auditors were overstated, this too is an optimistic view. The best slave narratives were useful for allowing black rhetors to present their version of events and portray themselves without the immediate threat of physical harm. They also had a strong sentimental appeal. But the supreme power to change votes was not in them. As I have suggested, the measure of a person at the time, of whether he or she deserved all the rights and privileges of the citizen, was action in the public sphere. Writing an autobiography was a sign of learning and so, with a proper number of poignant scenes, worked toward establishing the slave as a feeling and thinking individual in the same category as white men. In the early nineteenth century, though, only participation in public arguments would serve as evidence that blacks had the stuff of citizenship (and, by extension, could not be slaves). By entering the public sphere the black orators themselves provided the best response to the attempts to oppress their race. The white construction of blackness, then, needs to be approached as an effort primarily to restrict ethos.

The popular image of blacks came most powerfully in the form of various pronouncements about black inferiority from ideologues and, more significantly, from official branches of the U.S. government. At crucial moments, U.S. policies were set that accomplished one of three purposes: affirming the value of slavery by expanding its geographical territory, circumscribing the freedoms of "free" blacks, especially in the north, or defending slavery from criticism or attack by ideological opponents. The discourse of the government could impinge on the image of blacks explicitly by directly describing their debased nature or implicitly by suggesting that slavery was them.

In addition to generating all manner of negative expectations, the doctrine of inferiority made blacks rhetors feel as though they had to argue against their reputation before their other arguments would be heard. Always having to make a case for one's own humanity devolved into further problems, such as a lack of time to address other issues, and the natural weakness that comes from arguing against pre-sumption. In the final analysis, though, some answer was incumbent on black orators because of the seriousness of the defamation and the institutional authority of its source. The list of insulting official documents and acts is quite long, but a few examples related to major aspects of character are especially significant.[10]

The Franchise and Phronesis

One primary political concern was no less a document than the U.S. Constitution, for Garrisonians interpreted it as clearly pro-slavery. They pointed out that it nowhere called for the ouster of slavery, and its strongest "antislavery" provision was a far-off regulation of the foreign slave trade destined for 1808. In matters of *representation*, that hallowed ideal of republic governance, the Constitution's very first article assured the nation that slaves knew they counted only as "three-fifths" of a person and therefore should not expect the privileges extended by the rest of the document (regardless of whether this clause was intended to limit the voting power of slave states, it was usually understood as an assessment of the fitness of slaves for life in the public sphere).

True, voting and office-holding restrictions limited the representation of non-property-holding whites as well, but voting qualifications were being quickly eliminated in the early nineteenth century. Contrarily, northern blacks in the 1830s and 1840s found themselves arguing against laws in several states that would have increased restrictions on their political and social involvement.

The issue of the vote is an important one for understanding ethos in a democratic society. Offering the vote to a group of people confirms that they are trusted decision makers for the society. It admits that they are capable of judgment and suggests that they can put their own interests aside for the good of the nation. In so many words, the Constitution denied to African Americans two classical markers of ethos set down by Aristotle, good sense (*phronesis*) and good will (*eunoia*). As more lower-class whites were being told, "In you is represented the best this country has to offer," free blacks were told that they were incapable of using their votes properly, for the betterment of all.

As noted, there is in fact a strong connection between the broadening white franchise and the shrinking black one. Extending the franchise, in a very visible way, made the upper classes and the finer families equal with every fresh-faced youth straight from the family farm. To maintain the valued identity as the elite of society, the upper classes translated their disdain for the lower classes into a generic white male contempt for a "lower" race and rhetoric warning about the dangers of miscegenation.

Politics, Personhood, and Paternalism

The move to depersonalize and demonize the slavery class is, of course, as old as slavery; Aristotle himself did this in his *Politics*, and the elitism is apparent when he asserts that masters and slaves are types of people, not positions. In other words, slaves cannot, by definition, have the ethos qualities of a citizen — wisdom, good morals, and concern for the citizenry.[11] Even Aristotle's assumptions were not inviolate, though. When half the states began abandoning slavery as a system and allowed the "natural slaves" to walk among the citizens, it forced a problematic debate about the morality and utility of slavery to move into the public eye. It was problematic in two respects.

First, it brought the discussion of the slavery question from the moral into the political realm. Even though the motivations for northern withdrawal from slavery were economic and moral, and the arguments against it usually relied on charges of sinfulness, an entire region cannot adopt an economic policy in the American system of government without pitting states against each other. Whereas slave states could have squelched or ignored the rather meager opposition to slavery within their own borders, the arguments to justify slavery — which usually involved some disparagement of blacks — were drawn into national policy debates after northern emancipation. In fact, starting in the nineteenth century most major congressional debates would contain some discussion about slaves. This began in earnest the public, calculated, and organized refutation of black claims to full humanity.

The second problematic aspect of northern freedom was the creation of a false distinction between antislavery north and proslavery south. In the resulting political environment, while supporting northern interests in issues of expansion or commerce, northern politicians often found themselves maligning slavery and defending emancipation. The problem was that most northerners disliked the idea of sectional conflict more than idea of slavery. Whatever northern antislavery sentiment existed was more like a benighted and grudging application of uncomfortable enlightenment logic, rather than a deep respect for the humanity of the slaves. As Jefferson put it in his plea for colonization,

> Why not retain and incorporate the blacks into the state, and thus save the expence of supplying, by importation of white settlers, the vacancies they will leave? Deep rooted prejudices entertained by whites; ten thousand recollections, by the blacks, of the injuries they have sustained; new provocations; the real distinctions which nature has made; and many other circumstances will divide us into parties, and produce convulsions which will probably never end but in the extermination of one or the other race. — To these objections, which are political, may be added others, which are physical and moral.[12]

Thus in the course of defending their increasingly industrial economics, many public figures from the north were only mildly critical of slavery and careful not to credit the humanity of blacks for the change. The debate over slavery, where it existed, was constituted as a contest between two forces, one that approved of slavery in the strongest terms and one that disapproved in the mildest terms. Even slavery's detractors, were often cooperating in constructing black Americans as inherently inferior, their concern for the lot of blacks was a paternalistic, not a brotherly one. At the heart of the rejected *brother* metaphor are notions of working together and equality (well represented in the French slogan lauding *liberté, églalité, et fraternité*). Douglass and many other ex-slaves commented on the oppression that existed in the north long after emancipation, trying to disabuse audiences of the idea that freedom in northern society was an unqualified good for the black person.

The positive side of the politicization of the slavery debate is that northern freemen and ex-slaves were drawn into public sphere to confront their accusers. Benjamin Quarles, historian and author of one of the earliest Douglass biographies, argues that black activism was first motivated and united by their opposition to the colonization movement in the first decades of the nineteenth century.[13] Other authors locate the first organized agitation as far back as 1810 in opposition to a law that forbade the hiring of black postal workers.[14] Lacking representatives or newspapers, the black response was limited to public demonstration and conventioneering — gathering to give speeches and pass resolutions in support of anti-slavery and anti-discrimination activities. A coalition of political abolitionists and free northern blacks began a concerted effort to improve the political situation of blacks, agitating for everything from schools to voting rights. They also left behind the language of uplift and gentle reproof for vituperation and advocacy of policies and platforms.

Scholars have debated the relative merits of this kind of political action by Garrisonian abolitionists. Bormann, among others, is convinced that their extreme positions and rejection of compromises entrenched the opposition and alienated the very people they needed to reach to garner political power.[15] Strict rules against official political involvement and voting because of the supposed corruptness of the American government kept the swelling ranks of antislavery from having a voice in Congress. Nevertheless, Garrison and his allies may not have been so short sighted as they seem at first glance. The democratization of the rhetorical culture in the early part of the century certainly suggested to blacks that gathering to hear speeches was a powerful form of political action as well as a way of establishing their own identities as public actors. Perhaps, then, it is only that the notion of *voice* has been overrated as a political tool. Black abolitionists were convinced of the power of *presence*. The acts of meeting together, filling lecture halls, organizing lecture tours and societies were all parts of a strategy whereby blacks gave themselves a public presence that they believed would facilitate social change, even if they had no voice.

Since they lacked that official voice in the machinery of government, the black presence was still a purposefully political one. For instance, if the southern congressmen believed their own racist propaganda about the inherent maliciousness of blacks, one can only imagine their discomfort when they had to deliver speeches promoting the glories of slavery in halls filled to the brim with free blacks scowling at them. In some parts of the south blacks could be punished and even killed for gathering in groups larger than seven. (Douglass, citing this fact from Weld's *American Slavery As It Is* would use it as proof of the vileness of a society based on slavery, and suggest that southern society was based on fear.) Without uttering a word or casting a vote, being very visible in public activities revealed how capable of citizen-like actions black Americans were. Without resorting to violence, or even technically breaking decorum, black public activity challenged the premise that whites were the natural masters.

Before long, a political response met the increasingly political challenge of antislavery. In several northern states where antislavery work was becoming most active, assemblies wrote laws to restrict the public activities of blacks, and to settle the issue of the rightful place in society by writing into law the exclusion of blacks from voting and property owning. Still the agitation continued, increased even, in the face of the Missouri Compromise of 1820, a congressional act designed to give more *Lebensraum* to slavery. Even the Mexican-American war was protested because it was seen as nothing more than a national effort to extend slavery into Mexican territory. At each juncture, slavery was justified against its critics on the grounds that slaves needed and even appreciated their captivity because on their own they were incapable of living above barbarity, that, as Calhoun argued, Congress had no right to extend protection to blacks in the territories because Constitutional provisions applied only to white men, and that Congress was foolish for even desiring such a course of action inasmuch as slave labor was the best way of assuring equality among whites *as the rightful co-masters of blacks.*[16]

Despite the moves to expand and protect the slavery empire in the 1820s, John Quincy Adams's voice was one of the very few from "the establishment" questioning the underlying premises of American race-based slavery. When Missouri's statehood was granted and its constitution was approved by Congress, it included an explicit provision rejecting citizenship for free blacks. Adams's response shows how even genuine concern for the humanity (and therefore human rights) of blacks was mixed with denigrating assumptions about their relative quality. Adams's argues that the provision that denied blacks citizenship:

> would change the terms of the federal compact — change its terms by robbing thousands of citizens of their rights. And what citizens? The poor, the unfortunate, the helpless. Already cursed by the mere color of their skin, already doomed by their complexion to drudge in the lowest offices of society, excluded by their color from all the refined enjoyments of life accessible to others, excluded from the benefits of a liberal education, from the bed, from the table, and from

the social comforts of domestic life, this barbarous article deprives them of the little remnant of right yet left them — their rights as citizens and as men.[17]

He means to arouse pity, but it doesn't seem to occur to him that his description of such a genuinely pathetic people may reinforce the need to keep them segregated from any political power. Therefore it was not hard for those who disagreed with him to merely extend Adams's logic. One of his correspondents responded to this request for pity by running through a serious of familiar allegations, including the assertion that nine-tenths of all petty thievery was committed by blacks.[18] Incipient in the claim of their need was the counterclaim of their lack of merit.

Unlike President Adams, most northerners lacked even a patronizing concern for the full humanity and citizenship of blacks, although they may indeed have pitied them. Northern politicians tolerated the expansion of slavery as long as similar gains in territory were given to the north so they wouldn't be at a political disadvantage. The effects of slavery on American society were tolerated until the imposition of the slavery power inconvenienced them personally. In this regard, the northern mind is revealed well in their self-interested responses to the most notorious dehumanizing discourses, the Fugitive Slave Law of 1850 and the Dred Scott Decision of 1857.

The national Fugitive Slave Law made it possible for any white person to detain a black man or woman on suspicion of being a runaway slave. It then became the burden of the accused to prove he or she was not a slave, without the opportunity of testifying in his or her own defense at the hearing. The law also authorized officials to deputize any northern man in the hunt for a fugitive slave. This effectively turned the whole of America, in Douglass's apt phrase, into a "nation of slave catchers."

Prior to the introduction of this latest southern affront to northern self-governance, the north had already fought its share of battles with proslavery ideologues. One of the most famous, George Fitzhugh, argued that the chattel slavery of the south was infinitely preferable to the wage slavery of the industrializing north.[19] Northern rejoinders always relied on an enlightenment logic that people should be free to choose their careers and free to advance in society according to their potential and willingness to work. Their ideology of moral uplift and personal responsibility was in conflict with the southern method of "improving" and "protecting" the slaves by placing them in their proper roles and in close contact with the "superior" white race. Northern insistence that their economy held the greatest promise of uplift led to a certain pride about the freedoms blacks enjoyed to succeed or fail. They felt that they could take care of their own residents, especially their most "helpless" and pathetic ones, the ones most in need of parental concern and moral uplift.

So the conscription of northern men in the support of a law that was clearly hurtful to their already demoralized residents, and all for the sake of the South's archaic institution, rankled many a northerner. Several northern states had already passed "personal liberty laws" which legalized noncooperation with slave catchers and legitimized freedom of conscience. The new national legislation was designed to nullify such state laws, in effect overriding the popular will and removing a northern freedom. With it in place, northerners were starting to feel the power of slavery as a force that could override their own laws and as a threat to their liberty in a very concrete way.

To northerners, the law represented an illegitimate — indeed, paternalistic — authority and so kindled conscious resistance. Many captured slaves were freed, occasionally through violent conflicts with law officials. Many officials refused to prosecute anyone involved in noncompliance or fugitive rescue efforts. Along with these spontaneous reactions, the Fugitive Slave law inspired legal efforts to solidify a state's rights to determine its own policies on white duties and rights in relationship to slaves and free blacks. This inspired a measure of hope in the abolitionists, who lent their voices to the calls for equal protection under the law for all people and for the right of the states to make laws that reflected their attitude toward slavery and slaves (however paternalistic). In less than a decade, though, their hopes were quickly snuffed by Judge Taney's declarations in writing the Dred Scott decision for the Supreme Court.

Public Association and Moral Virtue

Dred Scott, who had petitioned the courts for his release from slavery on the grounds that being brought by his master into a free state turned him into a free man, was more than rebuffed by the Court. Chief Justice Taney made several points that directly countered every effort of black orators for full and equal citizenship. Among other things, the court decided that,

> [The black race] had for more than a century before [the Declaration of Independence] been regarded as beings of an inferior order, and altogether unfit to associate with the white race, either in social or political relations; and so far inferior that they had no rights which the white man was bound to respect; and that the Negro might justly and lawfully be reduced to slavery for his benefit....
> [I]t cannot be believed that the large slave-holding States regarded them as included in the word citizens.

And he concluded that, "The right of property in a slave is distinctly and expressly affirmed in the Constitution."[20]

This solemn declaration from the highest levels of government that a group of people is "so far inferior" as to be unfit for both rights and mere *association* with another has to be considered one of the most severe strangleholds on ethos ever faced in this country. How could an orator expect an audience to rely on his ethos as proof of his argument when they thought they were too good to even be seen with him in public? Adams was concerned that blacks could not share a table with whites; Dred Scott applauded it. And this was not just Taney's opinion. His words mollified a number of northerners who favored neither slavery nor social and political equality.

Because even associating with blacks was offensive to refined tastes, social ostracism haunted freemen and the white antislavery activists associated with them. In 1844 the reform-minded Lewis Tappan remarked how things were slowly changing but also the depth of the racial animosity:

> A friend of mine, now on a visit to Washington, writes that when he was there a few years since most Northern men hesitated about even speaking to a man of color, lest he should be taken for an abolitionist and be "lynched," but now abolition is the topic of conversation in all the boardinghouses, hotels, parties, &c., and that [sic] the House of Representatives appears to him like an Anti-Slavery Convention.[21]

The taboo against association was so strong that some attendees of abolition meetings could see little else. On the stage white men and women mixed with black male and, occasionally, female orators. Many workers in antislavery were white women; many of those in the audience were black men. The whole thing seemed like a "semi-flirtation" to some reporters, and they often laced their reviews with sexual innuendo.[22] When the public work of abolition could be perceived in salacious terms, when the desire of women to perform public duties like male citizens and the need for black men to gather to alleviate their condition became part of the mythos of illicit interracial sexuality, Dred Scott, far from being the source of the problem, was only a symptom.

About Dred Scott, officially at least, northern Democrats were chagrined and the Republicans were outraged. State and territorial sovereignty over the slavery issue had, in effect, been brushed aside in a single pronouncement. Dred Scott's extremism bolstered the Republican party, and so did play a part in the eventual election of Abraham Lincoln, overt sectional conflict, and by chain of inference, to the end of American slavery.

However, none of the uproar should be taken to mean that northern whites were, as a group, willing to grant free blacks equal political or social standing. Northern hostility was aimed at the infringements of their own rights and, to a lesser degree, the expansion of slavery in the southwest territories even while slavery had long been viewed as an archaic system sure to deteriorate and become obsolete in the radiance of the Enlightenment. The idea that gag rules could be put in place in the United States Congress to stave off all discussions of slavery was, along these lines, another straw on the camel's back. It should have forced people to question the extent of the "slave power." Yet none of these conflicts initiated anything like a northern movement of white civic leaders to recognize the rights and personhood of the black person. That more fundamental battle was carried on by black rhetors, as represented by their famous slogan, "Am I not a man and a brother?" To put it another way, as late as 1858 during the Lincoln-Douglass debates, Senator Douglass was extremely successful in arousing fear and anger in audiences by accusing the Republicans of favoring racial equality.

While it is true that many northerners rejected the control of the slave states in their lives, they agreed with one of Dred Scott's premises — the idea that blacks were from an "inferior order" of mankind. They concurred with Stephen Douglass when he said that blacks were incapable of enjoying independence, being so "degraded by ignorance, superstition, cruelty and barbarism."[23]

But Dred Scott was more than a debating point; it was the law of the land. Because of it, in the eyes of the court (and, of course, such people as agreed with it), ex-slave Douglass's denunciations of slavery had the same official weight as a trained parrot speaking the same words; the slave, the fugitive and the freeman were considered no better than chattels. Moreover, as a legitimate piece of property, Douglass confronted a basic ethical challenge when he was advertised or announced himself as an ex-slave orator, for he had "stolen" himself from his rightful owner. Under cover of darkness, and by lying to many white authorities, he and all fugitives had disobeyed the laws of the land and usurped the "natural order" by seeking liberty and equality in the North.

Attacking Colonization and the Loss of Good Will

Many northerners, unwilling to let blacks slowly work their way to equal citizenship status, and some with a genuine concern for the difficult life awaiting blacks in a country hostile to them, participated in the colonization movement. Garrison himself spoke out against the American Colonization Society as little more than thinly disguised racism, and a non-solution to the problem of slavery.[24] Removing free blacks to Africa was widely viewed in Garrisonian circles as an admission that blacks were incapable of succeeding in American society. It was based on the well-intentioned but thoroughly parental logic shown in Adam's plea for the country's most "miserable" citizens.

Unfortunately, the movement was highly reputable. It was not as controversial or as difficult to implement as immediate abolition, and its supporters, including its president, Henry Clay, were clear that they were against any kind of amalgamation of the two races. Douglass snidely remarked, "That Society is an old enemy of the colored people in this country. Almost every *respectable* man belongs to it, either by direct membership or by affinity."[25] By extension, the abolitionist was part of a radical and unrespectable movement; its agents were troublemakers. Another abolitionist pointed out, "It was a constant ruse with the orators of Colonizationism, to declaim against *slavery*, in order to enlist and use up the energies and means of philanthropists, while, in almost the same breath, they would justify *slaveholders*, and denounce '*incendiary abolitionists*.'"[26]

The rhetoric of the colonization societies, and their policy of removing the "problem" to Africa, bolstered the supposition that slaves and their abolitionist apologists were ultimately at fault for the strife in the glorious project that was American society (an argument that began as the southern response to Nat Turner's rebellion, David Walker's incendiary pamphlet urging revolution, and the mailing campaigns of anti-slavery literature). Only the wicked or the criminal would launch any criticism of fellow white men, even slaveholders, when it would encourage armed insurrection, especially when an attractive alternative could handle any problems caused by slavery or the exodus of blacks to the North. Thus, the project of the black abolitionists presented them with a dilemma: how does one attack slavery and the colonization plan without being identified as a treasonous rabble-rouser? Quarles is accurate in summarizing the general view that abolitionists were "sappers of the social order who incited slaves to rebel and the free Negro to seek intermarriage. And almost as bad, they endangered property rights, enfeebled the church, and subverted the Constitution."[27]

In addition, since white males had convinced themselves of their brotherhood and equality with each other and superiority over blacks, the abolitionists came across as obsessively committed to an agenda that hurt his fellows for a devotion to what one opponent called an irrational "niggerism."[28] In other words, for a white person, being an abolitionist meant being identified so completely with blacks, the wholly Other, the identification overrode the abolitionist's capacity for identifying himself as white. Most whites were unable to see abolitionists as bearers of good will, at least not toward them, since an abolitionist's warped mind was so occluded with a love for blacks.

THE IDEOLOGY OF INFERIORITY IN RHETORICAL PRACTICE

In general, the therapy-minded American populace resented abolitionists because they did not want to be bothered. They did not like the calls to sacrifice. On the other side, the pro-slavery rhetors did a fair job of portraying plantations as idyllic scenes of cooperation and uplift for blacks, but most people were probably not fooled; lash marks, manacles, and other kinds of physical evidence for the cruelty of slavery are hard to ignore (eventually Douglass would simply stop arguing that nearly all slaveholders, not just the bad ones, mutilated and starved their slaves, feeling that those whom the preponderance of evidence did not convince simply could not be convinced). Despite their awareness of the evils of slavery, people remained unmoved because they lacked what George Campbell would have called a "sympathy" with the dehumanized slaves. It is troubling to know that a neighbor beats his dog, or even that dogs are generally mistreated in a section of the country, but is it worth starting a war that would injure *people*? As a species of property in both sections of the country, the slave was only one step removed in many people's perceptions from other chattel.

All of this meant that many northerners were simply apathetic about slavery. Nathan Sargent the nineteenth-century journalist also suggests that the abolitionists should have realized early on that their primary obstacle was not economics, censorship, or misinformation about slavery, but apathy:

> at that time [of the start of the movement] probably four-fifths, if not nineteen-twentieths of the people of the non-slaveholding States, however opposed to slavery in the abstract, were equally opposed to any interference with it, not believing they had any right to meddle with it, and not thinking such interference calculated to preserve harmony or good feeling between the two portions of the country.[29]

As a result of apathy, abolition oratory had no use value for such people. It offended their sensibilities and concerned a topic that was better left undisturbed. They knew that slavery itself was bad, but they had more immediate concerns. Thus Wendell Phillips argued in 1853 that abolitionists needed to disabuse themselves of enlightenment thinking, noting there were "far more dead hearts to be quickened, than confused intellects to be cleared up"[30]

No program for abolition, much less equality, could be successful without somehow establishing the humanity and personhood of black persons, that there were, in W. E. B. DuBois's terms, souls in black folks. The character ascriptions had to be dealt with before they could successfully pursue any other point. Without ethos of some kind, there can be no persuasion or identification, and ultimately no reason to risk one's self and way of life.

Without any ethos relationship, Douglass's speeches could not be received as speeches. They seemed to some more like the ravings of a maniac, for someone who accepted the inferiority argument filtered all of the speech through that screen. An excellent example of this process is found in the Oswego [New York] *Daily Advertiser*, from a review of a Douglass speech that won the admiration of British audiences during his famous tour to raise support for American abolition. To the New York reporter, Douglass's speech tour is "lowering in the eyes of English courtesy and intelligence, the character of our slave population, though, perhaps, ignorance, rudeness, fanaticism, and an unthinking hatred of American, may loudly cheer him on." That is, Douglass's rhetoric was actually shaming the good name of slaves! An excerpt from the article is worth a lengthy citation because it reveals how someone can attend an otherwise eloquent speech, have a real disdain for slavery and its debilitating effects, and yet undercut every strength of the speech because of a racist logic that cannot see the man as an orator.

As a runaway slave, fleeing from bondage to liberty, Mr. Douglass was entitled to, and did receive our sympathy. And when, after he had obtained a smattering of education we heard him speak, and read his letters, characterized though his productions were by all the bad taste, bad grammar, and bad rhetoric, incident to acquirements as superficial as his must necessarily have been, we felt disposed to admire the mental power which would so well withstand the degradation of Slavery. But if the lash of the master has not broken his mind, it has driven from his heart every high moral trait. His whole course of freedom has been a career of indelicacy, falsehood, and abuse.... When his race was run here; when his darkey eloquence had ceased to be a novelty, he crossed the water there to make himself a raree show — to promote the ignorance, and pander to the vilest passions of the vilest Englishmen.... [Because] Irishmen and Englishmen have turned out as they would turn out to see an ourang-outang, or hear the bray of a wild ass, to see of what material a runaway slave is made, and how a thick-lipped orator can talk, his conceit knows no bounds.[31]

Several things are worth noting here. There is a clear distinction between the rhetorical proofs Douglass offers and those he does not. He is capable of using his "mental power" and the author already grudgingly admitted that the crowds were moved by Douglass's words to "loudly cheer him on." Logos and pathos are not at issue, then. Despite admitting that Douglass used them successfully, this is still "bad rhetoric" because it is lacking "every high moral trait." Such antagonistic critics could use the classical character-based standards to invalidate what was otherwise widely regarded as a resounding rhetorical success.

The review lists several more examples of Douglass's bad character at even greater length than I have excerpted here, all to counterbalance the apparent power of the ex-slave's oratory. In light of his estimation that this is "darkey eloquence" — and the adjective completely denudes the meaning of the noun — he has to conclude that British audiences are receptive for one of two reasons: either they are the "vilest Englishmen," in which case their approval of his poor character is a further indictment of Douglass; or, the audiences have turned out in droves merely to hear a novelty, a freak of nature, the beast who speaks, which puts us (at best) in the realm of personality-based ethos. Either way, the otherwise meritorious speech could not overcome the racist expectations the reviewer had, the firm conviction that a slave could not achieve true character. His belief is independent of any pity he has for Douglass or admiration of his intelligence, and even independent of his dislike of slavery and full acknowledgment that slavery caused all sorts of degradation and limitations.

Douglass quickly got used to such evaluations, and recognized that hatred of himself, his style or his topic was usually fueled by hatred of his race. The enormous contrast eventually wore on him, the vast gap between slavery as "the sum of all villainies"[32] described to them so earnestly by ex-slaves and the lackadaisical response of the American public. In Huggins's biography of Douglass, he notes that on the eve of the Civil War Douglass was "gloomy" about the future of antislavery. "Thirty years of intense labor had nearly succeeded in enlightening the public to the enormities of slavery, but there were few practical results. The moral conscience of the public had not been aroused." Or, as Douglass put it, "The grim and bloody tragedies of outrage and cruelty are rehearsed day by day to the ears of the people, but they look on as coldly indifferent as spectators in a theatre."[33]

A more appropriate comparison could not have been made, for Douglass's audiences were acting *exactly* as spectators in a theater. The black abolitionist, on stage with white women, giving speeches about beatings and rapes, was a titillating spectacle for white audiences to observe and enjoy. But get involved? That was too much commitment for a mere entertainer to ask and certainly not their reason for attending.[34]

If Douglass was depressed by this state of affairs prior to the election of 1860, Lincoln's election is evidence that he and his allies had made some inroads with the voters. On the other hand, Wendell Phillips's comments indicate that he and other white abolitionists seem to have been taken by surprise by the realization that a true understanding of slavery would not lead to universal calls for emancipation. Perhaps it was an evangelist's zeal for simple moral conversions or an enlightenment-induced fallacy that led the anti-slavery leadership to misunderstand their task as a social reform effort or an educational endeavor. More likely, though, it was the presence of racism within the ranks of the white leadership itself that blinded them to the need to construct blacks as fully, equally human outside of any mention of slavery.

Racism, the Enemy Without and Within

That racism affected Douglass's ethos is certainly not a revelation. Churches, many of whom were arrayed against him, decried his morality and orthodoxy, lending their voices to the many authorities constructing blacks as a degenerate race and abolition as an immoral cause. Thoreau felt that a worse disservice was done to Douglass and other black agitators by the racist leanings of the press. The newspapers, he felt, exercised "a greater and more pernicious influence than the church" because "we are not a religious people, but we are a nation of politicians." He concluded, that "Almost without exception the tone of the press is mercenary and servile [to the slave power]."[35] And those are the Northern newspapers!

All this is to say that there were many other sources of the ideology of inferiority than the federal government and many ways to carry it to the people. So ingrained was the notion that blacks were incapable of acquiring higher moral and intellectual states, Douglass felt that he was not much better off under Jim Crow in the North than he was under the whip of slavery in the South. This impulse led him to rebuke northerners for supporting segregation and intolerance. Rebuke rhetoric put a strain on his ability to reach democratic audiences for whom *good will* was best shown by offering an audience a therapeutic benefit. Wisely, when Douglass was still building his reputation, he saved his harshest words about northern hypocrisy and racism for predominantly black audiences and antislavery conventions rather than public lectures.

Prejudice affected Douglass's ethos in more subtle ways too. Recently scholars have scrutinized the white leadership of the antislavery movement for attitudes of superiority and even for evidence that they did not ascribe an equal and full humanity to the blacks who worked alongside them.[36] According to personal letters and some public proclamations, several workers in the abolitionist cause gave their time and energy because they were troubled by the numbers of escaped slaves moving in to northern territory. "Western Reserve Anti-Slavery convention had once, in 1842, declared that abolition was the one way to keep the North from being flooded by Negroes," Filler reminds us. "Slavery they equated with runaway slaves headed North, and in need of aid and co-operation. Emancipation alone 'could relieve them of the presence of a class whose contiguity was so offensive.'"[37]

Douglass's frequent companion in antislavery work, Wendell Phillips, had a more nuanced attitude toward race which was never expressed in overt acts of oppression or slanders of black orators. He did, though, mention to his wife that he was uncomfortable having to "sleep with the cause" when he and Douglass traveled together and had to share a room.[38] He was uncomfortable associating with a black man, which for the aristocratic Phillips was undoubtedly a matter of class difference as well as race.

Sometimes, though, the petty biases of the leadership of the National Anti-Slavery Society were translated into public acts. During his tour of the British Isles, Douglass was angered at being assigned a white companion, James Buffum, by Maria Chapman on behalf of the American Anti-Slavery Society to keep track of money. Douglass read into Buffum's assignment a statement about his own ability to handle money, or if not ability, his trustworthiness. This sort of slight may have given him sufficient reason to confront his paternalistic handlers in a more direct way, for shortly after his triumphant tour and return to America, he put plans in motion to start his own newspaper, a direct competitor to Garrison's *Liberator*. More than this, in his day to day activities for the cause, Douglass's recurrent confrontations with whites who assumed they were superior to him, or expected him to play the typical subservient roles of blacks and slaves, must have been on his mind rather frequently as he spoke. As much as his frustration with political acts of bigotry, these informal interactions demonstrated the extent to which the inferiority ideology had infiltrated American society. They probably also strengthened his resolve to "be a man and not a slave" at every moment given Douglass's stubbornness. His defiant bearing so obvious on the platform as well as when he was walking down the street with white female companions, was often commented upon (usually with disapproval), and may have been a part of Douglass's compensation for the tendency of his close allies to demean him.

There is a legitimate question here, though. How much did the racism inside the movement alter the nature of antislavery meetings and change expectations for Douglass's ethos? The most likely answer is this: the affect was noticeable by perceptive blacks and whites, especially early on. The entire antislavery structure was dominated by white philanthropists and leaders. The newspapers were run by whites and the lectures and tours planned by them. The structure of an antislavery event was itself a subtle indication that a distinction had been made between wise leaders and humble followers, a distinction that corresponded with racial lines much more so than gender.

Although Douglass was keenly aware of how beholden he actually was to white benefactors, how, among other embarrassments, he had to request that they send money to his wife when he could not support her, his monetary subordination was not publicized outside the movement. The pro-slavery ideologues and the apathetic public were shocked with the racial cooperation they saw at work in antislavery movements, and little evidence remains that whites outside antislavery ranks were privy to, or influenced by, its stratifications. Their expectations would have been set by the publicized view of antislavery as miscegenationists. Their interest in hearing a black orator speak would have been piqued by seeing him share a podium with white men and women. For most people, in other words, the internal hypocrisy of the Antislavery Society itself would not have established a lower expectation for a black speaker.

But from time to time, we can see instances where internal racism altered Douglass's ethos. Criticism of Douglass within the movement and during some public meetings was inspired by racial biases rather than the merit of his arguments. From very early in his oratorical career Douglass was willing to contradict white members of the Societies. At an antislavery meeting in 1843, he and a local politician spoke on different sides of a debate on the pro-slavery nature of the Constitution. Apparently, the other man left the meeting rather than dignify Douglass with a reply; he refused to have a black man talk back to him.[39] To some audience members, blacks perhaps more than others, this incident would have strengthened his reputation as someone who lived out the doctrine of equality. But for whites it also represented a viable reaction to Douglass's attempts to prove his arguments with ethos qualities that were normally reserved only for white males.

The most famous instance of prejudice within the ranks affecting expectations occurred in his early days lecturing with the Massachusetts Anti-Slavery Society. Although showmanship motivated him as much or more than racism, Garrison's famous ironic introduction of Douglass as a "miracle," and a "beast" who could speak severely constrained Douglass's ethos.[40] To be sure, introducing him with the affectations of a carnival barker in no way aided Douglass's ability to establish the traits of character a white orator might naturally assume. But it also limited the effectiveness of his personality by taking the spectacular and foreign elements of a black man speaking in public and bracketing them within the confines of the white leader's showcase. Rather than allowing Douglass himself to be the purveyor of exotic goods in the form of his speech, Garrison adopted the showman's role and constructed Douglass as one of his wares, as *the show itself.* Fortunately for Douglass and the movement, these sorts of introductions were relatively short lived and after a year or so on tour, Douglass could be confident of getting more respectful introductions.

Discourse about Racial Economics

The ideology of inferiority had at least three results, then: 1) it created a set of negative expectation for blacks as orators; 2) it created a general apathy about slavery that discouraged attendance at abolition rallies except for the express purpose of watching black orators parade their scars and life stories across the stage, and; 3) the ideology influenced the workings of the antislavery movements themselves. This last effect, though, may have acted as a prod to Douglass to strengthen his resolve and refuse the subservient place within the movement the paternalistic leaders wanted him to accept.

We should also note the construction of blackness as an inferior kind of personhood did not just occur in political and interpersonal discourse. Accompanying them there was a similar rhetoric in the economic sphere that characterized blacks as morally and intellectually inferior. In the success-driven society America was quickly becoming, the way the economic failure of blacks was constructed weighed more heavily on the minds of some their critics than any articulation of political policy.

The numerous ex-slaves making their way north in the 1830s and 1840s by escape or by purchasing their freedom quickly outstripped the few job opportunities for dark-skinned workers that existed in even the more enlightened cities. Illiterate, uneducated, and often skilled only for low-paying position, many simply gave up trying to make the American dream work for them. Resignation happened so often that neither of the most eloquent apologists for the race, Charles Lenox Remond nor Frederick Douglass, would argue against the generally degraded condition of their brethren in the North. Their apologies occupied a much weaker position in terms of ethos, namely, that the black man was indeed less of a man, but only because Southern slavery and Northern racism conspired to keep him that way. Arguing this, the black spokesmen were perfectly in step with their white counterparts in the abolition movement. What explanation can there be for this strategy, for the fact that abolitionists from both races failed to challenge the claim that blacks did not represent the best of humanity? Was it merely a lack of race pride?

Once again it helps to see the abolition movement in comparison to other reform movements of the nineteenth century. Presenting the many ramifications for blacks and for abolition of the reform impulse and the Second Great Awakening has already been the task of Walters, Banner, and others.[41] These authors point out that the belief in *perfectibility* as a goal attainable in this world inspired Christian reform efforts, especially in the matter of temperance. Humans were supposed to be able to improve themselves, especially if they would accept the help of God. Antislavery was fueled by the same notions as other reform movements and shared their membership rosters as well.[42] When antislavery speakers were unable to deny that sins of intemperate drinking and "slothfulness" (i.e. unemployment) were prevalent in the free black communities (the latter of which was also the result of racist hiring practices), they felt a moral duty to call for the uplift of blacks through education and Bible teaching. Their calls for help left the impression that the race was, as a whole, ignorant and un-Christian. The black enclaves were, at most, another mission field filled with savages. Fully cognizant of the double bind they were in, many blacks echoed Samuel Ringgold Ward's sentiments from his autobiography when he wrote, "I regard all the upright demeanour, gentlemanly bearing, Christian character, social progress, and material prosperity, of every coloured man, especially if he be a native of the United States, as, in its kind, anti-slavery labour."[43]

It is an odd sort of ethos offered by the orator who stands as a spokesman for an especially sinful race. The discourse of the abolitionists attempted to turn the discussion to their advantage, focusing on slavery as the root cause of the black person's degradation. Such speeches, though, (and Douglass made several of this type) amplified the slaves' lack of familiarity with scripture, and the sins the slave was forced to commit to survive (e.g. stealing food or lying to protect himself). On balance, these speeches probably had little ability to improve ethos expectations: whites were looking at the ex-slave speeches and autobiographies for reasons to disparage slavery *and* for reasons to dislike blacks; admitting moral problems but blaming them on slavery served both purposes. Meanwhile, black social problems continued relatively unchecked, especially since many reformers understandably directed their energies first against slavery rather than toward the welfare of northern blacks.

Putting these considerations aside for the moment, we can see that the Christian reform sentiment did afford blacks some unique opportunities for establishing character. At any number of reform meetings, the audience would expect to hear some version of an altar call where attendees were expected to declare that they were putting aside sinful behaviors because of the love and power in their hearts flowing from a conversion experience. A similar logic allowed blacks to repudiate slavery as merely the *scene* of their moral diminishment in a Burkean sense, much as a reformed drinker would denounce the tavern. A certain measure of moral standing always accompanies the public rejection of the sins of a past life, especially when one can blame the sin on a context, in this case, the desperate poverty and oppression of the plantation.[44]

Again, though, this rhetorical success was limited by the omnipresence of the inferiority ideology. The story Douglass often told about segregated communion (cited in the first chapter) is representative of how blacks' participation in revivals and temperance movements was segregated from whites'. The two groups were separated in physical space by sitting in different sections of the audience, and they were separated in time by allowing white responses to altar calls first. The separation signified that black character, regardless of how Christian and sinless it may declare itself to be, was somehow of a lower order, the result of a supposed limited capacity for intellection and moral choice. Through this process white audiences were inured to attempts of blacks to establish their good moral character, even if they performed the necessary public acts to redeem themselves from their "sinfulness."

Blacks' Limited Routes for Establishing Ethos

This brings us to the second result of the way whites constructed blackness, the denial to blacks of certain routes for establishing character. For the above reasons, and more, white audiences were situated to think of black orators as morally suspect. The concern about black men having predatory sexual appetites evident in all the talk about miscegenation was prevalent in the minds of upper-class white men.[45] Moreover, blacks had, it was widely believed, a violent nature that should keep them out of polite society. Even the apologetic slave biographies contained more than their share of criminal acts on the slaves' part as Andrews has explained.[46]

The power of whites to limit Douglass's effectiveness was extensive. Many of those most threatened by his presence on the platform were desperate to maintain the hierarchy and so felt justified in enforcing their superiority rather than relying only on words. Since, in their way of thinking, blacks were natural-born slaves and little more than chattels, it was appropriate to treat them that way even in the free states. They saw no problem with using physical violence to modify their behavior.

The very dangerous constraints on their speaking separate black antebellum orators from the Websters and Emersons. Among many examples, we could consider that Douglass couldn't speak in certain buildings in some towns by law, merely because he was black. And, even if he were legally allowed to use the place, a manager or owner might refuse him due to fear of mob violence, vandalism, or arson. The mobs were perfectly willing to attack him physically with fists, eggs and bricks. Douglass describes one incident from upstate New York in his first letter to the *National Anti-Slavery Standard* in 1841: "I spoke only for a few moments when through the windows was poured a volley of unmerchantable eggs, scattering the contents on the desk in which I stood, and upon the wall behind me, and filling the room with the most disgusting and stifling stench." He goes on to describe a group "howling with fiendish rage" assaulting him and injuring several of his protectors when he left the building.[47] Henry Clay himself might not have been so "magnanimous" faced with this barrage.

THE REHABILITATION OF MORALITY

Far beyond all the false images the attitudes about black morality penetrated into white consciousness, even affecting the efforts of blacks to rehabilitate their tarnished reputations. The inferiority motif was *overdetermined* in the sense that an entire network of social and symbolic relationships conjoined to cause a particular element of social life.[48] The many other ways blacks and whites related were therefore read into the act of black conversion and confession, such that a morally good act from a black person was re-interpreted to have less significance, so as not to count as morally proper. Repentance from someone who is morally and intellectually inferior cannot count as much as the deep grief a repentance white male was capable of, especially in an era when deep feeling was a sign of deep character.

Insidiously, a black orator who implied that his repentance, his beliefs, or his life in general was as worthy as any white man's could be immediately labeled "uppity." The same was true of someone daring to criticize the institutions of the country, from the Constitution to the church. Where a white rhetor might be labeled a radical and dismissed, or even a philosopher and quietly admired for his passive resistance (e.g. Thoreau), Douglass was risking his life when he rebuked whites.

A correspondent in Hartford, Connecticut, recorded the events at one of Douglass's early appearances where he "addressed a large audience, on the moral character of slavery, and the support it received from Church influence especially." His "application of the truth" was so thorough "as to call forth hissings" from pro-slavery elements in the crowd. The reviewer is clear that Douglass's logic, his truthfulness, was not at question, for two white men, Stephen Foster and John Wattles, spoke before him on "practical Christianity," a topic that necessarily critiqued the inaction of the church on the slavery debate. Rather, the reviewer thought, his "rebukes were insufferable, coming from a 'nigger!'"[49]

Such stories dispute the notion that Douglass's great eloquence and stature "overwhelmed" the prejudices of those who denied full humanity to all black persons. The crowds that responded so violently to him certainly did not think so. After Douglass's brazen censure of white Christianity, the antislavery forces were met with eggs and bricks the rest of that stay in Hartford. Whatever else Douglass did to establish his ethos, he had to adopt the roles of a Christian leader and a citizen to respond to the political and theological charges leveled against him and his brethren. In other words, he offered criticisms of the church from a stance of moral superiority, and in the mold of Martin Luther, he dared to carry his complaints to the public for discussion.

That stance of superiority and the assumption of the right to bring issues to the public sphere was a more egregious offense than *appealing* for political or social equality, much as if a London chimney sweep would have presumed to lecture parliament a century earlier. For the punishment to fit the crime, the response to forgetting his "place" was what it would have been on the plantation — physical violence was employed to stop the rebellious behavior. In the antebellum South, physical cruelty toward slaves was allowed and even supported because there was a widespread acknowledgment that keeping the slaves completely broken and fearful would keep the slave class in check, even though they were numerically superior to their masters.[50] Significantly, these northern mobs were reluctant to throw bricks at mixed groups of white men and women and blacks. The Hartford gang waited until Douglass was surrounded only by black companions to attack. In their restraint, choosing not to attack fellow white men and women, they proved that the message was not nearly so troubling as the messenger, for Phillips and Douglass spoke many of the same words but only one was a legitimate target for violence.

But the charge of "uppityness" had other uses when force was not an option. As one of Douglass's masters warned, "if you give a nigger an inch, he will take an ell." The master class was on the lookout for ways that blacks, allowed outside their proper positions, would abuse their freedom. One tactic of pro-slavery critics was to accuse the ex-slave orator by his own words whenever they asked for more than an end to slavery. Just so, Douglass's criticisms of America in England were deemed a breech of decorum and therefore a sign that he had gotten full of himself. Another common reproach was to take the most distinctive elements of the orator's appeal — the tale of his escape from slavery — and describe how much he relished in telling it. Any criticism of torture or cruelty on a plantation could be sabotaged by changing the issue to the ex-slave's pride and delight in criticizing his social betters.

For a proslavery ideologue, a speech could be evaluated solely on the issue of pride. "This fellow," one critic says of Douglass, "styles himself a fugitive from slavery, he undoubtedly is a fugitive from justice, and prides himself so highly on his escape, that he openly declared he would keep company with only a choice assortment of the blacks, and not with more than one in every nine, of the whites."[51]

This was in 1842, early in his career when his place in the movement and his reputation were not yet assured. At that time, if Douglass actually made such a declaration about the company he kept it was probably meant as a joke; ex-slaves frequently used ironic reversals in their discourse to question the social hierarchies. Still, the review forces us to consider: when condemnation for pride was not sufficient, or when the critic really wanted to make a point, Douglass's enemies were not above fabricating accusations. The evidence of this is earlier in the same review where a summary is given of Douglass's remarks that is at best a gross misrepresentation and almost surely a complete invention by the reviewer as it stands:

> [Douglass] lamented exceedingly that he had been refused the sacrament in some Methodist church, which he thought a burning shame, as he was ready to prove that *Jesus Christ, the Saviour of the world, was a Negro.* This was the highest flight of fancy we heard on the subject, and which if sufficient to deprive him of communion here, should entitle him to full communion in a much warmer region.

Since Douglass was having some success on this 1842 lecture tour and was showing himself competent in eloquence, he was performing the roles of white orators and was in danger of achieving their kind of influence. He had power over the audience and impressed them with his compelling stories of escape and northern racism. To counteract this kind of success, as we have seen, critics sometimes chided the audience for participating in the debauched antislavery spectacles. This reviewer, though, attempts to undercut Douglass's authority without even mentioning the audience by reconfiguring his courage and willingness to tell his life story as uppityness. The implication is that, given the opportunity, the Negro orator will get full of himself, revel in being above the law and in telling his silly little tale of escape as though it were great literature. The Negro who was allowed to address the public was prone to such pride that he had no compunctions about blaspheming, to making himself and his color the center of the moral universe. Finally, the reviewer levels the ultimate challenge to his morality, the indictment that he will burn in hell for his speaking.

THE REHABILITATION OF WISDOM

If black orators were constrained in rehabilitating their good morals, there were even more barriers to their ability to shore up their good sense or wisdom. Any given speech may have contained solid reasoning, but the delivery of the speech militated against the audience's perception of good sense. Audiences based their assessment on the subtle cues of accents (stereotypically presented in the dialogue of slave characters in *Uncle Tom's Cabin*) which revealed an uncultivated mind. In an age of acute attention to elocution, the ex-slave's questionable grammar and distinctive accent were ample evidence of ignorance, for those looking to find it. On the other hand, ex-slave orators whose diction revealed more of the academy than the plantation were suspected for making false claims. Douglass himself was charged with never having been a slave because he was too eloquent. To complete the chain of logic, if a slave were then to try to prove he had come up from slavery, he would have to mention his original name, the name of his master, and the location of his enslavement. Every item could be verified, but they also revealed the identity of the orator to any slave catchers. Since the orator would have already admitted to being an escaped slave as was readily identified by a specific slave owner, the ex-slave had little hope that a jury trial would save him from being sent South.

If an orator could get past this series of stumbling blocks, he could attempt to prove his practical wisdom through making sound observations about policies and procedures. In the early days of political antislavery in the 1830s and 1840s, leaders argued at every convention about the priorities of the movement and the most effective strategies for attacking slavery. During these arguments, personal experience and expertise contributed to one's ethos, and when ex-slaves spoke about the welfare of slaves still in bondage. Again, though, these qualities are individuating; they distinguish the person from the normal knowledge of the community. As Clark and Halloran suggest, personal expertise is antithetical to the republican norm of communal wisdom and morality.[52] This is why Aristotle suggests the best way to prove *phronesis* is by using maxims that the audience will know and agree with. Expertise, then, has more to do with personality than character.

Nevertheless, it is interesting that for Douglass personal experience does become a matter of practical wisdom. This is possible because he relays more than first hand account of slavery. He parlays his knowledge into arguments about how policies would change the life of the slave, and provides evidence for his assertions from the lives of slaves. For example, in one of his first recorded speeches we see him offering a first-hand account of what sorts of activities were beneficial to those trapped in slavery:

> I well remember getting possession of a speech by John Quincy Adams, made in Congress about slavery and freedom, and reading it to my fellow slaves. Oh! what joy and gladness it produced to know that so great, so good a man was pleading for us, and further, to know that there was a large and growing class of people in the north called abolitionists, who were moving for our freedom. This is known all through the south, and cherished with gratitude. It has increased the slaves' hope for liberty. Without it his heart would faint within him; his patience would be exhausted. On the agitation of this subject he has built his highest hopes. My friends let it not be quieted, for upon you the slaves look for help. There will be no outbreaks, no insurrections, whilst you continue this excitement: let it cease, and the crimes that would follow cannot be told.[53]

The key elements of the argument here are the warrants for continuing the petition drive in Congress. The hope of the slaves is first mentioned and used for a sympathetic appeal. Then Douglass builds to his strongest point, the argument that petitions to Congress shore up the dam that holds back a tidal wave of violent slave crimes. His knowledge of the character of slaves and their motives for suffering hardship is translated into practical information for his audience. The logic is based on a notion that all people, even slaves, will revolt if they see no other way of gaining their liberty. In American political argument from that era, this "maxim" would be irrefutable. Douglass shows good sense by drawing on his experience but relating it to what "everybody knows" about human nature.

In spite of this kind of good advice, in the earliest days of the antislavery societies contributions from ex-slaves were usually invited at the meetings, not freely given. Reading accounts of the meetings there is sense that ex-slaves are never fully in control of their own voices, never free to speak when they wish. Instead, they are called on for their wisdom on the sole issue of the character and thinking of the slaves. Their close connection with this one kind of knowledge may have precluded them being considered in other areas.

Other problems also plagued the ex-slaves who relied on their personal experiences to show their reasoning abilities. First, the emphasis of ex-slave orators on first-hand knowledge in debates over policy coincided with a general inattention in their speeches to lofty, abstract arguments in favor of simple life stories. The orator who was unable to act as Douglass had and draw significant conclusions from first-hand knowledge was not seen as wise, but as someone who could *only* make sense of things from everyday life. Children, critics knew, are capable of that level of thought. Second, recollecting a life in slavery focused attention on the speaker's Other-ness. It was not the testimony of an expert who had studied slaves in the South — those early sociological studies were usually done by proslavery ideologues — but the words of someone who lived it. The whole purpose of blacks participating in public arguments was to prove their equality with whites, when at the time "different" essentially meant "worse." The third problem is related to the second. Expertise about the best method for subverting slavery when it came from a slave exaggerated the revolutionary element of antislavery reform. At least in Douglass's early career, he was disinclined to advocate for a slave rebellion. Fomenting insurrection was also the last thing most white audiences wanted to hear, and would have been grounds for mob action against a speaker.

Self-centered, therapeutic listeners perceived the interests of the slaves to be in conflict with the interests of whites, especially wageworking whites who would have to compete with freemen for jobs.[54] It was hard for them to see his expert advice as sound for anyone but his brethren in chains. With black so alienated from white, an identification with both was difficult to achieve. Therefore, the ex-slave's expertise was contrived to be the advice of a traitor to his collaborators about starting a slave insurrection.

THE REHABILITATION OF AMITY

At this point we have begun to touch on the black orator's ability to establish good will. I have argued that to the therapy-seeking minds of white popular audiences the best evidence of good will was the promise of uplift, and the most disastrous move was to offer a rebuke. Insofar as a black orator could establish it, good will meant appealing amicably to white audiences for help and sympathy in fighting the slave empire. It was hard to argue that any other appeal for an end to prejudice by a black person was not self-serving.

The alienation of black from white was so complete that white readers of slave narratives identified with the white slaveholding characters rather than the heroic slaves. For narrators, writes Foster, "[i]t became almost axiomatic that for every two or three bad experiences related, one good experience must be recounted." This was at best a mediocre solution to a difficult problem: "They wished to contradict the masters' version of slavery by presenting the black slave's views, and they wanted to do this with an audience and with supporters who were more closely related by culture and vested interests to the masters than to the slaves."[55] The white northerner felt attacked not only when America was attacked for being racist, but when the slave holder was being vilified. When the South proved intransigent on the issue and the only resolution seemed to be through warfare, many whites thought the best solution for "us" was to allow slavery to continue.

BLACK RESPONSES TO THEIR NEGATIVE CONSTRUCTION

Despite all the rhetorical pitfalls and physical dangers, black orators did not shrink from opportunities to express their views. They participated in almost all of the rituals necessary to introduce themselves into the traditionally powerful social position of public orators. Not having access to Congress or the bar, their lectures nevertheless ran the gamut of speaking situations from lyceum lectures to political conventions, and in Douglass's case, to solo lecture tours where he had to arrange his own housing and venue.

Most white Americans would not attend rallies with black speakers and definitely would not subscribe to an abolitionist journal. Without this grounding, they had little else to base their judgment of black Americans on other than the political and economic discourse of the country and the racist logics that supported them. They never had the chance to respond to the impressive characteristics blacks displayed in their rhetorical efforts to establish themselves as Persons in political, economic, and moral spheres. This pattern, one that would have ended all hopes of rebutting the inferiority ideology, continued until whites began to see something valuable and therapeutic in attending abolitionist rallies.

Wisely realizing that many of the attributes of character had been denied them, black rhetors adopted one of two positions to draw and influence audiences. Some decided to stop trying to rehabilitate and establish their good character, opting instead for bald declarations of black personhood and white depravity. These rhetors were willing to suffer the consequences for this bold stance, believing that sometimes the best defense was to be as offensive as possible to the corrupt system. Another group, far more numerous, took advantage of the opportunities of the age and attempted to establish their ethos through personality. They built entire speeches around a glorification of their sentiments and retellings of tawdry details of their previous lives. For the most part, they also attenuated the force of their appeal by offering it and themselves as a commodity: since ex-slave oratory was primarily an exercise in autobiographical speaking, the ex-slaves were, in effect, selling their life stories, their most intimate memories. By hawking their autobiographies, they were effectively selling *themselves* to white audiences in the north rather than to masters in the south. In this way the master/slave relationship was perpetuated even in antislavery rhetoric.

Personality and Property

What other ways to identify themselves did black rhetors find when the constraints on their ethos proved to be too severe and audiences too obdurate? A very common method used by ex-slaves drew on the theatrical elements of the sideshow. Blacks would present themselves as curiosities for onlookers. Sometimes this involved saying a few words about slavery. At other times, fugitive slaves would be silent objects for viewing. The forums for this type of appeal could range from the typical speaker's platform to the living room of a worker on the Underground Railroad. Levi Coffin, for instance, invited prominent citizens to his house to view his recently acquired "curiosity from the South."[56] The curiosity was a couple of fugitives, a mother and son on their way to Canada. More dramatic, but equally demeaning, on Ohio clergyman gave a stirring antislavery speech, then drew back a curtain to reveal a family of fugitives. The audience "was surprised and horror stricken. Many eyes were filled with tears."[57] The congregation immediately took up a collection to help the family.

A far more notable way for an ex-slave to participate in the movement was offering a simple retelling of their lives, saying, in effect, this is simply me, what I have seen and felt and thought. Most of the recorded speeches of ex-slave orators as well as many of the slave narratives fall into this category.

What these rhetors were doing is not the same as using expertise to support universal claims the way Douglass did. This style of communication is very connected to an oral mindset, what Ong calls the condition of primary orality.[58] To describe the condition of primary orality, Ong posits nine "psychodynamics of orality." These characteristics reveal how a culture based on spoken language creates a specific kind of mental state in its people. Literate cultures, especially those with printing presses, are less hampered by the ephemeralness of spoken discourse whereas oral cultures orient their lives to spoken sounds that immediately go out of existence. Communication of primary oral cultures therefore must include internal memory aids (such as redundancy), since a text is not available for future reference. In this and other ways a society's primary method of communication has a great impact on the way people relate and on the structure of society.

One psychodynamic Ong describes is that oral communication tends to be additive, rather than subordinative. Oral narratives sound like near-endless streams of events because oral discourse lacks the kinds of logical subordination of ideas that literate communication thrives on. Oral communication is also "close to the lifeworld" rather than involved in abstractions. Many ex-slave orators used a straightforward oral style in their rhetoric by recounting events and experiences without a great deal of additional comment or argument. It is the kind of speech that Douglass rebelled against when his white handlers advised him to merely "give us the facts" because they would "take care of the philosophy."[59]

This is not a question of finding an afrocentric voice that repudiates the language and genres of the white power structure. The type of rhetoric that skirted many of the issues about black personhood was identified by its features, its unique plainness. It was designed to present the black orator in clear terms as a person, by sharing his or her most undeniable features such as when and why beatings were given (the scars from which were still visible) and most intimate features such as sexual liaisons, half-crazed reactions to one of slavery's many indignities, and grinding despair over their fate. The claims about physical abuse were supported by with the slaveholders' own words. Quoting announcements about runaway slaves collected from southern newspapers, the audience heard slaveholders coldly describe their property's branding marks, broken bones, and bullet wounds.

Character was not a real issue for orators employing this style of rhetoric. In every respect the rhetors (and their white mentors) were using accounts of intimate moments as a way of cutting through the veneer of character that was denied to them, in hopes of establishing a *real* and *believable* personhood even if it was not contrived to match popular taste. Their emotions were not socially sanctioned and their acts of criminality were not publicly commendable. They were, though, quite marketable to the prurient interests of therapeutic audiences.

The mode of simple retelling was therefore connected to the other method black rhetors used to persuade with personality: peddling their own lives for entertainment. According to Foster, "Utilization of the traditional literary forms and exploitation of current sensational, sentimental, and political shibboleths was often necessary to achieve the condemnation of the slave system."[60] So black orators offered themselves as storytellers, and their autobiographies as melodramas: They were heroes fighting against a clear enemy, slavery. Out in public to be entertained without having to get involved in difficult political or moral issues, many more white citizens would attend this version of antislavery rhetoric. What Winks says of fugitive slave narratives holds true for such rhetoric. Both were "the pious pornography of their day, replete with horrific tales of whippings, sexual assaults, and explicit brutality, presumably dehumanized and fit for Nice Nellies to read precisely because they dealt with black, not white, men."[61]

Given the motives of audiences, the speaker himself or herself was treated a consumable, another object sought for its use value in offering a night's entertainment. Maintaining *power* over an audience is difficult for a rhetor whose person, not just his speech, is being offered to audiences. Any emotions caused by hearing the graphic tales had a finality to them; they ended when the performance did. Presumably there could be a temporary identification, such as happened with the log-cabin bred corncob pipe-wielding political orator who needed to be likable enough to get votes, but to move from consumption to sacrifice, for an orator to inspire allegiance to a cause greater than themselves of their country, entertainment was insufficient. The impotence of this kind of appeal was especially poignant for slave orators. By letting market forces control their self presentation, they were essentially offering themselves as property, this time for proper white northern audiences and only for the length of the performance. However useful for bringing in crowds, the consumer/object relationship mired in hypocrisy the slaves' contempt for the practice of buying and selling humans.

Proclamations of Black Character

The option of "selling out" had its share of problems for the orator's ethos. Another route was followed by Charles Lenox Remond. As an orator, Remond was not the imposing physical presence Douglass was. He did not come out of a life of harsh physical labor since he was born a free man and received a good education. More than Douglass, Remond was able to fit in with white society. In fact, after ending his speaking career, he worked as a clerk. Given all this, it is most remarkable that this smallish man would take the formidable stand he did in loudly condemning white character and lauding black. Through his speech he attempts to reconstitute black personhood as fully human by denying or ignoring all claims to the contrary and repudiating the social structure that made such judgments in the first place.

We can see Remond's strategy in a speech before the New England Anti-Slavery Convention. His topic is slavery, but he tackles it from the peculiar angle of black Americans' patriotism and manliness, affirming that both have a great history.[62] He then asserts that white people know this, but consider black contributions and sacrifices of a lower order than white ones. Contradicting some white speakers at the convention who were afraid of the ramification of secession, he challenges the crowd, "Why is it that men stand aloof from this subject? Why do they look coldly upon the discussion of the question of the dissolution of the Union? I think I may safely say, Sir, that the courage and patriotism of the colored man is of a higher character than that of the white man." The black man, he explains, has always fought for the country though he had none of the material and political benefits to gain whites had, and would be willing to do so again in the event of a war.

After calling the heroes of the Revolution to witness against white American apathy, Remond all but dismisses the white population of the country. "I have said before, and I repeat it again, even in view of the humble position I occupy as a black man in the State of Massachusetts, I would rather be ten thousand times blacker than I am than to be the proudest pale face that walks State Street to-day, doing the bidding of the slaveholder." He then continues by listing some of the degradations from the inferiority ideology: "It has become not only a part of our education, but almost part and parcel of our nature, to look upon the colored man in this country as born to the vile inheritance of slavery… to do the bidding of the pale face; to go and come at his call." The purpose of the list is to continue his subversion of the white-established hierarchy; by calling white people "pale faces," he is *marking* white color and not allowing it to be the neutral standard against which black color and character is judged. The speech is constructed around this one idea.

Throughout he tells white audience members (both immediate and those who might later read the speech) that if they could put themselves in the black person's place, if they could think like him, act nobly as he does, *be more black*, then they would do the right thing with regard to slavery. Remond does more than ignore the ideology of inferiority. He reverses it, and uses the new higher position of blacks to condemn the white populace.

His speech reaches a climax in a section where he acts as a negotiator rather than a supplicant, and even proffers a veiled threat:

> Friends! God has made us men. If you will recognize us as such, we will conduct ourselves in a manner worthy your regard and protection. All we want is a fair chance; and just in proportion as this is granted will this recognition be made. I ask no man for his sympathy. I am simply asking of the majority, because we are a minority, an opportunity to develop the faculties which the Creator was given us. I tell you, my friends, if we were equal in numbers to-morrow, we should not ask your aid; into our own hands we would take the vindication of our rights.

What is accomplished at the end of the speech is a frontal assault on the denial of black character. Remond doesn't even stop there, however. He allows himself, at the last moment, to also support his argument with a wink at a personality appeal:

> I know, Mr. Chairman, that I am not, as a general thing, a peacemaker. I am
> irritable, excitable, quarrelsome — I confess it, Sir, and my prayer to God is, that
> I may never cease to be irritable, that I may never cease to be excitable, that I may
> never cease to be quarrelsome, until the last slave shall be made free in our
> country, and the black man's manhood is acknowledged.

By choosing the word "peacemaker," Remond denies one of the most famous of
Jesus' beatitudes, and the blessedness that goes along with it. He lists his character
flaws — even confesses them as sins — but ultimately depicts them as justified. His
most audacious move is to ask God for to grant him the ability to be sinful, since this
is what is necessary to win the fight.

PROCLAMATION OF CHARACTER AS A RHETORICAL STRATEGY

In Bormann's rhetorical analysis of abolitionist rhetoric, Remond and Garrison,
along with Douglass are labeled "agitators." The type of insulting, assaulting speech
that we see here from Remond was, in Bormann's account, a serious hindrance to the
abolition cause. "The rhetoric of agitation," he writes, "served... as a divisive force
within the movement as well as a repelling agent for those whom the movement
might have radicalized."[63] The most infamous piece of rhetoric on this count was
David Walker's *Appeal*, which openly called for the revolt of the slaves and argued
from the premise that whites were morally corrupt and violent by nature. Evidence
affirms that Walker's pamphlet did repel some potential allies. Its strong emphasis on
vengeance even bothered Garrison.[64] As moving as a reading of it is today, direct confrontation of white supremacist logic was limited in its ability to mobilize blacks or
whites against slavery in a concerted way.

    Bormann concludes that the "evangelist" branch of abolition was far and away
more successful than the agitators. The evangelists, such as Theodore Dwight Weld,
were growing the antislavery movement by leaps and bounds by accepting the positive myths about America, and working within the culture to critique slavery with
America's own values and "convert" people to antislavery. Their effectiveness was
limited by the irascible rhetors who refused to kowtow to popular tastes. They ended
up dividing and diminishing the movement.

    I have argued, though, that rhetoric of accommodation ("evangelism") was clearly
ineffective because it did nothing to change the underlying assumptions on which slavery
was based, namely the inferiority and immorality of blacks. In contrast, Remond's speech
shows definite promise. He was, after all, the second most famous and popular black
speaker after Frederick Douglass. From his speech we can see why. His ardent refutation
of white myths, and his overturning of the hierarchy circumvent many of the constraints
on black ethos. This is accomplished without a direct rebuke of white America. Rather,

he offers a radical promise of uplift, assuming whites are willing to imitate their superiors, black Americans.

Clearly, then, he is not trying to win approval for his morality by going through a public conversion ceremony. Instead, his "claim" to morality avoids white approval altogether as he addresses God directly. His Judge is higher than any merely human arbiter.

Although he is undermining the social hierarchy in these ways, he does not base claims on any privileged knowledge about slavery that would identify him as an Other. Instead, he adopts a strategy that integrates himself and his people with the best of American history. In William Andrews's volume on slave narratives, *To Tell a Free Story*, he relates a similar strategy as a characteristic of the very best slave narratives. These "more thoughtful narratives" argue that "far from being the radical alien, the slave was actually a fundamental component of the social structure. Indeed, the slave was literally the basis on which the entire class and case structure rested."[65] He adds, "Slave narratives like Douglass's, [William Wells] Brown's, and [Josiah] Henson's portray the black other's divestiture of his own marginality through autobiographical acts designed to reidentify him as a fulfillment of the essence of Christian American selfhood."[66]

Remond's speech goes farther than this too. He does align himself with America's highest ideals, but he manages this with more than simple autobiography. He appeals to a grand tradition, and resorts to thought exercises with the audience so they imagine themselves as the other. He also allows himself to be a full man in the American tradition by acknowledging his flaws. Like Franklin before him, he admits his sinfulness. That is, he tempers the claims of absolute character with moments of personality.

A parallel strategy can be found in later slave narratives as authors discovered that they could not rehabilitate their humanity by offering themselves as paragons. Andrews remarks of the black author's credibility,

> For decades the slave narrator had asked to be believed on the basis, at least in part, of his ability to restrain himself, to keep to the proprieties of discourse that required the ugliest truths of slavery to be veiled. At mid-century, however, the black autobiographer would begin to claim credibility *because* he or she had violated those same proprieties of discourse. The further this new autobiographer placed himself or herself outside the conventions of the standard discourse on slavery, the more truthful this autobiographer claimed to be. I am to be trusted, this new black narrator seemed to be saying, because what I tell you is shocking and ought not to be said.

This is the type of self-identification that I have labeled a personality-based appeal. Remond's limitation is that he constructs this identity outside the bounds of propriety only at the end of his speech, and only briefly. Douglass would learn this lesson, both in his second autobiography, and earlier in his speaking career up through mid-century. What for Remond is almost an afterthought — the integration of character and personality — is the key to Douglass's success in using ethos proofs. It is to his speeches we must now turn.

CHAPTER FIVE
Douglass as an Exhibit of Ethos

The title of this chapter has a double meaning. Frederick Douglass was frequently lauded by his allies and reviewers as an "excellent specimen" of his race. His life, represented in his ethos, served several closely related functions: he was a representative *example* of other blacks in slavery, he was an *exemplar* of the highest of society's virtues, but he was also an *exhibit* of a dangerous and exotic kind of manhood that thrilled antebellum audiences and enticed them into the hall to hear abolitionist speeches. How Douglass managed to portray himself in such diverse ways, as typical yet exceptional for both his character and personality, and the power that came from doing so, are the subjects of this chapter.

Douglass's ethos can best be appreciated with an understanding of the social forces that shaped the antebellum audience, an account I tried to give in the previous chapters. When Enlightenment ideals met Jacksonian politics, audiences were willing to listen to speakers of questionable character who had a powerful personality. The qualities of character — the moral rectitude, social refinement, and worldly wisdom — were associated with being one of society's elites, and democratic audiences were reluctant to submit to those elites. Personality on the other hand offers itself to the audience for consumption in the hope that the consumer/audience will find something useful in the orator's presence that will warrant a hearing. Where character is sure of its intrinsic merit and its "use value" as a guide for society, in many ways, claims used to establish the fleeting, flawed-but-entertaining appeal of personality are antithetical to character traits such as stability, gravity, and habituated morality.

As I have illustrated, several nineteenth-century orators recognized the need to identify themselves with shifting, interior personality traits rather than relying on the bedrock foundation of publicly proven character. American politicians along with entertainers of all kinds drastically changed the way they went about their business in order to take advantage of the appeal of personality. Using both character and personality, though, was very rare because it was difficult to balance the conflicting identity they work to create: it is difficult to sound logical presenting oneself as highly moral and deeply flawed. The great advantage to presented the audience with contrasting aspects of identity is that they must judge the different qualities in by different standards. Community well being is more important for character, for instance, while personal desires are at the heart of personality.

Yet only by recognizing both sets of identity markers does it become possible to explain why Douglass, as a person, stood out from other orators, even from antislavery orators with the same opportunities for using their ethos as support of their antislavery arguments. The best metaphor to describe Douglass's ethos is a hall of mirrors. Various sets of ideas — the hierarchical ethos of a Republican orator and the subversive pronouncements of a tantalizing, subversive personality, reflect off each other. By presenting himself this way, he creates productive conflicts, ironic turns, and ambiguities of identity and morality that, kaleidoscope-like, fascinate the spectator with their dancing interaction and rarely give a solid foothold for judgment.

Judgment, as we have seen, was a major concern of antebellum theorist, critics, and audiences alike. All the major rhetorical theories of the time aim to develop the faculty of judgment so the audience is best able to penetrate anonymity and false images. Campbell, Priestley, Whately and Blair all offer the reader a plan for improving their judgment and applying sound principles of discernment to public arguments. Campbell advocates intuition and common sense as reasonable measures of an argument and orator (respectively). Priestley uses most of his lectures to teach criticism, but also warns readers about the states of mind that induce belief and therefore inhibit judgment. Whately bases his whole theory of argument on the idea that people can learn to be reasonable so they can know when the burden of proof has been met. Judgment, specifically as it applies to aesthetic creations and to people, is the subject of Blair's entire rhetorical textbook. It could be argued that improving the judgment was the central idea of the modern rhetorics.

As always, the change in rhetorical theory was a response to social needs. Judgment was a necessity in the realm of ethos as much or more than anywhere else. For, in the absence of standardized patterns of behavior and normalized codes for expressing oneself, modern orators and audiences were largely mysteries to each other. Anonymity was a major concern, especially in an increasingly democratic, urban rhetorical culture where all sorts of "riffraff" might take it upon themselves to speak to the people.

Also problematic was the escalating number of people using rhetoric to present an *image* of themselves to the audience. The elocutionists, for instance, promised to teach the mannerisms of refined speakers to anyone. The aristocratic Henry Clay was tapping into the same fascination with changing one's image when he offered himself as a rough and tumble stump speaker. To counter the ubiquity of images and anonymity, nineteenth-century audiences were told to refine their faculty of judgment so they would have the ability to pierce any facade.

Rhetorical theory developed along these lines largely as a reaction to other popular philosophies. The operative definition of judgment in the antebellum rhetorical culture came from faculty psychology which is predicated on passivity.[1] Faculty psychology, especially as it was translated into rhetorical theory, suggests that the human mind consists of series of abilities that are waiting to be activated by a stimuli, be they a speaker's words our visual perception of a sunset. Campbell's rhetorical theory, the clearest example of a rhetoric based on faculty psychology, is also clearly inclined to characterizing people as receptors waiting to have their imagination, passions, and memory aroused by the well-chosen words of the orator. In Campbell and the other modern rhetorics (in varying degrees) the faculty of judgment is just as passive as any other faculty. There is no sense that audiences are co-creators of meaning along with the rhetor.

In other rhetorical theories prior to faculty psychology, the audience was construed as a much more active agent. The classical notion of *phronesis* or practical wisdom was always an active trait in Greek thought. One cannot have *phronesis* without years of experience in the real world, and one cannot simply "have" *phronesis*. One must show it through choosing wise actions. It is less an ability to criticize and more an ability to act in useful ways at the right time.

Another term that might be confused in the twentieth century as a rough synonym for the "faculty" of judgment is *expertise*. Expertise does require a practical ability to apply knowledge. But Whately correctly delineates the difference: expertise is much more limited in scope than *phronesis* because it is knowledge about specific subjects. *Phronesis* applies to all of life's activities.[2] Expertise is not a passive trait because it is only gained through committing oneself to a particular activity.[3] Specialization of knowledge into areas of expertise in the eighteenth and nineteenth centuries coincided with the division of livelihoods into "professions," and of universities into departments.[4] In distinction from the judgment "faculty," expertise is more like something you acquire by living. It is something you profess as a skill that others can see and measure, not something you activate at moments of decision making.

In practice these distinctions matter a great deal to the way Douglass manages his ethos. The *phronesis* and expertise he exhibits are intended to bolster his character, but a large part of his rhetorical power comes from his ability to stymie the faculty of judgment. That is, he keeps audiences effectively passive and makes them more receptive to his appeals by not "setting off" their faculties of judgment. Usually this is accomplished by keeping them entertained. In his more serious moments when the entertainment ends (and, often, the rebukes begin) Douglass shifts from one type of ethos appeal to another so seamlessly and quickly the audience is unable to find a firm ground upon which his identity stands and so are unable to successfully criticize his person. If they fault him in one area he is able to offer an opposing characteristic that silences their criticism. And, wherever successful assaults theoretically could be launched against his ethos, when his critics have the authority of the church or the constitution on their side, Douglass incapacitates the audience's ability to judge him by directly challenging and subverting those authorities. [5]

THE APPEAL OF DOUGLASS'S PERSONALITY

In some ways the separation of Douglass's ethos appeals into two categories is misleading. One instance of self-characterization may serve many functions and reveal a variety of qualities. Nevertheless, for purposes of analysis and to highlight some of the more prominent qualities Douglass adopts for his rhetorical identity I have decided to categorize appeals by personality and character. Inside each section are sub-categories that deal with one major quality or relationship to the audience developed by Douglass. However, with his complex identity and his equally complex relationships to black and white audiences, it often happens that an appeal that mostly falls in one category subtly reinforces something in the other category and I will mention it in both sections. In other words, the sections, much like the qualities they discuss, are closely related to each other.

Douglass's Representativeness as a Personality Appeal

The early eloquence and later fame of their new star orator were put to good rhetorical use by the antislavery societies. Douglass was portrayed in their newspapers and speeches as a "representative man," a typical example of the kind of person you are likely to find among the slaves. If all slaves did not exhibit the same outstanding qualities, it was argued, it was only because their meager existence in slavery had kept them from developing according to their potential.

Douglass also incorporated this image into his rhetoric. "I am the representative of the slaves," Douglass would tell audiences when he wanted to address them as a spokesperson for the enslaved race. [6] This way he could establish his expertise on matters affecting slaves and as a spokesman for their interests.

He could also make arguments about the injustice of slavery by depicting himself as the typical slave. We can see this in his tour of Britain. His major effort there was aimed at Scottish churches. After a denominational split, the Free Church of Scotland found itself without sufficient funds to build church buildings, and had appealed to brethren across the Atlantic for financial help. As the church's fundraising agents canvassed American churches, they found southern churches were wealthier and more willing to give. In an effort to defame and isolate southern religion, Douglass linked the donation to the issue of slavery. He urged the Scottish churches to "give back the money" often by getting his audiences to chant those very words in unison. [7]

A typical appeal on this topic is found in a Glaswegian newspaper where Douglass gets the audience to imagine the church representatives coming to collect:

> Had I been at the South, and had I been a slave, as I have been a slave — and I am a slave still by the laws of the United States — had I been there, and that deputation had come into my neighborhood, and my master had sold me on the auction block, and given the produce of my body and soul to them, they would have pocketed it, and brought it to Scotland to build their churches, and pay their ministers. [Cries of "No," "Yes, yes," and applause.] Why not? I am no better than the blackest slave in the Southern plantations.[8]

The real power of Douglass's representativeness evolves from the audience's obvious liking of their speaker. They had been laughing along with him about the foolishness of slaveholders and the hypocrisy of American churches. They were enjoying his presentation and people were clamoring for his company throughout Britain. Then, as we can see, he drives the point home: your money could just as easily have come from selling my body.

The argument hinges on the tension of the last statement. Douglass is, in very significant ways, "better" than other slaves. In the immediate context, the difference is that he is better than most other people, black and white, at public speaking. That difference in talent is what makes the audience face the idea that anyone's body could be sold for their coffers, even someone they enjoy as much as Douglass because he is representative or typical of slaves. To further emphasize the point of what they could lose by losing him, the representative black man (and what they have already potential lost to hideous deaths and confinement), Douglass has the audience enjoying his talents again, shortly after making the above statement, eliciting "cheers" and "great laughter."[9]

As can be seen here, as a matter of ethos Douglass's position as representative black man is complicated.[10] Two things are especially worth noting. First, the "representative man" label was only attached to Douglass because he was suitably distinguished for his character. Abolitionists would only want to separate out someone as a representative that they expected to bring praise and glory to the cause. Second, the representative status itself was highly constraining and would not allow Douglass to develop his character traits because it highlighted his similarity to other blacks. The traditional ethos of a leader is based on elevation in wisdom and virtue. Logically, Douglass cannot embody the *typical* qualities of a group of people and still be revered for his *superior* qualities.

Because of all the pressure to disprove the inferiority ideology, Douglass therefore had to portray himself corporately. It would not do to claim that he had risen out of the dregs of slave society because he was an exceptional figure. This would do his brethren in slavery actual harm by attesting their inferiority by their very inability to rise up. The representative man was forced to sublimate his individual claim to excellence to counter proslavery rhetoric.

One of Garrison's introductions of Douglass at an antislavery rally (before their estrangement) makes what is actually a very common argument based on Douglass's representativeness. Douglass "is not a picked man sent to show off," Garrison asserts, "he is the creature of accident, one who has had no previous advantages, and who is but a specimen of what thousands, now bound down by the yoke of oppression, might be, if they were only blessed with the precious boon of liberty." Note, anything special about Douglass is a result of "accident" and the determining force of "liberty." Therefore, unlike an orator of truly noble character, Douglass cannot take credit for developing his eloquence, wisdom, or excellence. He is figured by Garrison in the strange position of having character *because* of personality factors, that is, accidents of fate. He has been made into something good purely by osmosis and not through any work of his own.

Applying judgment to this quality is, accordingly, rather difficult for the audience. Can they legitimately fault Douglass for not being better than his fellows (as Garrison depicted him), for being typical and for not contributing to his own excellent character? At the same time, how could they not notice that he handled himself well? Torn between the overt characterization of his typicalness and a self-presentation that made him stand out, the audience is forced to choose between two standards for judging him, both contained in the image of his representativeness. His charm mixes with his close identification with the slaves to create cognitive dissonance. Further complicating the situation, Douglass offers no help to the person attempting to judge him for being a representative black man. Sometimes he speaks of the slaves using "us" and "we," but in the same speech he will also refer to them as "they" and distance himself from the plantation.

Douglass's Flaws as Personality Appeals

Sennett suggests that personality became such a commonplace in Anglo-American discourse because the general attention of American culture was turning inward. Once that interior turn is made, people began to see the inconsistencies and uncomfortable truths about themselves that could have remained unacknowledged in a society measured by public performance. Whately, who was the writer from this period most sensitive to the interior turn, also recognized that the preoccupation with interior states heightened the situational elements of rhetoric. Or rather, it heightened people's own sense of their tendency to act differently in different situations.[11]

When only public actions "count" I can take pride in the consistency of my actions; habit and character can be closely associated as they are for Aristotle. But when my personal desires and private acts are measured *against* my public deeds I find it difficult to claim that all my actions are motivated by habits of character. I may publicly act politely toward an enemy, but in my heart I find the blackest hatred. To a society in which character, virtuous action, and social elevation still have enormous cachet, acute awareness, and even careful study, of all one's flaws and inconsistencies (as we see in Montaigne and Benjamin Franklin, among others) can be very discomforting.

Yet, as happened in the nineteenth century, once the populace accepts the idea that everyone is flawed in some way, it becomes possible for orators to create a bond between themselves and their audience by admitting mistakes. Moreover, when the important part of a person is the interior and hidden aspects, the very process of revealing these flaws becomes exciting. We can watch a public figure shuck the image he or she has worked to construct as a protective barrier against the appraisal of others. As a rhetorical commodity, publicly admitted flaws are valuable because they are scarce.

Originally it seems only the most notable and otherwise praiseworthy fellows of the society could admit their sinfulness. Benjamin Franklin certainly suffered little harm to his status when his autobiography admitted several faults. Henry Clay escaped most of his bouts with criticism and scrutiny unscathed. Of course, they both operated in the end of the Republican era when public deeds silenced private peccadilloes. Frederick Douglass assumes to right to mingle in this lofty company by presenting his flaws in public. It was quite a powerful move to do so without the obligatory scraping for forgiveness expected of slaves who were caught red-handed. Of course, any orator, black or white, could assume some level of protection from condemnation by getting right with society by confessing flaws, by calling sin, sin, and admitting that the dominant morality was preferable to any self-gratifying escapades or foibles he or she may have shown, but Douglass rarely adopts that stance toward his flaws. He presents them as one part of his persona, then quickly moves on to assure the audience of his goodness, integrity or courage.

Admissions of Cowardice

The most noticeable flaws Douglass owns up to might be classified "flaws of courage." These usually occur when he admits his fear at some aspect of his antislavery service. In his first speech for which we have a good record, he begins by saying, "I feel greatly embarrassed when I attempt to address an audience of white people. I am not used to speaking to them, and it makes me tremble when I do so, because I have always looked up to them with fear."[12] Similarly, on the day he first announces the name of his owner and the verifiable details of his life in slavery, he is keenly aware how much this will increase his risk of capture and return to the south. He opens that speech with this admission: "When I came in this morning, and looked at those massive pillars, and saw the vast throng assembled, I got a little frightened, and was afraid that I could not speak; but now that the audience is not so large and I have recovered from my fright, I will venture to say a word on slavery."[13]

Now, in the Golden Age of American oratory, it was common enough to see an orator admit to feeling inadequate to some great task. Fourth of July speeches, for instance, nearly required that the orator admit an inability to capture the greatness of the commemorated event. This move by Douglass is something different. He is admitting actual squeamishness about his personal safety, not just humility about tackling a lofty topic.

More unusual still is his admission of fear to a friendly crowd in 1860. He bemoans the fact that he lacked courage to stand with John Brown's insurrection; he admits that cowardice clouded his judgment.[14] Of course, the audience stands ready to forgive him and the effect of the confession is actually a strengthening of the audience's resolve to participate in radical antislavery activity as everyone agrees that not helping Brown was wrong. This shows that Douglass was ready to admit to inferior qualities to achieve a particular result with an audience. On the other hand, admitting fear, though not considered a manly or honorable thing to do, was not as damaging as some other flaws could be. In relationship to the traditional ethos ideals of Christian charity and self control, a lack of goodness was at least as damaging to his character than the loss of honor, but Douglass readily admits these types of flaws too. The most striking instances occur when Douglass admits to harboring violent hatred toward enemies, and even promises them harm.

Sometimes he tempers his disclosures by merely aiming his threats at anyone who dares to cross him and by singling out those who would seek to re-enslave him. Thus he declares, "You may put the chains upon me and fetter me, but I am not a slave, for my master who puts the chains on me, shall stand in as much dread of me as I do of him."[15] Building on the account in his autobiography where he stood up to the "slave breaker" Covey and fought for his dignity, this remark promises Douglass will attempt physical harm to anyone who dares call him their slave. This stance was particularly problematic for the workers in the staunchly pacifistic anti-slavery movement. He no doubt repeated this threat to many front-row rowdies throughout his lecture circuit who hoped to disrupt abolitionist meetings, or even earn a large monetary reward for returning Douglass to his former master.

While we might explain away his violent threats as a matter of self defense, there are more serious lapses in Douglass's character. A good example is found in 1860, on the same day Douglass declared his cowardice during the John Brown raid. The outrageous events from earlier that same day had inspired that admission, for they brought him to the point of such anger at racism he actually felt remorse that he could not die for the opportunity of striking a blow against the south. Earlier in the day he had tried to speak at an anniversary service for John Brown and in favor of the dissolution of the union. However, pro-union forces had dominated the meeting and when he was reluctantly recognized to speak, several gentlemen of standing blocked his way to the rostrum. Douglass pushed through them, covering up, the newspapers wrote, like a "trained pugilist." Then during his speech the same men repeatedly tried to cut Douglass short and heckled him mercilessly. Finally, when he heard one antagonist sarcastically encouraging him to continue his speech with, "Go on nigger!" he completely forgot the rules of decorum. McFeely's account reads this way:

> At this point, Douglass's temper broke totally. 'If I were a slave-driver, and had hold of that man for five minutes,' he pealed, pointing to the culprit, 'I would let more daylight through his skin than ever got there before.' [Chair of the meeting Richard] Fay responded, 'He has said the truth, for a negro slave-driver is the most cruel in the world.' Douglass, up out of that gutter, shouted above it all, 'It seems to me as though some of the white men of the North [have] gone to the devil. They'd murder liberty — kill freedom.'[16]

As far removed as we are now from the passion of this moment, it seems downright indecent for Douglass, the bitterest opponent of the cruelty and inhumanity of slavery, to wish slavery on anyone else and then promise them a violent beating. Douglass highlights the discontinuity even more by referring to the devil and the murderous nature of some of his opponents, calling Christian morals to bear on their interaction. For a man who spent years advocating nonviolent and even nonpolitical solutions to slavery by winning over hearts with a Garrisonian version of tough love, promising violence raises serious issues of character. On two counts, then — one of morality and one of hypocrisy — Douglass's character-based ethos was marred by this sort of outburst.

How can such incidents be passed over by writers who perpetuate the standard story about his preeminent character? In any normal rendering of the qualities of ethos, this kind of exchange with an audience fails miserably. An argument based on effectiveness is equally shaky because this eruption only caused the meeting hall to be cleared of Douglass's party and the meeting to break down into chaos. Perhaps because of our sympathy for Douglass it is easy to read this utterance as deserved or forgivable. To prove the harshness of his remark, we might consider what the ramifications would be for, say, Reverend Jesse Jackson if he threatened a heckler with a slave-like beating.

Perhaps courage is a type of "character" Douglass shows during the times he engages in fisticuffs or threatens violence on people. But lowering himself to the level of his opponents actually works with modern audiences because they see responsiveness to unique situations as a more important trait than stability of character. Rather than sublimating his rage to keep some pretense of humility or nobility, Douglass gives it full vent. It would have been inappropriate in this situation to simply rise above the fray and remain serene. Douglass also knew when to stop himself: there were no blows landed at the John Brown service. Even if Douglass or someone else had started swinging, there were enough pacifists on the stage and in the crowd to separate them. The appeal for audiences was knowing that they were probably safe, and that violence would probably not happy, but the *possibility*, however unlikely, made the atmosphere electric. It was equally unlikely that Northerners would allow the high profile orator to be shipped back South to slavery so that Douglass would have to make good his threats to beat his captors. The talk of violence was the kind of melodrama audiences knew and craved and it was made all the more exciting by being grounded in reality and by Douglass assuming the place of power as the initiator of the threats.

Douglass physically wrestling with opponents and the scene at the John Brown service both make for compelling stories. The account was carried in prestigious newspapers such as the New York *Tribune* and the Boston *Post* and probably had audiences paying closer attention to this antislavery meeting than any other in recent memory. Potentially this incident could have doubled the audience for the next appearance of "Fightin' Fred Douglass" because of his sensational image. Next time, the proper people in the audience would wonder with a thrill, will the conflict end in physical violence?

Family and Infidelity

Aside from questions of honor versus pugnaciousness, there was also a series of improprieties related to women and family that Douglass allowed in his life even though they made it impossible for him to claim the *vir bonus* standard. A notable one has to do with the lack of genuine concern he apparently shows for his family still trapped in slavery. Although he lamented that slavery destroyed the natural bonds between parent and child or husband and wife, Douglass's own family is virtually absent from his early rhetoric. There is little evidence that he attempted to secure the freedom of family members still trapped in slavery, although his fame could have done much for them. He makes it clear that we was worried for his safety if details of his former life were known, but opponents could have faulted him for putting his self interests above his family's needs. Critics over the years have found much to dislike in his treatment of his immediate family in the north, with his lecturing duties making him a virtual absentee father.[17] He did, however, include notices in his paper if an illness in the family kept him from writing more editorials, but for reasons I will explore below, he was not particularly concerned with cultivating the image of the caring father and husband in his rhetoric.

Worse still, Douglass scandalized the antislavery hierarchy and set off a storm of reaction when he began a close affiliation with British abolitionist Julia Griffiths. Although there is scant hard evidence that their relationship was anything but friendly, simply allowing her to move into his house and being alone with her in his office spurred rumors of his infidelity. Garrison implied as much in his paper, and the disruption deeply damaged the two men's relationship. The uproar only began to die down after Douglass's wife Anna wrote a public letter to Garrison stating that "the presence of a certain person" did not cause her family unhappiness.[18] Douglass refused to address the moral charges, and when he did finally reply to Garrison he focused on their ideological differences.

All in all, it is amazing the anti-abolitionist press did not play up this story more. Douglass surely would not have wanted to gain a public reputation for adultery. However, the relationship with Griffiths did play a significant role in establishing his ethos. By ignoring the advice of friends about the image he was creating for himself Douglass was showing his independence. In abolitionist circles public debate raged over the propriety of his deeds and over the charges from the Garrisonians that he could not participate in such behavior and still appreciate the demands and philosophy of abolitionism. Since Griffiths also encouraged Douglass to break away from Garrison's non-political brand of abolition and start making political allies, he was seen as apostate by his former mentors. He shortly became an "enemy" of true abolition in the eyes of Garrisonians and even had his editorials reprinted in the *Liberator* in the column normally reserved for scorning pro-slavery rhetoric.

As Douglass weathered the storm and defended his choices rhetorically he also drew blacks to his side of the debate. This further incensed Garrison and "by 1860 he declined even to sit on the same platform with this 'thoroughly base and selfish' man who was 'more and more... destitute of every principle of honor, ungrateful to the last degree, and malevolent in spirit."[19] Douglass remained unmoved because he had a point to make: alleged impropriety and ideological independence were somehow worse crimes for a black man than a white one. The proof cost him dearly though. He sacrificed a measure of character, of principle and selflessness in Garrison's estimation, to secure the right to associate as he pleased. And too, by following Griffiths's advice and becoming more political, Douglass was showing a willfulness in choosing his political associations despite the debt he owed to the Garrisonians for starting his professional career and providing for him financially for years. For pragmatic reasons, as his fame grew, he allied with parties and candidates who were only marginally anti-slavery, including the Free Soil party, which only desired to restrict the growth of slavery.

In all this, why was he successful with the anti-slavery constituency? At meetings across the northeast, blacks gathered to pass resolutions in support of Douglass, even lauding his readiness to "crucify all personal considerations" for his people.[20] Their support ignored the issue of fidelity in marriage and focused instead on his faithfulness to improving their lot. They saw him as living out his commitment to racial equality by treading on the very hazardous ground of black men's relationships with white women. Garrison's and his allies' racist attempts to put Douglass "back in his place" through insulting personal attacks also added to Douglass's appeal. He was suffering racist attacks, and as a sufferer deserved the support of the black community. Because the blacks at the heart of the movement sided with one of their own, Garrison's name would never again receive the same respect from the black community. Still, Garrison was right in saying that Douglass's actions would hurt the cause of abolition. The debate over his behavior directed the energies of abolition's greatest rhetors toward petty infighting. The obvious question is, why would Douglass tarnish his image knowing that every act detracted from his ability to maintain the *wholly good man* standard?

Fidelity and Sexuality

The illogical and even bigoted response of Garrison makes this a difficult issue to sort out. Reconstructing its history, though, one key factor had to be Douglass's public appearances, arm in arm, with Griffiths, her sister, as well as with other women. At the time, we must remember, he was still a married man. Would it have been proper for any man of that day to escort women in that way? Would popular morality even today allow a married man to escort various women around touching each other intimately?

We have to consider, therefore, the matter of Douglass's sexual attractiveness, most certainly a part of his personal appeal. Male and female commentators noticed his fine looks, but female admirers also sometimes sexualized the relationship. One remarked that "the play of his fine features made a little thrill run through me. The dignity of his attitude, the majesty of his stature made Frederick Douglass look every inch a man."[21] The orator always in control of his self presentation and keenly observant of the reactions of others to him could not have been unaware of sexual tensions in his presence. The willingness of Douglass to continue his public shows of friendliness toward women must go down as part of his ethos. If slave oratory was a kind of "pious pornography" suitable for public consumption, Douglass's looks and sexual gaucherie established a sexual identity for himself. He was, in so many words, allowing himself to be objectified as a sexual object all the while decrying the objectifying effects of slavery to his audiences.

Fulkerson handles this topic well when he describes Douglass's "glamour" as a key element in his British image.[22] Although his statements refer to the British tour, they apply equally well to Douglass's stateside rhetoric. "At twenty-seven," Fulkerson remarks, Douglass "was a public figure in his own country, handsome, well-dressed, charming as a conversationalist… [and so] his meetings often attracted a disproportionate number of women." According to the author, the fact that "British reform-minded females were doubly zealous under the spell of Douglass's virile appearance, rich voice, and refined manners was, in fact, so marked as to become a source of embarrassment to him."

No reconfiguration of the *vir bonus* ideal will account for sex appeal, but in Douglass's case (as in President Clinton's case, among others) it is a clearly a matter of ethos and factors into some people's judgments of his worth. This ethos quality, whether we want to call it glamour, allure, or sex appeal, is personality-based because it is predicated on the ability of the orator to fulfill a personal desire rather than a community-preserving function. The undercurrent of sexuality, like the hint of violence, gave certain audience members a reason to attend a lecture (although whether they were inclined to be moved by his logic is another matter). Additionally, an orator's or entertainer's identity as a sexually desirable object creates a fetish value and appeal that can only be fully realized in the presence of the person. In Douglass's era, which can be described at the beginning of the Age of the Consumable Subject, the oratory of the handsome or seductive was more appealing as an event and so competed better in the entertainment marketplace for attention, time and money. Unless they believed that beauty somehow equates with truth, sex appeal did very little to make the speaker more *credible*, even though it was clearly a part of the speaker's ethos.

Douglass, who was open with the fact that the British tour renewed his confidence and energy for abolition work, usually cited the relative lack of racial prejudice there. It was in England that he "saw in every man a recognition of [his] manhood."[23] If his public relationships with women after returning home are an indication, his was equally affected by the way British women recognized his masculinity. Although his recorded speeches are free of conspicuous sexual innuendo, it is possible that he related to the audience in less than neutral ways. We will never know the level of eye contact he made or how much he physically touched admirers before or after speeches. However extensively he did it, Douglass's willingness to develop — or at least not to squelch — his public reputation for being sexually desirable reveals the many ways he was willing to identify himself for audience effect, even when the trait was socially taboo and he was publicly chastised for it.

Douglass's Authenticity as a Personality Appeal

One of Douglass's primary means of establishing his identity is by sharing the secrets of his psyche. The interior domain is not always attractive for the audience or flattering of the orator, but that is precisely what makes it desirable. Sharing details of one's personal life can be embarrassing. If someone does it despite their embarrassment, the logic goes, then the details must be true. Would people would risk gossip and the scorn of society to present falsities about themselves? The power of establishing an aura of authenticity is partly in getting the audience to believe you are presenting your true, unexpurgated self. Where authenticity is not decidedly persuasive, it can at least be compelling. As Trilling argues in Sincerity and Authenticity, an authentic presentation of the self often weaves a rich tapestry that can be startling and endearing. It is a pleasure to share an authentic self when there is something deep there to be explored.[24] As the sense grew in the nineteenth century that the world of industrialization and impersonal labor was distastefully unauthentic, there is a certain heroism that attaches to individuals who dare to go against the grain and be themselves.

Audiences found Douglass interesting particularly for his detailed reports of pain and suffering.[25] They wanted to hear about the evil he had endured and the soul searching it had inspired regarding issues of humanity, including his own. For instance, according to abolitionist Maria Chapman, the British tour had roused some people "who never could have been influenced except by a person who had himself suffered." From another stop on the tour, one correspondent praised speaker Douglass, noting that his claims "have double weight, since drawn from his own painful experience: no Englishman however gifted could call forth the same kind of enthusiasm."[26] The same reports of the sufferings of slaves could not have the same impact on audience coming from a third party. Even a gifted orator, a master of vivacity and description, would have been helpless to elicit sacrificial donations and a willingness to work for emancipation the way Douglass could. Looking at the commentaries carefully, the difference is not principally one of credibility (although Fulkerson reads it that way). The Scottish churchgoers did not have to be convinced of the harsh conditions accompanying American slavery. They simply had yet to be *moved* by them, especially since caring may have required them to give back a huge donation from American churches in the south to their building fund.

A person who shared himself in authenticity was capable of moving passive or apathetic audiences and accomplishing something even greater, such as motivating them to return the money earned by the labor of slaves. Like the pastor who puts a large bill in offering plate before passing it, sharing authentically puts pressure on others to give of themselves. In this case, Douglass sacrificing his pride to talk about his formative years of humiliation and abuse implicitly calls his Scottish audiences to sacrifice their donations as a matter of reciprocity. The logic is similar to the idea covered in chapter two where the emotional displays of an orator warrant displays from the audience. A rhetor's authenticity, by breaching of decorum, makes the lecture hall a safer place for the audience to divest themselves of the enervating dictates of society.

Authenticity in the hand of a skilled orator is potent for several reasons. In the first place, material that may be damaging to one's reputation is bound to be interpreted by the audience as more true. Whately recognizes this in his discussion of "undesigned testimony."[27] Judged against the nineteenth century desire to conceal true feelings and build a successful image, any admission that seemed unplanned or even counter to one's interests would have a ring of truth. Being authentic also suggests to the audience that they can easily judge the rhetor. Authenticity admits no artifice, so even the uncultivated mind can assess the authentic person correctly. This is quite comforting to audiences who know they are supposed to practice careful, educated judgment but were not sure how developed their judgment faculty had become. Of course, for the crafty orator, authentic confessions are planned events for calculated effect; authenticity has to be faked very carefully.

If authenticity gives the impression that our critical faculties can relax, it also has a leveling effect in democratic contexts. Tocqueville see it as a powerful bonding element for society when he argues,

> When ranks are almost equal among a people, as all men think and feel in nearly
> the same manner, each instantaneously can judge the feelings of all the others; he
> just casts a rapid glance at himself, and that is enough. So there is no misery that
> he cannot readily understand, and a secret instinct tells him its extent."[28]

Authenticity can therefore be used to create sympathy with an audience; by clearly and unequivocally displaying the desired emotion, rhetors can easily inspire a like feeling in the audience because they are understood so well.

By this logic, we can see the reason behind Douglass's lament of hopelessness in his 1847 speech about the "Right to Criticize American Institutions."[29] Facing the weary warriors of abolition and hundreds of free blacks who had seen little improvement in their lives after a decade of abolition work, Douglass's downbeat mood at first seems inappropriate. Rather than inspiring his admirers, Douglass complains:

> We have been trying to make this thing appear sinful. We have not been able to
> do so yet. It is not admitted, and I hardly know how to argue against it. I confess
> that the time for argument seems almost gone by. What do the people want?
> Affirmation upon affirmation — denunciation upon denunciation, — rebuke
> upon rebuke?

His failure is disheartening to him, just as the failure of the movement must be hard on his listeners generally. He even hints at a desperation that will leave argument behind no doubt in favor of physical violence. And, in a moment of frailty, he despairs of affirmations, denunciations and rebukes, the standard repertoire of a Garrisonian. More importantly, by sympathy he brings the audience along with him into the depths of despair. But what possible reason could he have for creating despair?

The answer is found as we follow Douglass to the next section of the speech. He immediately moves to a discussion of "evangelical flogging" and switches into a mode of imitation. To show the absurdity of advocating whippings as a form of church correction, he "assume[s] a most grotesque look, and with a canting tone of voice" reads extracts from a published sermon on this absurd topic. He mentions that flogging is called a form of "correction" in the south, "and that word as it is understood at the North, is some sort of medicine." Douglass finally comes to the crux of the sermon's argument: it offers a warning to slaveholders that killing a slave is just as bad as killing a white person, unless the slave dies under "*moderate correction.*" Although this caveat is enough to discredit the argument, the reverend author goes on to remind the slave that his duty is to bear correction, whether it is deserved or not. He would have slaves happily bear their undeserved "moderate correction" even unto death!

Throughout this section of the speech, Douglass switches between sarcastic parenthetical comments and his hilarious imitation of the author. Attested to by the many notices of "laughter" in the speech text, he succeeds in moving the audience to hysterics over his reading of the absurd sermon. In less than ten minutes, then, Douglass has brought his audience from deep despair to delight. This is the kind of oratorical power that so many observers have recognized in Douglass's speech.

His purpose is greater than merely showing off, though. He continues, "I am glad you have got to the point that you can laugh at the religion of such fellows as this Doctor. There is nothing that will facilitate our cause more than getting people to laugh at that religion which brings its influence to support traffic in human flesh."[30] In lieu of the affirmation, denunciation, and rebuke that he just discounted, Douglass offers a new strategy especially for the blacks in his audience. He is encouraging them to mock the oppressing institutions. He is telling them that all the fiery reprimands had failed and Douglass presumes instead to make his major strategy the effort to make the proslavery church a laughingstock.

At the root of this appeal is authenticity, a characteristic of personality. Douglass began this appeal in weakness and soul searching. But he would not stay there. By admitting his despair, he effectively discredited the standard practices of Garrisonian agitation. At the same time, he created sympathy and promoted resignation in the audience, but only temporarily.

Then, like a Moses, who intended all along to bring his flock to a new place of power, encouragement, and renewed social action, he leads them out of the land of despair he himself guided them into. He models a new rhetorical strategy for his black audience by assuming a higher moral authority that can publicly mock the church. By this point his ethos has changed as well. The authenticity is gone and along with it the transparent, vulnerable self. In its place is an air of authority and nobility, and a clearly calculating speaker who as much as admits to making the audience laugh just to prove a point about its effectiveness in "facilitating our cause."

THE APPEAL OF DOUGLASS'S CHARACTER

Commentaries about Frederick Douglass rarely spend much time developing descriptions of his darker side. The way he ends the "Right to Criticize" speech is the way he is typically depicted. Even today, that imperial presence still reaches out to defend his reputation from attack. His great personal authority, has to be taken into consideration as a quality of ethos, for it is still the dominant one in determining how people approach him to this day.

Douglass's Authority as Character

In the classical Roman world view antebellum America was leaving behind, moral authority was found in a community, Clark and Halloran assert.[31] In Douglass's day, moral authority was shifting location to the individual's private convictions. Douglass takes advantage of this change by establishing himself as an authority. His authority is very personal, relying on no outside institution or public consensus for its legitimacy. In many of his speeches, he attributes moral authority to himself, usually to counter the illegitimacy of the current authority sources, namely the church and the government. His self-authorized authority relies on an unassailable hierarchy. Douglass does not use his superior status to promise uplift to his audience, nor is he only temporarily better than them as we would see if this were a personality appeal. His authority is meant to be inviolate.

We have already examined instances of Douglass establishing himself as a moral authority. In one he denied the right of his former friends and sponsors to judge the propriety of a relationship. In another, he assumed moral authority superior to the church's. This latter stance gives him something more than the right to merely criticize the church and rebuke it. The act of spreading evil forebodings about the church and its corruption has a long history in the prophetic tradition. The problem is that, historically, most prophets are ignored or killed. Rather than continue in an historically feeble role and repeat criticisms that had not worked, Douglass does what few would dare to do: he decides to make the church ridiculous. This was a more serious assault on its authority than any rebuke could be, for by suffering rebuke the church's importance and connection to God is confirmed by the effort to return it to a right relation. Making the church an object of folly (as Erasmus found out centuries earlier) is the kind of critique than cannot be tolerated.

Another key relationship of authority for Douglass is his superior stance toward white Americans. He accuses apathetic listeners of being "as bad as slaveholders" for not actively working for immediate emancipation.[32] Douglass even defends his criticism of America by announcing, "I do not flatter myself that there is moral power in the land sufficient to overthrow Slavery, and I welcome the aid of England."[33] His tone here is almost imperial. He knows the depravity of the land and the people so well that he feels justified in seeking outside help. Only someone who was moral in the extreme could brush aside an entire country's moral fortitude. And too, only someone of great authority can actually call upon *another country* for aid; that duty is usually reserved for the President. This is *dignitas* (or perhaps *hubris*) that would make even Cicero proud.

When Douglass can establish his own moral and even political authority this way, he manages to shield himself from another charge that could be laid against his character. As the prime arbiter of what is right for Frederick Douglass, he is free to change his mind and his public stances as he sees fit. There are no commitments to keep or parties to account to. So he can describe in an article from the *Liberator* the absence of Jim Crow laws and segregation in the south as a way to admonish northerners for their biases and hypocrisy, but he can contradict several parts of this account in his famous *Narrative* just three years later. In an even shorter time, he can change his public opposition to the attempt of a slave, Lunsford Lane, to buy himself and his family to protect them from being returned to slavery. As Lampe points out, no one reacted negatively to this major about-face.[34] In addition, as Kinney notices, Douglass switched from the Liberty Party to the Free Soil part in 1852 after strongly supporting the Liberty party in voice and pen.[35] Most famously, he abandoned Garrison's leadership and principles, yet most people admired him for it.

The list of deeds in this category could be quite long. And in response to all of them, Douglass is all but untouchable. He allows no one the right to impede him and only addressed criticisms in his speech when he has a plethora of counterarguments and evidence to present. Surely this imperial disregard for external authorities is one of the features of his presentation that causes some people to see Douglass's ethos as overwhelming. It is not even that case that he overwhelmed anyone else, but that he refused to be moved himself. It is the stubborn resistance to all encroachments on his self-determination that seems to make him so "majestic" and leads on-lookers to see in him something of the "African prince" or "lion." Grimké's eulogy, quoted in the last chapter, is significant here for its careful word choice: she says no one "*dared* to whisper" derogatory words about him. She would not assert that no one had bad things to say, just that people were to afraid to speak them because of Douglass's authority.

Expertise and Judgment

Although Douglass's ethos strategies make it hard for audiences to judge him, he presents himself as a person of powerful critical abilities. By portraying himself as an expert on slavery, he lends the weight of studied knowledge to his criticisms of the south. But because expertise is necessarily a narrow kind of knowledge, Douglass wisely builds his upon one of the widest possible applications of expertise — black and white racial relations. Extending the scope of his expertise to this general matter brings much of American politics and society within his purview as a commentator.

His expertise, then, is unlike the majority of slave orators who simplistically related their tales. His is designed to increase his authority as he speaks to white society. When, for instance, Douglass claims he can "distinguish a slaveholder or a slave by the very cast of his eye, the moment he sees one"[36] he is claiming more than a sensitivity to the haughty looks of slaveholders. He is branding them, trying to add to their shame. If he could, he would have all slaveholders wear a scarlet letter "S" on their clothing to remind them of their sin. Instead he confronts them with the idea that their sin follows them into the north and polite society. Any image of refinement or morality they might try to put on is thwarted. Douglass, who is something of an enigma on stage, claims he can pierce through other people's appearances and discern their true nature. He has access to some knowledge that allows him to read the signs that people give off unconsciously.

Douglass's expertise has another social function as well: it allows him to make assessments about white society they can not make on their own since they are too blinded by biases and false doctrines. His expertise in this matter functions as a critique of the ideology of inferiority, not by offering counter evidence, but by depicting whites as dupes of leaders with false ideas. Their mistaken opinions about blacks are not a result of poor reasoning that needs to be corrected or even of sinful race pride. Instead, Douglass takes the issue of inferiority out of the realm of debate where blacks had never been particularly successful. He locates the problem elsewhere by indicating that, in actuality, all whites are suffering from a kind of false consciousness. There can be no debating with them on this issue, for their minds are occluded. The problem can only be solved by getting them to accept him as the doctor of their ideas.

In a similar way, Douglass asserts his expertise by applying it to the church's role in race relations. He blames the "charm" of false religion has used its deceptive power to "overawe" most white people.[37] Thus his constant counter to the criticism he receives from the church is that he "loves the true religion of Christ" and again,

> It is the faithless and the recreant Priesthood I would hold up, not the true servants of an impartial God, who created us All in his likeness. I will never be driven off the platform of the Christian Religion in fighting slavery. But my heart goes out only toward a practical religion. I see in this Convention an exhibition of adherence to the vitality of religion. Christianity works thus not alone with the rich and the strong, but it reaches its long beneficent arm down to seize and bear upward the lasting of humanity. Such Christianity is embodied in the great anti-slavery movement of the nineteenth century.[38]

So he will defend his Christianity — that much was essential to anyone's ethos — but he rarely gets involved in proper theological arguments. It is enough for him to assert the blindness of his opponents, that it is due to powerful forces, and that he can explain the problem. If, as Campbell suggests, the lower classes do seek strong leaders because they have a sense that they cannot lead themselves, Douglass is meeting that need by portraying himself as an expert. Of all people, he alone can lead them out of the land of confusion. But the proof that their thinking is confused is ultimately only offered through ethos: their ideology is false because he can tell the difference and he has determined it is false.

Voice and Expertise

Douglass's method for acquiring and establishing his expertise is one of the most fascinating elements of his rhetoric. To be reckoned an expert, someone has to exhibit a precise knowledge of a subject matter. Now if he confined his claims of expertise to slave life, his autobiographical statements would act as sufficient proof. But professing a master about matters of race relations requires him to go farther, to prove his erudition regarding the lives, ideas, and habits of white people.

One way to do acquire such learning would be to take Tocqueville as his model and go on a tour of the country to study white people and their proclivities. Of course his dark skin would have made that method of study a dangerous, if not impossible one.[39] Even if it were possible, though, it would have been wrong for Douglass the ex-slave, because that is how a literate mind would approach the problem, attempting to gain knowledge through analysis of empirical, especially visual, data.

Douglass's method is, fittingly, that of an oral person. He learns about a subject through dialogue and proves his knowledge in discussion. In other words, his expertise comes from carefully listening to whites. That knowledge is exhibited without studies, essays or philosophy (until much later in his career), but by engaging in dialogue with the voices of whites *in the course of his speeches.* What I mean will be made clear by looking at his speech commemorating West India emancipation in 1847 (shortly after his return from his Tocquevillian "tour" of England). It offers a prime example of how he establishes his expertise and even reveals Douglass's attitude toward his own expertise.[40]

After an introduction celebrating the freedoms won in India, he moves into the body of his speech. He starts by responding to a challenge that has been leveled at him and the occasion, the propriety of "one nation celebrating the deeds of another." His concern is that it might show a lack of patriotism to celebrate the accomplishment of other countries — a very real concern for someone who had just spent several months praising England's stance on slavery. In his own defense he intones, "In celebrating his day, we place ourselves beneath the broad aegis of human brotherhood," and supports this claim in this way: "And, Sir, where is the man, of high or low standing, white or black, who would lift his arm, or raise his voice, to remove us from this place, or to silence our joyous exultations?" Through this, one of Douglass's customary figures, an apostrophe, the issue is constructed as one of competing voices. Foes are those who would raise their voices, friends are engaged in exultations.

He then connects his praise of India with an attack on American slavery by criticizing the treatment of slaves everywhere. At the heart of a list of indignities is the fact that slaves whether in India or America are "not permitted to give testimony in courts of law." In other words, one of the worst problems of slavery is the inability to defend oneself in words. If that one right were allowed to slaves, Douglass suggests, many of the other problems on the list would be lessened or disappear altogether.

The downfall of American slaves is that they are alienated from control over their speech. To make this point, his lecture is filled with references to speech. Slaves, he says, are unable to unite or to fight back because they are "strangers to the English tongue, their only language is that of the lash." Then they are "driven to market, and under the cry of the auctioneer, they are sold." Yet amid all this inability to speak and the perverted voice of the whip's crack, "scarce a voice" is heard against the oppression. Voices, then, are key to resisting slavery, and the slave's forced silence is a major reason for its perpetuation. The many slave narratives were intended as written testimonies about slavery for just this reason.

Douglass obviously shared the concern with having a voice. But he is not content to show his expertise merely by giving testimony about slavery. Since he deigns to speak as an expert on blacks and whites, he must show himself qualified to speak using the same logic that made him the voice of the slave. He represents and imitates white voices in his speech as much as he speaks from the perspective of an ex- slave. This is a major motivation behind several Douglass's better known rhetorical strategies; his famous imitation of the racist sermons he had heard, his mockery of the ignorance of plantation owners are proof of his intimate knowledge of their ways.

Although this is an unusual form of expertise, if his imitations had not had an element of truth in them, audiences would not have found them so amusing. They did, though, as this account shows:

> Here the Speaker [Douglass] assumed the attitude and drawling manner so characteristic of the American preachers, amid the laughter of all present, and continued — Thus do these hypocrites cant. They also tell the slaves there is no happiness but in obedience, and wherever you see poverty and misery, be sure it results from disobedience. (Laughter)

Douglass adds to this a story a slave being whipped for falling asleep where he can actually "quote" a white man:

> 'You servants,' continued the preacher, 'To what was this whipping traceable, to disobedience, and if you would not be whipped, and if you would back in the sunshine of your master's favour, let me exhort you to obedience. You should also be grateful that God in his mercy brought you from Africa to this Christian land.' (Great laughter.)[41]

Although the most obvious results of this strategy are entertainment and a mocking of the opposition, Douglass is indeed true to the purpose given in the title of his speech: "I Am Here to Spread Light on American Slavery." He reveals the nature of the white man, not by abstractions, but by imitating their foibles so perfectly his expertise about this type of man cannot be questioned. As one reviewer commented, his "graphic mimickry of southern priestly whining and sophistry was replete with humor and apparent truth, which elicited tremendous applause."[42]

How does one refute this type of expertise? Study can counter study and rules of logic, evidence or procedure may be applied to discredit a treatise. But when one's expertise is based on personal observation, and when it is presented so that it has the *ring of truth*, it does not matter, strictly speaking, if the claim or impression is accurate. Once again, then, audiences and opponents alike would have had trouble finding the grounds for judging or denying one of Douglass's ethos proofs.

Douglass's Manliness as Proof of Character

"I have been taunted," Douglass laments more than once, "with the want of valour: so has my race because we have not risen upon our masters."[43] On the other hand, one of his favorite features of England was that "I saw in every man a recognition of my manhood."[44] It is easy to see, then, that being a man, and a strong masculine one at that, was important to Douglass's presentation of who he was as a person. It was also a key rhetorical move to present himself as both "a man and a brother" "despite the statutes denying it" to show that he was not suitable material for slavery.[45] Critics responded as he wanted them to. They saw a Douglass who

> stood there in manly attitude, with erect form, and glistening eye, and deep-toned voice telling us that he had been secretly devising means to effect his release from bondage, we could not help of thinking of Spartacus the Gladiator.... A man of his shrewdness, and his power both intellectually and physically, must be poor stuff to make a slave of.[46]

The word choices here speak volumes about Douglass's decidedly masculine image. In fact, even Douglass's eloquence and diction were considered with an eye toward his gender. His companion on an early lecture tour offered this impression of the ex-slave:

> Though never been favored with the advantages of an education, his style of speaking is chaste, free and forcible — his enunciation clear and distinct — his manner deliberate and energetic, alike free from tameness and ranting vehemence. His descriptions of slavery are most graphic, and his arguments are so lucid and occasionally so spiced with pleasantry, and sometimes a little satire, that his addresses, though long, are seldom tedious, but are listened to with the

most profound attention. He is capable of performing a vast amount of good for
his oppressed race.

Notice here the qualifications on the compliments. Although his diction and delivery
are polished, they are not so careful as to suggest an effeminate speaker. He is
energetic, free from tameness, and from its opposite, rampaging emotion. That is, his
diction evinced the perfect amount of manly self-control.

Kimmel, for one, makes an excellent case that manhood was a major concern
for all men in the antebellum era. Exhibiting acknowledged traits of masculinity had
what I have called "therapeutic value." Masculinity was proven through self-control,
which is also a necessary trait for voting citizens. Valorizing the masculine allowed
men to brag about their achievements in a time when identity was defined by success in the marketplace.[47] It therefore shored up their identities in a time of change
from an agrarian to an industrial society. Leverenz makes the economic connection
even stronger, asserting that being manly primarily meant having dignity because of
one's labor, and that this connection allowed men to define themselves as the only
public actors.[48]

For Douglass, masculinity was essential because of his stance on women's rights.
The popular epithet for such people was "Aunt Nancy Men."[49] They were accused of
trying to create equality not by bringing women up to the stature of men, but by
feminizing men. White men, the only full citizens, saw this as akin to miscegenation,
an overturning of the social order that was also unnatural and immoral.

But establishing manhood was important for Douglass's ethos especially as a
matter of character. Hugh Blair is very clear on this issue. The word "virtue," he
notes, comes from the Latin for "manliness," and he lists the virtues an orator should
achieve by referencing a list of "manly virtues."[50] The orator here serves as a
synecdoche for all public actors. His virtues are the traits thought to be useful for
acting in the world. So, his ethos is a list of virtues that are actually markers of
masculinity. Against the intimacy and emotional exploration of the age, men opposed
counter-trends. Getting in touch with emotions and expressing them with sincerity
and authenticity was good enough for women, but men, it was decided, controlled
themselves. In fact, they were so much in control of their emotions they could express
them in powerful ways so that others would be infected by them and swept along in
the tide. Men also did not remain engaged overly long in the life of the mind,
choosing to participate instead in the *vita activa*.

Activity, self-control, and most of all, working to improve one's lot in life not
just to make a living: these were the elements of the antebellum *self-made man*.
Because there were assumed to be few external limitations on success (perhaps the
banking power or trade restrictions would count), no discrimination based on class
and no limitations on their right to hold and use property, the only things American

men thought could stand in the way of their success were any personal flaws they may have. Therefore the notion of self-made manhood linked one's moral and economic success.[51] Acquiring money through hard work was a proof of character and indicated that one had risen above any character flaws such as slothfulness that might keep one poor.

Douglass, eager to deny he was a natural-born slave, latched on to this idea. He developed his own version of self-made manhood, and even gave speeches advising others, whites as well as blacks, on how to achieve his kind of success. Leverenz argues that Douglass erased connections to his family and other women in his second autobiography in order to make himself look more self-reliant.[52] He would even chide fellow blacks on this standard: "I have often thought that what the colored people want most in this country is character," he would say. "They want manly aspirations and a firm though modest self-reliance, and this we must have, or be like all other worthless things swept away before the march of events."[53]

Being manly, showing his composure and control, was a way for Douglass to prove his worth. By tapping in to the methods white men were using as well, he ingratiated himself into mainstream American society. And since few people outside the inner circles of the anti-slavery societies knew how much support Douglass received from white men and even women during the early days of his career, his economic success and undeniably good work ethic did much to commend him to mainstream America.

DOUGLASS'S PERSONALITY AND CHARACTER: CONCLUSIONS

Because the grounds underlying his ethos proofs shift so regularly, it is useful to establish that Douglass was not acting haphazardly. The complex weave of appeals in Douglass's speeches can be verified as conscious, strategic choices in the way he presents himself to various audiences across time. Stepto, referring to Douglass's written autobiographies, celebrates his ability to resist the impositions of the culture and his white sponsors. He thoroughly "controls the presentation of his personal history"[54] by presenting his own thoughts in his own way. Moreover, he manages to turn the tables on his white sponsors by recognizing a white man's poem as a fair portrait of southern slave life. He *authenticates* the poem of the northern abolitionist whereas the normal course of events is to have an abolitionist patron guarantee the authenticity of the words of the ex-slave. Butterfield makes a similar case about Douglass's careful image construction:

> It is Frederick Douglass, among all the slave narrators, who made the best use of his materials, who mastered and assimilated the rhetoric of the literary mainstream, stamped it with his personality and experience, and most ably turned it to whatever purpose he chose: persuasion, propaganda, passion,

rational argument, narrative, and drama. In Douglass, the 'white influence' and the black experience make one continuous grain of accomplished artistry. He was able to dominate his influences where most of the narrators, in style at least, were dominated by them.[55]

With minor changes, the statement could refer equally well to Douglass's ethos. That is, he mastered and assimilated the character appeals of the oratorical mainstream, the "white influence," and stamped them with his personality and experience. The two do come together artistically as one grain.

Thinking of the rhetorical process this way, we can list Douglass ethos "materials." He started with the inferior qualities that were expected of someone of his race and with his background. Strong reactions to Douglass's performances were based on his exceptional acuity for exceeding the passionately held expectations of the listener. His personal qualities were always greater in some way than they expected and always used for his own purposes. People who came ready to dismiss him for his inherent depravity came away with an earful of his foibles, but with an enjoyable evening or even a sincere respect for his complex, authentic personhood.

After exceeding enough expectations over a long enough period of time, Douglass, in effect, raised his own standard. People began to turn out just to hear him speak. They brought with them a load of different demands that were as high as they had always been, but were changed to be more typical of those we place on a modern celebrity. Yet the limitations on his ability to persuade with ethos were undiminished; instead of being a sub-human chattel species of orator, he became an extra-human species of consumable object.[56] According to communal standards he exchanged his status as one type of property, wrongly owned by a southern master, for the status of a different kind of property that anyone in the north could use for their entertainment and therapy.

Ultimately, Douglass's struggle was to use his properties — the qualities the society would accept as a measure of ethos — to prove he was no one else's property, either in the logic of slavery or of capitalism.

Douglass as Spectacle

I have suggested throughout this book that Frederick Douglass's ethos can only be understood in light of the economic and social forces that were changing notions of personhood for his audiences and creating new opportunities and reasons for "consuming" oratory. Two of his major challenges, in light of overwhelming apathy and antipathy, were to get people to attend his lectures and to reduce their defensiveness to the appeals he would offer. Ethos served both purposes since audiences were following a consumer model. This makes sense if we extend the metaphor. How could Douglass get people to "buy" what he was saying? In terms of his apathy and antipathy, how did he get them in the "store" and get them to consider his pitch?

First he had to entice people to the event. For this, personality was called upon. He was exotic and a bit naughty. An evening with him promised to be entertaining, if nothing else. He allowed himself to be portrayed by Garrison, his de facto carnival barker, as a spectacle. He said he was "willing to be regarded as a curiousity, if I may thereby aid the high and holy cause of the slave's emancipation."[57]

Once inside, the "sell" had to begin since his most important audience, the white middling classes, came only to window shop. They did not want to expend themselves, just observe his wares. All their defenses would be up to resist committing to abolition or even admitting his humanity. At this point, his complex array of ethos appeals came to bear upon them.

His problem was essentially the problem of the first department stores and his response was similar to theirs. The first department stores had to stimulate people to buy in the midst of great surpluses — the kind of surplus of oratory that existed in the antebellum period. To start, the stores created a spectacle outside by using their display windows; Douglass's reputation, willingness to parade around town and call for attendance, and the patronizing introductions he received served this function admirably. So too did the accounts of him contradicting whites, heckling and imitating them, and sometimes even getting into fights.

The next move the stores made was to juxtapose objects randomly on the shelves so that, in Sennett's words, the "use character of the object was temporarily suspended. It became 'stimulating,' one wanted to buy it, because it became temporarily an unexpected thing; it became strange."[58] Moreover, "the stimulation produced by jumbling dissimilar objects together the retail owners reinforced by the continual search for exotic *nouveautes* to put on sale in the midst of the most prosaic wares." The strange displays of wares created a disorientation that mystified the objects, gave them an increased attractiveness, and reduced the consumer's defensiveness.

The responses of admirers prove that Douglass's many and varied ethos qualities functioned in essentially the same way. They list quality after quality, and as they describe him, they realize they haven't quite captured their impression, and so are forced to add an opposing notion. Just in the reviews I have already included in this chapter, he is neither vehement nor tame, pleasant but sarcastic, long but not tedious, graceful but powerful and overwhelming. As he depicted himself, he is a man of great character but also decidedly flawed according to moral and social norms. He is representative but the exception. He purports to be an expert, but there is no way to measure his claims which, regardless, come out in a very entertaining and non-threatening manner. He is identified with the slaves — his expertise and authority come partly from that aspect of his autobiography — but he is also a self-made man, representing an opposite extreme. He is a loyal Christian, against the church, but morally superior to it. He can incorporate the black experience into white language, and white personae into his own imitations. Perhaps most of all, he is free yet still a slave.

In short, Douglass's self-presentation is dazzling. The various voices he includes in his oratory only add to this image. It arrests the attention and stymies the judgment.

But, in all of this, he was not strictly speaking selling "himself." Another way to say it is that he constructs a multifaceted identity, then uses it to identify with all constituents of the audience. For those who merely want to use him for entertainment, he offers his properties, but he is still in control of them. They are clearly part of his crafted image. This, I believe, is what made Frederick Douglass so appealing.

Douglass's Impact on the Rhetorical Culture

In the opening chapter I argued that ethos cannot be understood apart from an appreciation of the notion of the self prevalent in the era in question. Douglass's example also encourages a reversal of the formula: the prevalent notion of the self cannot be fully understood in a given era with an appreciation for how selves were codified in ethos appeals at that time. What people take as constitutive of their personhood is not formed in a philosophical vacuum. Selves are always proven and tested in front of others when they are presented as identities. When selves are presented rhetorically, ethos appeals are the results. The kinds of identities — or better, the particular qualities of persons — that are deemed valuable in that public "trial by fire" become the significant ones, the ones people use to define themselves.

We could, for instance, consider the powerful part rhetorical culture plays in determining women's notions of their selfhood when only women who present themselves as submissive, emotional, and virginal are approved. For this example, adopting the terminology of ethos would call our attention to the expectations for women prevalent in the time, the resources present in the speaker's life, the identity the speaker tries to establish with the audience, and the audience's reaction to that identity.

If Douglass's example proves a serviceable model for feminists and other reformers, his rhetoric would suggest that reform sometimes needs to come at the expense of holding to all character ideals at all costs. Early in his career people responded primarily to the entertainment Douglass's presentation offered. It gave him the ear of the audience long enough to establish some character traits. The whole package was so subtle, that the power and eloquence, personality and character, are all but indistinguishable for the audience. Such is the case with the reviewer of an 1841 abolition meeting who reported to the Liberator's readers,

> Much interest was added to this occasion by the eloquent and thrilling re-
> marks of a fugitive slave the audience hanging with breathless silence on the
> lips of this faithful representative of lions in bondage. As he finished, many

were ready to exclaim — woe to the oppressor who would crush a spirit so full of heavenly fire.[59]

So there is a somewhat distasteful conclusion to be drawn from this study. As long as audiences remain therapeutically oriented in a consumer society, they can be reached by people who first offer themselves as commodities for consumption. The first step in changing the dominant ideology of personhood surrounding a group can be to inject members of that group in to the mainstream as entertainment. This worked to an extent with Harlem Renaissance poets and musicians in the early twentieth century. Thus, too, rap artists today have the potential to change dominant notions about black personhood by presenting particular versions of themselves for consumption.

Of course, Douglass's difficulties present the harsh realities that constrain this tactic. He had to put enormous effort into his self presentation. Every public act for him was a calculated decision. His most important, most difficult, and best decisions, were his meticulously crafted displays of traditional character qualities. These qualities, which previously had been reserved for leaders and decision makers, limited the cycle of consumption by establishing him as a Person, removed at some level from the act of entertaining. In this area, some of today's African American hip-hop stars may not be doing the same work as Douglass and may actually be enforcing notions that blacks are merely consumable objects, valuable only for their instrumental, therapeutic value.

This study also suggests several questions for future research. On a historical note, I have argued that the rhetorical culture of the antebellum period was therapeutic. This claim applies the terminology used by major theorists back over fifty years. Their work identified a problem that came about with Freudian psychology (Rieff) and the advertising culture (Jackson-Lears). Instead, I am suggesting that audiences had a consumer's mentality very early in the nineteenth century. The market metaphors and Marxist terminology that are woven throughout this paper are not, therefore, there as a result of any ideological commitment. "Commodity fetish," "use value" and the other terms are used because in my estimation they best reflect the actual workings of the rhetorical culture in an age of industrialization and democratization. The accuracy of this assessment needs to be tested.

Theoretical questions also arise. Particularly, the appeal of celebrity status is somewhat hard to account for using my terminology. Celebrities draw people to movies (say) because they are known quantities; people expect a certain level of acting ability or what have you and so are willing to spend their money on the "credibility" of those actors' cachet. Of the two kinds of traits I have referred to throughout the dissertation, character traits are supposed to be the bankable ones. Character, I have said, is based on a record of public deeds. On the other hand, celebrity clearly participates in the appeal of personality: celebrities are expected to be entertaining and to offer their lives as well as their performances for audience consumption. Perhaps other qualities need to be explored to see how well the character/personality terminology explains a person's ethos.

One last route for exploration would be the role of audiences in an era of changing notions of ethos. If audiences who appreciate personality are indeed witnesses rather than judges, this forces us to consider a reevaluation of Aristotelian theory where deliberative and forensic audiences are judges. Is a change in ethos sufficient to cause this degree of change, or are commensurate changes in pathos and logos required? This is a crucial question for a democracy where people who lack Douglass's good intentions can potentially dazzle audiences and stymie their judgment. What are the typical responses of democratic audiences to the spectacle of modern orators who can incorporate both personality and character traits into their rhetoric, and what should our responses be? These are crucial questions for the ongoing viability of the rhetorical culture going into the next century.

End Notes

NOTES TO CHAPTER ONE

1. Frederick Douglass, *My Bondage and My Freedom* (1855; New York: Dover, 1969) 353.
2. Female orators played an instrumental part in expanding the notion of ethos beyond those of ideal masculinity. However, in the American scene this did not fully happen for years after the time period covered by this work. Also, the question of the influence of female orators on the understanding of ethos is best handled by a separate, equally in-depth examination.
3. Plato, *Gorgias*, trans. Walter Hamilton (London: Penguin, 1981) 75.
4. The easy division of ethos into three characteristics probably contributes to Aristotle's preeminence in later scholarship. For those studying persuasion, or especially ethos, his clear divisions make obvious targets for challenges or extensions.
5. Aristotle 1356a. The translation I will use throughout the dissertation unless otherwise noted is *Aristotle, On Rhetoric: A Theory of Civic Discourse*, trans. George A. Kennedy (New York: Oxford UP, 1991).
6. Aristotle, 1378a; *Rhetoric* 121.
7. Jack L. Whitehead, Jr., "Factors of Source Credibility," *Quarterly Journal of Speech* 54 (1968): 59-63; Jesse G. Delia, "A Constructivist Analysis of the Concept of Credibility," *Quarterly Journal of Speech* 62 (1976): 361-375; Kenneth Andersen and Theodore Clevenger, "A Summary of Experimental Research in Ethos," *Speech Monographs* 30 (1963): 59-78.
8. The beginning paragraphs of studies in source credibility are remarkably similar. There is a customary mention of Aristotle's divisions of the modes of proof and tripartite division of ethos qualities. Then, there is a leap to the work of Hovland, Janis, and Kelly as the beginning of the modern study of ethos, followed by a brief review of the characteristics others have studied. See, for example, Delia, *Constructivist* 361.
9. William M. Sattler makes a similar argument for the Hellenistic period. See his "Conceptions of *Ethos* in Ancient Rhetoric," *Speech Monographs* 14 (1947): 55.
10. Quintilian, *Institutio Oratoria*, XII. 2.385; Cicero, 2.152; See also Richard Lee Enos and Karen Rossi Schnakenberg, "Cicero Latinizes Hellenic Ethos," *Ethos: New Essays in Rhetorical and Critical Theory*, ed. James S. Baumlin and Tita French Baumlin (Dallas: Southern Methodist UP, 1994) 197.

11. The perception of conflict is not quite accurate. Given Aristotle's strong definition of appearances as something akin to truth-as-we-can-know-it, his philosophy of character as something that requires a life time to inculcate, and his caveat that "the true and the just are by nature stronger than their opposites" (1355a, p.34), his position is much closer to Socrates's than Callicles's. However, it is possible to keep the same ideas about *how* ethos works, but combine them with a different set of assumptions about *what* works as ethos. Absent his ethical system and his definition of man [sic] as *zoon politikon* (which requires that a man be judged by his relationship to the community), Aristotle's rhetorical guidelines are quite relevant and helpful for understanding all sorts of rhetors.

12. Augustine, *De doctrina Christiana*, trans. D. W. Robertson, Jr. (Indianapolis: Bobbs-Merrill, 1958).

13. Douglas Ehninger, "Dominant Trends in English Rhetorical Thought, 1750–1800," *Southern States Communication Journal*, 18 (September 1952): 3–12; Vincent M. Bevilacqua, "Philosophical Influences in the Development of English Rhetorical Theory: 1748–1783," *Proceedings of the Leeds Philosophical and Literary Society, Literary and Historical Section*, 12, Part 6 (April 1968): 191–215.

14. Hugh Blair, *Lectures on Rhetoric and Belles Letters*, ed. Harold Harding (Carbondale: Southern Illinois UP, 1965); George Campbell, *The Philosophy of Rhetoric*, ed. Lloyd Bitzer (Carbondale: Southern Illinois UP, 1963); Adam Smith, *Lectures on Rhetoric and Belles Lettres*, ed. David Potter (Carbondale: Southern Illinois UP, 1971); John Ward, *Systems of Oratory* (London: 1759). For most of these authors, seeming good is more than sufficient for common audiences who are, in so many words, too stupid to follow complicated arguments and will follow anyone who impresses them.

15. Campbell 101.

16. Campbell 104.

17. Campbell 104-5.

18. William L. Andrews, "Frederick Douglass, Preacher," *American Literature* 54 (Dec. 1982): 592-97; Robert G. O'Meally, "Frederick Douglass's 1845 *Narrative*: The Text Was Meant to Be Preached," ed. Dexter Fisher and Robert B. Stepto, *Afro-American Literature* (New York: MLA, 1978) 192–211.

19. Charles Taylor, *Sources of the Self: The Making of Modern Identity* (Cambridge: Harvard UP, 1989).

20. My summary of the history of the discipline is indebted to Charles J. Stewart's "Historical Survey: Rhetorical Criticism in Twentieth Century America," *Explorations in Rhetorical Criticism*, ed. G. P. Mohrmann (University Park, PA: Pennsylvania State UP, 1973) 1–31.

21. The classic challenge to Aristotle's preeminence in rhetorical criticism is by Edwin Black, *Rhetorical Criticism: A Study in Method* (Madison, U of Wisconsin P, 1965).

22. Bernard L. Brock, Robert L. Scott and James W. Chessbro, *Methods of Rhetorical Criticism: A Twentieth Century Perspective* (Detroit: Wayne State UP, 1972) 28. These authors refer to neo-Aristotelian criticism as "speaker oriented," for several reasons, including a focus on the speaker's choice of strategies.

23. Stewart 11.

24. See, for example, the analyses of Clay and Calhoun in *A History and Criticism of American Public Address*, ed. William Norwood Brigance, vol. II (New York: McGraw-Hill, 1943).

25. Again, studies of Henry Ward Beecher and Theodore Parker in Brigance, vol I, provide good examples.

26. Cornelius Abraham Ladner, "A Critical Analysis of Four Anti-Slavery Speeches of Frederick Douglass," thesis, U Iowa, 1947. Another example is found in Lois Belton Kinney, "A Rhetorical Study of the Practice of Frederick Douglass on the Issue of Human Rights, 1840-1860," diss., Ohio State U, 1973.

27. Ladner 16, 25.

28. Ladner 29.

29. Ladner 29.

30. Part of the reason critical studies have followed this trail is the close link habit (εθος) and character (εθος) have in Aristotelian terminology. Because of his ethical philosophy Aristotle believed that the most persuasive speaker would have inculcated the traits of elevated character, so he emphasized the close etymological connection. Breaking this link does not entail eliminating the rest of his observations about ethos (e.g., that it is the most powerful element in the speech, it is built through the speech, and it is unseverable from a concern for particular audiences). That the *idea* of ethos needs to be separated from the idea of character to understand modern speaker's persuasiveness is one of the fundamental arguments of this dissertation, but I am in no way anti-Aristotelian.

31. David B. Chesebrough, *Frederick Douglass: Oratory from Slavery* (Westport, CT: Greenwood Press, 1998).

32. Chesebrough's discussion of Douglass's ethos covers pages 83-90.

33. Kinney 282.

34. See pages 148–156.

35. On patriarchy, see Deborah E. McDowell, "'Hear My Voice, Ye Careless Daughters': Narratives of Slave and Free Women Before Emancipation." *African American Autobiography: a Collection of Critical Essays*, ed. William L. Andrews (Englewood Cliffs, NJ: Prentice Hall, 1993); Kristin Hoganson, "Garrisonian Abolitionists and the Rhetoric of Gender, 1850–1860, *American Quarterly* 45 (December 1993): 558–595; and Jenny Franchot, "The Punishment of Esther: Frederick Douglass and the Constitution of the Feminine." *Frederick Douglass: New Literary and Historical Essays*, ed. Eric J. Sundquist (Cambridge: Cambridge UP, 1996) 141–65. For obeisance to whites, see William S. McFeely, *Frederick Douglass* (New York: Norton, 1991) 295.

36. Gerald Hauser, *Introduction to Rhetorical Criticism* (Prospect Heights: Waveland, 1986) 101, emphasis in original.

37. James Darsey, "The Legend of Eugene Debs: Prophetic *Ethos* as Radical Argument" *Quarterly Journal of Speech* 74 (1988): 434–452. Despite the title, this is a study of a prophetic persona. Insofar as it relates to ethos, it might be called a study of an ethos genre. That is, Debs's discursively presented qualities are compared to a Type of person, the biblical prophet. On the relationship of voice to ethos, see Margaret D. Zulick, "The Agon of Jeremiah: On the Dialogic Invention of Prophetic Ethos," *Quarterly Journal of Speech* 78 (1992). Note that both these works are still concerned with the speaker's relationship to biblical morality and thus are still operating on the assumption that ethos is related to character.

38. Carl I. Hovland, Irving L. Janis, and Harold H. Kelly, *Communication and Persuasion* (New Haven: Yale UP, 1953); Whitehead, 59; Delia, 361.

39. Helen Lewis, "Studies in the Principles of Language and Judgments and Attitudes: IV. The Operation of 'Prestige Suggestion,'" *Journal of Social Psychology* 14 (1941): 229–256.

40. Christopher J. S. Tuppen, "Dimensions of Communicator Credibility: Oblique Solution," *Speech Monographs* 41 (1974): 253–260.

41. Andersen and Clevenger; Kim Giffin, "The Contribution of Studies of Source Credibility to a Theory of Interpersonal Trust in the Communication Process," *Psychological Bulletin* 68 (1967): 104–120; William A. Phillips, "A Note on the Generality of Source-Credibility Scales," *Speech Monographs* 36 (1967): 185–186; Gary Cronkhite and Jo Liska , "A Critique of Factor Analytic Approaches to the Study of Credibility," *Communication Monographs* 43 (1976): 91–107; George E. Yoos, "A Revision of the Concept of Ethical Appeal," *Philosophy and Rhetoric* 12 (1979): 41–58. The most recent and succinct effort to redefine ethos studies is Cal M. Logue and Eugene F. Miller, "Rhetorical Status: A Study of Its Origins, Functions, and Consequences," *Quarterly Journal of Speech* 81 (1995): 20–47, although I disagree with several of their attempts at redirection as this chapter makes clear.

42. Whitehead 63.

43. Logue and Miller 24.

44. Logue and Miller (43) offer this summary of Delia's argument.

45. Nan Johnson, "Ethos and the Aims of Rhetoric," *Essays on Classical Rhetoric and Modern Discourse*, ed. Robert J. Connors, Lisa S. Ede, and Andrea A. Lunsford (Carbondale: Southern Illinois UP, 1984) 98–114. Johnson does not address the social scientific literature in Speech and Psychology studying credibility, but that research, which ends up with a related list of characteristics to the one she cites, would not have forced her to change her analysis.

46. Stephen Greenblatt, *Renaissance Self-Fashioning From More to Shakespeare,* (Chicago: U of Chicago P, 1980); John O. Lyons, *The Invention of the Self: The Hinge of Consciousness in the Eighteenth Century,* (Carbondale: Southern Illinois UP, 1978). For comparison's sake, a strictly Aristotelian theory of composition would focus on putting topoi into the text. His conception was very different from a composition textbook of today, because for him ideas existed in the world and society and were available for the rhetor to place into a text. *Self*-expression would be an almost incomprehensible effort for Aristotle's contemporaries; they were seeking to express *logos*.

47. I am grateful to Bruce Gronbeck for this example.

48. Blair 100.

49. On ethos as self-expression and self-esteem, see Walter S. Minot, "Personality and Persona: Developing the Self," *Rhetoric Review* 7 (1989): 352–361.

50. James S. Baumlin, "Introduction: Positioning *Ethos* in Historical and Contemporary Theory," *Ethos: New Essays in Rhetorical and Critical Theory*, ed. James S. Baumlin and Tita French Baumlin, (Dallas: Southern Methodist UP, 1994) xi–xxxi.

51. 1356a4; Kennedy, *Rhetoric* 38.

52. Speaking in Congress is a slightly different matter. Congressional speeches received a great deal of attention in the antebellum press because of the weight of the issues being discussed, and were often noted or panned for their logical cogency. In the halls of government, overwhelming emotion or being "overpowered" (except by outrage at an opponent's speech) was virtually unheard of. While there were certainly

elements of ethos when a Clay or Webster stepped up to speak, logic seemed to be both the goal and standard.

53. It is Bakhtin in "Epic and Novel" and "Forms of Time and Chronotope in the Novel" who points out the uncomplicated and unchanging nature of epic heroes, and contrasts that image to the complex individuals that emerge in Douglass's time period, though novels. M. M. Bakhtin *The Dialogic Imagination*, ed. Michael Holquist, trans. Caryl Emerson and Michael Holquist (Austin: U of Texas P, 1981).

54. Edmund Quincy to [Caroline Weston?] July 30, 1847, Weston Sister Letters: qtd. in McFeeley 147.

55. McFeely 148.

56. Warren I. Susman, *Culture as History: The Transformation of American Society in the Twentieth Century*, (New York: Pantheon, 1984); Christopher Gill, "The Character-Personality Distinction," *Characterization and Individuality in Greek Literature*, ed. Christopher Pelling (Oxford: Clarendon, 1990): 1–31.

57. Trevor Parry-Giles, "Character, the Constitution, and the Ideological Embodiment of 'Civil Rights' in the 1967 Nomination of Thurgood Marshall to the Supreme Court," *Quarterly Journal of Speech* 82 (1996): 377, 376.

58. William M. Sattler, "Conceptions of *Ethos* in Ancient Rhetoric," *Speech Monographs* 14 (1947): 55–65.

59. Harvey Yunis, *Taming Democracy: Models of Political Rhetoric in Classical Athens* (Ithaca, NY: Cornell UP, 1996); Josiah Ober, *Mass and Elite in Democratic Athens: Rhetoric, Ideology, and the Power of the People* (Princeton, NJ: Princeton UP, 1989); ed. J. Peter Euben, John R. Wallach, and Josiah Ober, *Athenian Political Thought and the Reconstruction of American Democracy* (Ithaca, NY: Cornell UP, 1994).

60. Besides the three autobiographies that Douglass wrote, he was eulogized and re-presented almost without end, every ten years or so since his death. Booker T. Washington and W. E. B. DuBois argued about the meaning of his life for black Americans and about who should inherit his legacy. His major biographies are included in my bibliography. The best discussions of his rhetorical career are found in Blassingame's introduction to his five-volume collection of Douglass's oratory, and in the following dissertations: Gerald Fulkerson, "Frederick Douglass and the Anti-Slavery Crusade: His Career and Speeches, 1817–1861," diss., U of Illinois at Urbana-Champaign, 1971; Gregory P. Lampe, "Frederick Douglass: Freedom's Voice, 1818–1845," diss., U Wisconsin, 1995.

61. The dissertation by Lampe offers an excellent investigation of Douglass's oratorical experiences as a youth and young adult that clearly reveal that he protested too much about his lack of education. He had been, for a dozen years, a public speaker or sorts before the fateful day he stood up to speak, was heard by Garrison, and invited to join the antislavery cause "officially."

62. Lampe 51.

63. I will discuss this in chapter four in a section on the "standard story" about Douglass's overwhelming ethos.

64. Jean Baudrillard, *Simulacra and Simulation*, trans. Sheila Faria Glaser (Ann Arbor: U of Michigan P, 1994). The application of some classical theories of ethos, which presume that the person of the speaker is at least as important as his/her discourse is not the only way in which my approach differs from some of the *avant-garde* work in rhetorical/literary studies. As the differences seem relevant, I will try to address

them; but this work is not an apologia of modernist methods either and so cannot respond to every challenge.

65. John Paul Akin, *Fictions in Autobiography: Studies in the Art of Self-Invention* (Princeton: Princeton UP, 1992).

66. Cal M. Logue and Thurmon Garner, "Shift in Rhetorical Status of Blacks after Freedom," *Southern Communication Journal* 54 (Fall 1988): 1–39.

67. Michael Leff offers a nice analysis of Douglass's authoritativeness at the dedication of the Lincoln memorial. See "Lincoln Among the Nineteenth-Century Orators," *Rhetoric and Political Culture in Nineteenth-Century America*, ed. Thomas W. Benson (Lansing: Michigan State UP, 1997) 142, 151.

68. Exile as Emergence: Frederick Douglass in Great Britain, 1845–1847," *Quarterly Journal of Speech* 60 (1974): 69.

69. I have addressed this topic in a paper entitled, "Frederick Douglass and the Consciousness of Orality," paper to the Speech Communication Association, San Diego, CA, November 1996.

70. Garrison, humorously described Phillips's many "corrections" to his speeches before publication in a letter to Oliver Johnson, qtd. in Ernest G. Bormann, ed., *Forerunners of Black Power: The Rhetoric of Abolition*, (Englewood Cliffs, NJ: Prentice-Hall, 1971): 93.

71. Hereafter these works will be referred to as *Bondage* and *Narrative*, respectively.

72. Robert Gray Gunderson, "The Magnanimous Mr. Clay," *Southern Speech Communication Journal* 16 (1950): 136.

73. This account of the transformation of the standards of personhood, and therefore ethos, as a glorification of everyday life, and a focus on interiority is based on Charles Taylor's philosophical history in *Sources of the Self.* Bakhtin traces similar developments in his essay "Forms of Time and Chronotope in the Novel."

74. Douglass's account of the constraints put on him by the abolitionist hierarchy is probably overstated. Douglass did not "stick to the facts" and leave the philosophizing for the whites, even in his early career as Lampe clearly shows. Wilson J. Moses argues convincingly that white abolitionists had little motive to limit their best speaker or to make him seem in any way less of an orator in "Writing Freely? Frederick Douglass and the Constraints of Racialized Writing." *Frederick Douglass: New Literary and Historical Essays*, ed. Eric J. Sundquist (Cambridge UP, 1990) 99–117.

75. Richard Sennett, *The Fall of Public Man* (New York: Knopf, 1977), 153.

76. Sennett 152.

NOTES TO CHAPTER TWO

1. Gladys L. Borches and Lillian R. Wagner, "Speech Education in Nineteenth-Century Schools," *History of Speech Education in America: Background Studies*, ed. Karl R. Wallace (New York: Appleton-Century-Crofts, 1954) 282.

2. On the importance of the common person's own theories of rhetoric, see Ernest Bormann, *Communication Theory* (New York: Holt, Rinehart, and Winston, 1980); Tamar Katriel and Gerald Philipsen, "What We Need is Communication: Communication as a Cultural Category in Some American Speech," *Communication Monographs* 48, 301-17; and Christine Oravec, "The Sublimation of Mass Consciousness

in the Rhetorical Criticism of Jacksonian America," *Communication*, 11 (1990), especially pages 291-2.

3. The idea that every person acts as an incipient scientist is based on Kellian psychology, as described in his works: George A. Kelly, *The Psychology of Personal Constructs* 2 vols. (New York: Norton, 1955). Kelly refers to people as "incipient scientists" in describing a fundamental human quality—our constant habit of predicting the outcomes of our actions, acting on the basis of our predictions, and testing our hypotheses after we have acted. Because Kelly's formulation is such a compelling explanation of the way audiences would approach a rhetorical situation, I have started my analysis with audiences' expectations. Kelly's terminology is nowhere present in the dissertation, but his influence is strong.

4. On the idea of social practices that contextualize rhetoric as a "rhetorical culture," see Thomas B. Farrell, *Norms of Rhetorical Culture* (New Haven: Yale UP, 1993). The argument is extended by Robert Hariman, Dilip Parameshwar Gaonkar and Maurice Charland, "The Forum: Norms of Rhetorical Culture," *Quarterly Journal of Speech* 80 (1994): 329–342. A similar idea is pursued by in *Oratorical Culture in the Nineteenth Century: Transformations in the Theory and Practice of Rhetoric*, ed. Gregory Clark and S. Michael Halloran (Carbondale: Southern Illinois UP, 1993).

5. Terry Lovell, qtd. in John Storey, *An Introductory Guide to Cultural Theory and Popular Culture* (Athens, GA: U of Georgia P, 1993) 196.

6. Celeste Michelle Condit and John Louis Lucaites, *Crafting Equality: America's Anglo-African Word* (Chicago: U of Chicago P, 1993).

7. Terrence Ball and Richard Dagger, "Fascism" *Political Ideologies and the Democratic Ideal*, (N.Y.: Harper, 1991)176–198; Jesse G. Delia, "Rhetoric in the Nazi Mind: Hitler's Theory of Persuasion," *Southern Speech Communication Journal* 37 (1971): 148; Haig A. Bosmajian, "Nazi Persuasion and the Crowd Mentality," *Western Speech* 29 (1965): 68-9.

8. See Richard Lee Enos and Jeanne L. McClaran, "Audience and Image in Ciceronian Rome: Creation and Constraints of The *Vir Bonus* Personality," *Central States Speech Journal* 29 (1978): 98–106.

9. Thus, as Enos and Schnakenberg illustrate, Cicero had to "Latinize" the Greek conception of ethos to account for its long-lasting effects on the orator's public position: "For Cicero, *ethos* was not only a 'proof' created within the discourse [as it was for Aristotle]; indirectly, *ethos* was manifested in the development of personal power and public glory." Richard Lee Enos and Karen Rossi Schnakenberg, "Cicero Latinizes Hellenic Ethos," *Ethos: New Essays in Rhetorical and Critical Theory*, ed. James S. Baumlin and Tita French Baumlin (Dallas: Southern Methodist UP, 1994) 206.

10. Samuel Cooper Thatcher, "Who Gave Up to Party: The Case of John Quincy Adams," *The Federalist Literary Mind*, ed. Lewis P. Simpson (Baltimore: J. H. Furst Co., 1962) 90-1.

11. Edward G. Parker, *The Golden Age of American Oratory*, (Boston: Whittemore, Niles, and Hall, 1857). The phrase is also used in Robert T. Oliver, *History of Public Speaking in America*, (Boston: Allyn and Bacon, 1965) 316, and Barnet Baskerville, *The People's Voice: The Orator in American Society*, (Lexington: UP of Kentucky, 1979) 33.

12. Clark and Halloran 9–17.

13. John W. Blassingame, *The Slave Community: Plantation Life in the Antebellum South* (New York: Oxford UP, 1972) 64-66; Eugene D. Genovese, *Roll Jordan Roll: The World the Slaves Made* (New York: Random House, 1974) 161-225.

14. Arthur L. Smith [Molefi Asante], "Socio-Historical Perspectives of Black Oratory," *Quarterly Journal of Speech* 56 (1970): 264.

15. For Douglass's early experiences listening to oratory see "Boyhood in Baltimore: An Address Delivered in Baltimore, Maryland, on 6 September 1891," *The Frederick Douglass Papers, Series One, Speeches, Debates, and Interviews,* vol. 5, ed. John W. Blassingame and John R. McKivigan (New Haven, CT.: Yale UP, 1992) 25-33, and Douglass, *Bondage* 168. The best commentary on the importance of these early oratorical experiences is found in the first two chapters of Lampe's dissertation.

16. Stephen Chambers and G. P. Mohrman, "Rhetoric in Some American Periodicals," *Speech Monographs* 37 (1970) 111.

17. Frank Luther Mott, *A History of American Magazines, 1850-1865* (Cambridge, MA: Harvard UP, 1938) 423.

18. Oravec, "Sublimation" 292.

19. Oravec too comments on this ("Sublimation" 293) although her point is to show the degree to which audiences were socially controlled by the commentary. My emphasis is almost the opposite. I interpret the critic's focus on the audience's character and reaction as a recognition of their importance, and as a way of exalting the power of the orator, and only secondarily as a commentary on their rustic behavior.

20. Edward O. Pessen, *The Many Faceted Jacksonian Era: New Interpretations,* Contributions in American History 67, (Westport, CT: Greenwood, 1977).

21. Alexis de Tocqueville, *Democracy in America,* Trans. George Lawrence. Ed. J. P. Mayer. (Garden City, NY: Anchor Books, 1969) 499.

22. Plato, *Gorgias,* trans. Walter Hamilton, (London: Penguin, 1971).

23. *New York Review and Monthly Atheneum,* July 1825, 125.

24. Myron Matlaw, *American Popular Entertainment,* Papers and Proceedings on the History of American Popular Entertainment (Westport, CT: Greenwood, 1979) 189-190.

25. "Everett's Orations" *New York Review,* Oct., 1825, 334.

26. Mott, I, 452.

27. "Mr. Webster's Speech," *The Pathfinder,* 27 May 1843: 1, quoted in Christine Oravec, "The Democratic Critics: An Alternative American Rhetorical Tradition of the Nineteenth Century," *Rhetorica* 4 (1996): 410.

28. In "The Democratic Critics," 401 Oravec asserts that the Whig intellectuals "engaged in political and intellectual controversy as a leisure and specialized pursuit."

29. Qtd. in Oravec, "Sublimation" 305.

30. For a discussion of the "star quality" of the contestants and the national following of the proceedings of the Webster-Hayne debate, see Lloyd E. Rohler, "Robert Hayne," *American Orators Before 1900,* ed. Bernard K. Duffy and Halford R. Ryan (New York: Greenwood, 1987) 215-6; and Robert T. Oliver, *History of Public Speaking in America,* (Boston: Allyn and Bacon, 1965) 94-5. On the Brownlow-Pryne debate, see Gordon F. Hostettler, "The Brownlow-Pryne Debate, September, 1858," *Antislavery and Disunion, 1858-1861,* ed. J. Jeffrey Auer (Harper, 1963) 1-28.

31. Baskerville, *The People's Voice* 33.

32. Borchers and Wagner 290.
33. Rosmarie K. Bank, *Theater Culture in America*, (New York: Cambridge, 1997) 113.
34. Oravec, "Sublimation" 294.
35. David Grimstead, "Uncle Tom from Page to Stage," *Quarterly Journal of Speech*, 56 (1970) 243.
36. Grimstead 243.
37. The literature on domesticity and "cult of true womanhood" in antebellum culture is large. Barbara Welter "The Cult of True Womanhood," *American Quarterly* 18 (1966): 151-174 is at least a good starting place.
38. Upper crust socialites in New York such as Horace Greeley were so concerned about how the middling and lower classes might behave in public as theater audiences—especially if they were only provided giant and dwarf shows or (actual) dog and pony shows—they launched a press campaign in the 1840s to establish moral standards for theaters. It was, though, no more successful than a more radical call by clergy in the 1820s to shut the theaters down altogether for similar reasons. See Bank 111-113.
39. William Lee Miller, *Arguing about Slavery: The Great Battle in the United States Congress*, (New York: Alfred A Knopf, 1996) 4.
40. Bank 114.
41. Bank 113.
42. Lois W. Banner, "Religious Benevolence as Social Control: A Critique of an Interpretation," *Many-Faceted Jacksonian Era*, 309.
43. *National Anti-Slavery Standard*, 14 May 1846.
44. Blassingame, *Papers* I, 15–16.
45. Blassingame, *Slave Community* 19, 67-8; Molefi Kete Asante [Arthur L. Smith], "Some Characteristics of the Black Religious Audience," *Speech Monographs* 37 (1970): 207–210.
46. Marion M. Miller qtd. in Robert T. Oliver, *History of Public Speaking in America*, (Boston: Allyn and Bacon, 1965) 92.
47. Pessen, *Multifaceted* 194; Oliver's commentary on the debate is revealing, for at one point he states that the "star performers had played their roles" (95).
48. Philip Rieff, *The Triumph of the Therapeutic: Uses of Faith After Freud*, (New York: Harper, 1966) 5, 13.
49. Richard Wrightman Fox, and T. J. Jackson-Lears, eds . *The Culture of Consumption: Critical Essays in American History, 1880-1980* (New York: Pantheon Books, 1983).
50. Frederick Douglass, *Life and Times of Frederick Douglass, Written by Himself* (Hartford, CT: Park Publishing Co., 1881) 227-8.
51. Jackson-Lears 4.
52. C. W. Janson, *The Stranger in America, 1793-1806* (New York, Press of the Pioneers, 1935) 88
53. David Brion Davis, *Antebellum American Culture: An Interpretive Anthology*, (Lexington: D. C. Heath, 1979) 68.
54. Gunderson 138.
55. Oravec's point, in both her articles on antebellum criticism is to argue that Whigs tried to limit the revolutionary potential of oratory. Therefore, they praised oratory that controlled its audience, but only praised audiences who remained passive respondents to oratory. Whiggish oratory, then, constructed its audiences as sublimated object of oratory, made to feel, but left ultimately impotent as a part of the *scene* of

the oratory, not as actors. On the other hand, the purpose of this chapter has been to argue that neither "Whig" nor "Democrat" critics had to worry much about audiences being moved to revolution by oratory. That type of rhetoric was extremely rare, the Douglass's type of rhetoric being the exception rather than the rule. In line with her Whig/Democrat duality, Oravec argues that Democrats constructed the audience as active, co-creators of rhetoric to empower the masses. I, on the other hand, think it just as likely that the Democratic critics were political opportunists who were able to praise audiences for their sensitivity to "the truth" of Democratic oratory because their side was winning the major elections. Had the audiences been flocking to vote for Whigs, I doubt the Democrats would have been so fulsome in their praise of the discerning audience. It could also be argued that the democratic rhetoric was more popular because of its therapeutic benefit (its entertainment value, emotional power, and simplistic morality) not merely, as Oravec implies, because it was a rhetoric of empowerment that resonated with egalitarian audiences.

56. Joseph Stevens Buckminster, "The Dangers and Duties of Men of Letters," *Federalist Literary Mind*, ed. Lewis P. Simpson (Baltimore: J. H. Furst Co., 1962) 96.

57. *Hazard's Register*, 6 August 1831: 90, qtd in Oravec, "Sublimation," 299.

58. *New Englander*, January 1844: 108, qtd in Oravec, "Sublimation" 299.

59. See Oravec, "The Democratic Critics," 415.

60. Smith and Campbell are only the most famous of the many modernist rhetoricians to advance the idea that an orator had to express a certain emotion before that emotion could be aroused in the audience.

61. Barnet Baskerville, "Some American Critics of Public Address, 1850-1900," *Speech Monographs* 17 (1950) 18.

62. *New England Magazine*, February 1832: 95.

63. *American Quarterly Review*, June 1837: 196

64. Another paper could be written on they ways reform rhetoric met the therapeutic needs of wealthier Americans as they "made the difficult transition from traditional ethics to tough-minded capitalist egotism," according to Charles Sellers, *The Market Revolution: Jacksonian America, 1815-1846* (New York: Oxford UP, 1991) 216. Sellers adds that support of benevolent societies "satisfied the most pressing psychic needs of Christian entrepreneurs . . . businessmen who sold ever more commodities in an ever larger market found their special skills irresistibly challenged by the gradualist millennial mission of national conversion. From their radical new commitment to life by calculation, they brought to the evangelical movement their unique experience in projecting, organizing, and managing large schemes to yield large results over long periods." Again, we see that a "spirit of calculation" was an important prop for benevolent reform rhetoric.

65. Hugh Brogan, *The Penguin History of the United States of America* (London: Penguin, 1985) 281.

66. Bormann 20-25. He makes the distinction between abolitionists who were "agitators" (the Garrisonians) and those who practiced a less confrontational "rhetoric of conversion" such as Beecher and Stanton.

67. The antagonistic response to Garrison and his followers is well documented. See Friedman, *Gregarious Saints: Self and Community in American Abolitionism, 1830-1870* (New York: Cambridge UP, 1982), and Gilbert Hobbes Barnes, *The Antislavery Impulse, 1830-1844* (Gloucester, MA: P. Smith, 1957).

68. Henry Steele Commager, *The Era of Reform, 1830-1860* (New York, Van Nostrand Reinhold, 1960).

69. J. L. Austin, *How to Do Things with Words* (Oxford, 1962).

70. I am loosely following Burke's rhetorical analysis of the speech act of scapegoating in the *Grammar of Motives*, 1945. 3rd. ed. (Berkeley: U of California P, 1969).

71. Oliver 229.

72. Sacvan Bercovitch, *The American Jeremiad* (Madison: U of Wisconsin P, 1978).

73. Hocmuth and Murphy, *History of Speech Education in America* (New York: Appleton-Century-Crofts, Inc., 1954) 158.

74. Hugh Blair, D. D., *Lectures on Rhetoric and Belles Letters*. Ed. Harold Harding. Carbondale: Southern Illinois UP, 1965.

75. Richard Whately. *The Elements of Rhetoric*. 1855. Carbondale: Southern Illinois UP, 1963.

76. "Pulpit Eloquence," *American Monthly Magazine* Aug, 1824: 131.

77. Ralph Waldo Emerson, *Complete Works*, vol. VII (Boston: Houghton Mifflin, 1903) 128.

78. Qtd. in Rush Welter, *Mind of America, 1820–1860* (New York: Columbia UP, 1975) 335-6.

79. Qtd. in Charles Sellers, *The Market Revolution: Jacksonian America, 1815–1846* (New York: Oxford UP, 1991) 234.

80. Russel Hirst, "The Sermon as Public Discourse: Austin Phelps and the Conservative Homiletic Tradition in Nineteenth-Century America," *Oratorical Culture in Nineteenth Century America: Transformations in the Theory and Practice of Rhetoric*, ed Gregory Clark and Michael Halloran (Carbondale: Southern Illinois UP, 1993) 78–79.

81. Some of the more successful revival speakers did critique individual sin by putting certain audience members in "anxious seats" and beckoning them to leave their sinful ways. However, this was done with an eye toward personal change—a saved soul—not with the goal of social upheaval. The method of reaching those souls was through strong emotions and flamboyant presentation, just like other popular forms of entertainment of the era.

82. Smith and Windes, "Symbolic Convergence and Abolitionism: A Terministic Reinterpretation," *Southern Communication Journal* 59 (1993); Sellers, *The Market Revolution*, 30–33 makes a similar analysis.

83. Lois Banner, "Religious Benevolence as Social Control: A Critique of an Interpretation," ed. Edward O. Pessen, *The Many Faceted Jacksonian Era* (Westport, CT: Greenwood, 1977) 302-321; Perry Miller, *The Life of the Mind in America: From the Revolution to the Civil War* (New York: Harcourt, Brace & World, 1965).

84. Smith and Windes 57.

85. Marvin Meyers, *The Jacksonian Persuasion: Politics & Belief* (Stanford: Stanford UP, 1957).

86. Kenneth Burke addresses this issue in *Grammar of Motives*, 406–408, among other places.

87. Nathan O. Hatch, *The Democratization of American Christianity* (New Haven: Yale UP, 1989); Hirst 102-6.

88. Hirst 96-100.

89. Qtd. in *Liberator* 14 May 1846.

90. Condit and Lucaites 96.

91. Dillon 44.

92. Although, it must be said, that the increased used of African American, especially ex-slave orators was increasing in the 1830s. While the arguments of these rhetors may have many superficial similarities to those used by Garrison and other white orators, the fact of having a black person mouthing the arguments is a fundamental difference in the argument, because of first-person experience, and other ethos issues involved. All this will be discussed in chapter four.

93. Leonard Richards, *"Gentlemen of Property and Standing": Anti-Abolition Mobs in Jacksonian America* (New York: Oxford UP, 1970).

94. Richards 166.

95. "My speech and teaching were not with enticing words." I Cor. 2:4; "[H]e who is foolish and abounds in eloquence is the more to be avoided the more he delights his auditor with those things to which it is useless to listen so that he thinks that because he hears a thing said eloquently it is true," Augustine, *De doctrina Christiana*, trans. D. W. Robertson, Jr. (Indianapolis: Bobbs-Merrill, 1958) 121.

NOTES TO CHAPTER THREE

1. Warren Guthrie, "The Development of Rhetorical Theory in America," *Speech Monographs* 13 (1946): 14–22; "The Development of Rhetorical Theory in America, 1635–1850," *Speech Monographs* 14 (1947): 38–54; "The Development of Rhetorical Theory in America, 1635–1850," *Speech Monographs* 15 (1948): 61–71.

2. Messieurs Du Port Royal, *The Art of Speaking Written in French by Messieurs Du Port Royal: In pursuance of a former Treatise, Intitled, The Art of Thinking* (London, 1696) 283–284.

3. John Ward, *Systems of Oratory* (London, 1759) 141-2.

4. Carl R. Burgchardt, "Henry Clay," *American Orators before 1900: Critical Studies and Sources*, ed. Bernard K. Duffy and Halford R. Ryan (New York: Greeenwood Press, 1987) 93.

5. Qtd. in Herbert L. Curry, "John C. Calhoun," *A History and Criticism of American Public Address*, vol. 2 ed. William Norwood Brigance (New York: McGraw Hill, 1943) 644.

6. Classical studies continued to be a part of rhetorical training, even as consideration for elocution and composition grew. See Hocmuth and Murphy 163-4.

7. Johnson 107-8.

8. Campbell 97.

9. Campbell 97–98.

10. Campbell 98.

11. Charles Dickens chastised Americans for their distrusting natures and the "national love of trade" that caused it. "It has rendered you so fickle, and so given to change, that your inconstancy has passed into a proverb; for you no sooner set up an ideal firmly, than you are sure to pull it down and dash it into fragments: and this, because directly you reward a benefactor, or a public servant, you distrust him, merely because he is rewarded" *American Notes for General Circulation* (1842; New York: Penguin, 1972) 285.

12. Campbell 97, emphasis mine.

13. Clark and Halloran 15; Borches and Wagner 290.
14. Henry Louis Gates. Jr., *The Signifying Monkey: A Theory of Afro-American Literary Criticism* (New York: Oxford UP, 1988) 6.
15. John P. Hoshor, "American Contributions to Rhetorical Theory and Homiletics," *History of Speech Education in America*, ed. Karl R. Wallace (New York: Appleton-Century-Crofts, 1954) 129.
16. Richard Whately, *The Elements of Rhetoric* (1855, Carbondale: Southern Illinois UP, 1963) 208.
17. Whately 215.
18. Whately 204. Campbell, too, makes a gesture toward this idea (103ff), but his unequivocal statements about sympathy and democratic audiences suggest otherwise.
19. Whately 224.
20. Hocmuth and Murphy 157.
21. Borchers and Wagner 290; Guthrie, "Development" (1948) 70.
22. Paul Reid, *The Philosophy of American Rhetoric as It Developed in the Boylston Chair of Rhetoric and Oratory At Harvard University*, diss. Ohio State U, 1959 (Ann Arbor: UMI, 1960) 175.
23. "Alliances of Literature," *The Knickerbocker*, 15 (March, 1840) 176, qtd. in Chambers and Mohrmann, "Rhetoric in Some American Periodicals, 1815–1850." *Speech Monographs* 37 (1970) 118.
24. Walter Ong, *Orality and Literacy: The Technologizing of the Word* (New York: Methuen, 1982), 96–100.
25. Sellers 365-6.
26. Ong 43-4.
27. Ong 45-6.
28. Reid 102–104.
29. Qtd. in Chambers and Mohrmann 118.
30. Warren Guthrie, "Principle Themes of Nineteenth-Century Critics of Oratory," *Speech Monographs* 19 (1952) 13.
31. *National Anti-Slavery Standard*, 14 May 1846: 1.
32. Baskerville, "Principal Themes" 20.
33. Baskerville, "Some American" 13.
34. Lewis Perry, *Intellectual Life in America* (Chicago: U of Chicago P, 1989) 174.
35. Sennett 49.
36. Sennett 145.
37. Sennett 151-2.
38. Cicero's three purposes of rhetoric were to teach, to move, and to delight.
39. Frederick J. Antczak, *Thought and Character: The Rhetoric of Democratic Education* (Ames: Iowa State UP, 1985) 9–10.
40. Oliver 148.
41. Nathan Sargent, *Public Men and Events in the United States*, vol. 1 (1875, New York: Da Capo Press, 1970) 171.
42. Qtd. in Glen Mills, "Daniel Webster's Principles of Rhetoric" *Speech Monographs* 9 (1942) 129.
43. Mills 130.
44. Robert Gray Gunderson, "The Magnanimous Mr. Clay," *Southern Speech Communication Journal* 16 (1950) 136.

45. Carl Burgchardt, "Henry Clay" *American Orators before 1900: Critical Studies and Sources*, ed. Bernard K. Duffy and Halford R. Ryan (New York: Greeenwood Press, 1987) 89, 93-4.

46. Burgchardt (87) comments, "While he never obtained his most cherished prize of the presidency, his rhetoric was perfectly attuned to the voters of Kentucky, who gave him unwavering support on nearly all of his positions."

47. Qtd. in Oliver, 156.

48. Qtd. in Bradley and Tarver "John C. Calhoun's Rhetorical Method in Defense of Slavery" *Oratory in the South 1828-1860*, ed. Waldo W. Braden, Jeffery Auer, and Bert E. Bradley (Baton Rouge: Louisiana State UP, 1970) 170.

49. Curry 645-5.

50. Sargent I, 28

51. Curry 646.

52. Curry 643.

53. Sargent I, 26.

54. Qtd. in Curry 647.

55. James Darsey, *The Prophetic Tradition and Radical Rhetoric in America* (New York: New York UP, 1997) 27–31.

56. Darsey 72; Curry 643.

57. Warren I. Susman, *Culture as History: The Transformation of American Society in the Twentieth Century* (New York: Pantheon, 1984) 273 .

58. Gill, Christopher, "The Character-Personality Distinction," *Characterization and Individuality in Greek Literature*, ed. Christopher Pelling (Oxford: Clarendon, 1990) 1-31; and "The Question of Character and Personality in Greek Tragedy," *Poetics Today* 7/2 (1986): 251–273.

59. Gill, "Distinction" 23.

60. Gill, "Distinction" 2.

61. D. A. Russell, "Ethos in Oratory and Rhetoric," *Characterization and Individuality in Greek Literature*, ed. Christopher Pelling (Oxford: Clarendon Press, 1990).

62. 1.9.32; *Rhetoric* 82.

63. (§ 8, § 54) I have argued that Aristotle is in fact aware of personality-based ethos: "The Character/Personality Distinction in Aristotelian Ethos" presented at SCA, 1996.

NOTES TO CHAPTER FOUR

1. The story of the change is given in much greater detailed in Taylor's *Sources of the Self,* and in Bakhtin's essays "Epic and Novel" and "Forms of Time and Chronotope in the Novel," in *The Dialogic Imagination,* ed Michael Holquist, trans Caryl Emerson and Michael Holquist (Austin: U of Texas P, 1981).

2. Blassingame I, 28.

3. Douglass, *Narrative* viii.

4. *Herald of Freedom,* 11 Feb. 1842: 202, qtd. in Lampe 202.

5. Qtd. in Benjamin Quarles, *Frederick Douglass,* Great Lives Observed (Englewood Cliffs, NJ: Prentice Hall, 1968), 123–24.

6. George Asher Hinshaw, "A Rhetorical Analysis of the Speeches of Frederick Douglass during and after the Civil War," diss., U of Nebraska at Lincoln, 1972, 151.

7. James C. McCroskey, *An Introduction to Rhetorical Communication*, 3rd ed. (Englewood Cliffs, NJ: Prentice Hall, 1978) 71–83. McCroskey actually uses the term "credibility" instead of ethos. His tripartite distinction is still useful, since any rhetor must direct the audience's previous knowledge during the process of identifying him- or herself in the speech.

8. Cal M. Logue and Thurmon Garner, "Shift in Rhetorical Status of Blacks after Freedom," *Southern Communication Journal* 54 (1988): 1–39. Logue and Garner's article is one of the few exceptions to the rule that no one looks at race, definitions of personhood, and ethos. However, their work alters the terms of the discussion from ethos to "rhetoric status." See also Molefi Asante, "The Rhetorical Condition as Symbolic Structure in Discourse," *Communication Quarterly* 34 (1986): 170–77.

9. Qtd. in Foster 20.

10. I have found *They Who Would be Free* the most useful summary of the various arguments about race in antebellum America: Jane H. Pease and William H. Pease, *They Who Would Be Free: Blacks' Search for Freedom, 1830–1861* (Urbana: U of Illinois P, 1990).

11. 1255b20.

12. Thomas Jefferson, *Notes on the State of Virginia* (New York: Norton, 1982).

13. Quarles, *Black Abolitionists* 8.

14. William Goodell, *Slavery and Antislavery: A History of the Great Struggle in Both Hemispheres; with a View of the Slavery Question in the United States*, 1852 (New York: Negro UP, 1968).

15. Bormann 18–20.

16. For insight into Calhoun's racist logic, Miller's *Arguing about Slavery* has an excellent section on the diaries of John Quincy Adams's diaries detailing private conversations the two had about the Missouri question.

17. Qtd. in Miller, *Arguing* 192-3.

18. Miller, *Arguing* 193.

19. George Fitzhugh, *Cannibals All! Or, Slaves without Masters*, ed. C. Vann Woodward (1856, Cambridge: Harvard UP, 1960).

20. Dred Scott v. Sanford, Justice Roger B. Taney, March 6, 1857.

21. Tappan to John Beaumont, 20 Jan. 1844, qtd. in Louis Filler, *Crusade against Slavery*, (Algonac, MI: Reference Publications, Inc., 1986), 210.

22. McFeely 99 quotes some reporters' comments along these lines.

23. Kinney 30.

24. William Lloyd Garrison, *Thoughts on African Colonization* (Boston: Garrison and Knapp, 1832).

25. Blassingame II, 206-7.

26. Goodell 437.

27. Quarles, *Black Abolitionists* 37.

28. A pro-slavery article reproduced in the *National Anti-Slavery Standard*, 14 May 1846, from the Geneva, Illinois, *Advocate* makes this case.

29. Sargent I, 295.

30. Huggins 141; Wendell Phillips, *Speeches, Lectures, and Letters*, (Boston: Lothrop 1891) 106.

31. Article reproduced in the *National Anti-Slavery Standard*, 29 Oct. 1846: 1.

32. Foner II, 506.

33. Huggins 70.
34. Today the conditions have reversed as both the therapeutic condition and personality appeals have become more familiar to Americans. Celebrities regularly promote causes and invite social action whereas similar calls from politicians are fairly suspect and easier to ignore.
35. Qtd. in Filler 194.
36. Merton L. Dillon, *The Abolitionists: The Growth of a Dissenting Minority*, (De Kalb: Northern Illinois UP, 1975). This book does a good job of analyzing the various degrees and affects of racism within the antislavery ranks. McFeely catalogs Douglass's responses, both public and private to conscious and unconscious prejudice from his fellow reformers. Perhaps the most sensitive account is given by Quarles in his *Black Abolitionists*. Quarles reveals various ways an attitude of superiority on the part of white leaders angered and alienated black leaders.
37. Filler 268.
38. McFeely 94.
39. Lampe 269.
40. Blassingame I, 15.
41. Lois W. Banner, "Religious Benevolence as Social Control: A Critique of an Interpretation," *The Many Faceted Jacksonian Era: New Interpretations*, ed. Edward O. Pessen (Westport, CT: Greenwood, 1977) 302–321; Ronald G. Walters, *American Reformers, 1815–1860* (New York: Hill and Wang, 1978).
42. Pro-slavery, on the other hand, was not tied to this faith. Its advocates often acknowledge that there were problems and "evils" associated with slavery, but that everything human has such flaws. See Faust's introduction to *The Ideology of Slavery*, 5–6.
43. Qtd. in Foster 67.
44. Charles J. G. Griffin, "The Rhetoric of Form in Conversion Narratives," *Quarterly Journal of Speech*, 77 (1990): 152–163.
45. In *The Arrogance of Race*, (191–196) Fredrickson speculates about the origins of the imputation of sexual immorality and enormities on blacks. In general, he and Winthrop D. Jordan, *White Over Black: American Attitudes Toward the Negro, 1550-1812* (Chapel Hill, U North Carolina P, 1968) offer the most complete accounts of the ideology of inferiority.
46. See Andrews, especially chapters two and three.
47. *National Anti-Slavery Standard*, 19 August 1847; Foner I, 256-7.
48. Louis Althusser, *Reading Capital* (London: New Left Books, 1970) 186-9. A useful reading of Althusser's and Hegel's concepts of determination and causality related to the topic of identity construction is found in Ernesto Laclau, ed. *The Making of Political Identities* (London: Verso, 1994) 52–53.
49. *National Anti-Slavery Standard* 6 Aug. 1843.
50. Genovese 72-3.
51. Qtd. in Lamp 220.
52. Clark and Halloran 2.
53. Blassingame I, 4.
54. McFeely (135) is one who argues the benefits antislavery would have received from aligning itself with labor movements.
55. Foster 14.

56. Larry Gara, "The Professional Fugitive in the Abolition Movement," *Wisconsin Magazine of History* 49 (1965) 198.
57. Qtd. in Gara 198.
58. Ong 36-57.
59. Douglass, *Bondage* 361.
60. Foster 59.
61. Qtd. in Foster 20. For further analysis of the sexuality and "spectacality" of slaves and slave orators, see Maurice O. Wallace, *Constructing the Black Masculine: Identity and Ideality in African American Literature and Culture, 1775-1995* (Durham: Duke UP, 2002).
62. Quotations are from Bormann, *Forerunners* 169–173.
63. Bormann, *Forerunners* 20.
64. Pease and Pease 111.
65. Andrews 175.
66. Andrews 176.

NOTES TO CHAPTER FIVE

1. The most visible feature of the way audiences are treated as passive spectators rather than co-creators of meaning is in the emphasis of the so-called "New Rhetorics" on description. See Gerald Hauser, "Empiricism, Description, and the New Rhetoric," *Philosophy and Rhetoric* 5 (1972): 24–44, especially his analysis of the ways description functions on the different faculties.
2. Whately 230-56.
3. In fact, Whately suggests that expertise can masquerade as *phronesis*. The audience must not be foolish enough to assume that knowledge of one subject matter gives an orator authority in all matters.
4. In medieval times, the abilities we associate with the term "expertise" would have been categorized under "memory." Memory was the ability to acquire knowledge, recall it, and synthesize it to accomplish various tasks. Writing was viewed as a process of drawing on elements of one's memory to create a new whole. See Mary Carruthers, *The Book of Memory: a Study of Memory in Medieval Culture* (New York: Cambridge UP, 1990).
5. Others have noted that Douglass had a tendency to turn confessions of moral lapses or inferiority into arguments of strength. See, for example, Scott C. Williamson, *The Narrative Life: The Moral and Religious Thought of Frederick Douglass* (Macon, GA: Mercer UP, 2002).
6. For instance, in Blassingame I, 36 and the introduction to his famous Fourth of July speech where he exhaustively details the way he is a typical slave and thus an unfit orator. Rafia Zafar catalogs several other instances in "Franklinian Douglass: The Afro-American as Representative Man" *Frederick Douglass: New Literary and Historical Essays*, ed. Eric J. Sundquist (New York: Cambridge UP, 1990) 99–117.
7. A fine account of Douglass's rhetorical successes in charming Scottish and English audiences is found in Gerald Fulkerson's "Exile as Emergence: Frederick Douglass in Great Britain, 1845–1847," *Quarterly Journal of Speech* 60 (1974): 69–82.
8. Foner I, 176.
9. Foner I, 177.

10. The complex issues surrounding the status of "representative black men" is discussed in Robert S. Levine, *Martin Delany, Frederick Douglass, and the Politics of Representative Identity* (Chapel Hill: U of North Carolina P, 1997).

11. Whately 221–227.

12. Blassingame I, 3.

13. Blassingame I, 30.

14. McFeely 210–262.

15. Blassingame I, 33.

16. McFeely 209.

17. Quarles, *Black Abolitionists* 109.

18. The relationship and resulting uproar is covered in Benjamin Quarles's *Frederick Douglass* 106–110 and in Nathan Huggins, *Slave and Citizen* 66–70.

19. Garrison qtd. in Jane H. Pease and William H. Pease. *They Who Would Be Free: Blacks Search for Freedom, 1830–1861* (Urbana: U of Illinois P, 1990) 90.

20. Qtd. in Pease and Pease 89.

21. Qtd. in Waldo E. Martin, Jr. *The Mind of Frederick Douglass* (Chapel Hill, NC: U of North Carolina P, 1984), 43.

22. Fulkerson, "Exile" 71.

23. Blassingame II, 59.

24. Lionel Trilling, *Sincerity and Authenticity* (Cambridge, MA: Harvard UP, 1972), 112–113.

25. Fulkerson 70-1.

26. Lucy Brown, qtd. in Fulkerson, "Exile," 71.

27. Whately 230–235.

28. Alexis de Tocqueville, *Democracy in America*, trans. George Lawrence, ed. J. P. Mayer (Garden City, NY: Anchor Books, 1969) 564.

29. Bormann 159.

30. Bormann 160-1.

31. Clark and Halloran 2.

32. Blassingame I, 33.

33. Foner I, 238.

34. Lampe 176–177.

35. Kinney 87–88.

36. *Liberator*, Dec. 3, 1841.

37. Bormann 161.

38. Blassingame II, 344-5.

39. As Fulkerson (1974) clearly shows, Douglass's tour of England gave him a renewed confidence and vigor. Fulkerson argues this as a result of the attention he received and the celebrity status he attained. In addition, though, he could have been free for the first time to mingle amongst whites without fear of slave catchers or corrupt law enforcement. He was among them in a way that increased his knowledge of them. His post-England speeches seem to have an increased breadth to them. He seems more like a student of the world than a slave looking out at whites from the plantation.

40. Blassingame II, 69–84.

41. Blassingame I, 45.

42. *Liberator* 2 September 1842: 138.

43. Bormann 159.

44. Blassingame II, 59.
45. Blassingame II, 131.
46. *Liberator* 3 Dec. 1841: 193.
47. Michael Kimmel, *Manhood in America: A Cultural History* (New York: Free Press, 1996) 77.
48. Leverenz 364.
49. Kimmel 71.
50. Blair 232.
51. Martin 256.
52. David Leverenz, *Manhood and the American Renaissance* (Ithaca: Cornell UP, 1989) 134.
53. Foner II, 150.
54. Robert Stepto, *From Behind the Veil: A Study of Afro-American Narrative* (Urbana: U of Illinois P., 1979) 25.
55. Stephen Butterfield, *Black Autobiography in America* (Amherst: U Massachusetts P, 1974) 64.
56. Although he doesn't focus on ex-slave orators, a useful account of celebrities feeling as though they might be "eaten alive" is found in Michael Newbury's "Eaten Alive: Slavery and Celebrity in Antebellum America," *ELH* 61 (1994): 159–187.
57. McFeely 114.
58. Sennett 144.
59. 10 September 1841, p.146.

BIBLIOGRAPHY

Althusser, Louis. *Reading Capital.* London: New Left Books, 1970

Andersen, Kenneth and Theodore Clevenger Jr. "A Summary of Experimental Research in Ethos." *Speech Monographs* 30 (1963): 59–78.

Andrews, William L. ed. *African American Autobiography: A Collection of Critical Essays.* Englewood Cliffs, NJ: Prentice Hall, 1993.

Andrews, William L. ed. *To Tell a Free Story: The First Century of Afro-American Autobiography, 1760–1865.* Urbana: U of Illinois P, 1988.

Antczak, Fredrick J. *Thought and Character: The Rhetoric of Democratic Education.* Ames: Iowa State UP, 1985.

Aptheker, Herbert. *Abolitionism.* Boston: Twayne Publishers, 1989.

Aristotle. *Aristotle on Rhetoric: A Theory of Civic Discourse.* Trans. George Kennedy. New York: Oxford UP, 1991.

Asante, Molefi Kete. *The Afrocentric Idea.* Philadelphia: Temple UP, 1987.

Asante, Molefi Kete. "The Rhetorical Condition as Symbolic Structure in Discourse." *Communication Quarterly* 34 (1986): 170-77

Asante, Molefi Kete.[Arthur L. Smith] "Socio-Historical Perspectives of Black Oratory." *Quarterly Journal of Speech.* 56 (1970): 264–269.

Asante, Molefi Kete. [Arthur L. Smith] "Some Characteristics of the Black Religious Audience." *Speech Monographs.* 37 (1970): 207–210.

Auer, J. Jeffery, ed. *Antislavery and Disunion, 1858–1861.* New York: Harper, 1963.

Augustine, *De docrtina Christiana,* Trans. D. W. Robertson, Jr. Indianapolis: Bobbs-Merrill, 1958.

Bakhtin, M. M. *Art and Answerability: Early Philosophical Essays by M. M. Bakhtin.* Ed. Michael Holquist and Vadim Liapunov. Austin: Texas UP, 1990.

Bakhtin, M. M. *The Dialogic Imagination.* Ed. Michael Holquist. Trans. Caryl Emerson and Michael Holquist. Austin: U of Texas P, 1981.

Bakhtin, M. M. *Rabelais and His World.* Trans. H. Isowolsky. Cambridge, MA: MIT Press, 1968.

Bakhtin, M. M. *Speech Genres and Other Late Essays.* Ed. Caryl Emerson and Michael Holquist. Trans. V. W. McGee. Austin: Texas UP, 1986.

Ball, Terrence and Richard Dagger. *Political Ideologies and the Democratic Ideal.* New York: Harper, 1991.

Bank, Rosemarie K. *Theater Culture in America, 1825–1860.* New York: Cambridge, 1997.

Barnes, Gilbert Hobbes. *The Antislavery Impulse: 1830–1844.* Gloucester, MA: P. Smith, 1957.

Baskerville, Barnet. *The People's Voice: The Orator in American Society.* Lexington: UP of Kentucky, 1979.

Baskerville, Barnet. "Principle Themes of Nineteenth-Century Critics of Oratory." *Speech Monographs* 19 (1952): 11–26.

Baskerville, Barnet. "Some American Critics of Public Address, 1850–1900." *Speech Monographs* 17 (1950): 1–23.

Baudrillard, Jean. *Simulacra and Simulation.* Trans. Sheila Faria Glaser. Ann Arbor: U of Michigan P, 1994.

Baumlin, James S., and Tita French Baumlin, eds. *Ethos: New Essays in Rhetorical and Critical Theory.* Dallas: Southern Methodist UP, 1994.

Benoit, William L. "Argumentation and Credibility Appeals in Persuasion." *Southern Speech Communication Journal* 52 (1987), 181–197.

Benson, Thomas W., ed. *Rhetoric and Political Culture in Nineteenth-Century America.* East Lansing: Michigan State UP, 1997.

Bercovitch, Sacvan. *The American Jeremiad.* Madison: U of Wisconsin P, 1978.

Bercovitch, Sacvan. *The Puritan Origins of the American Self.* New Haven: Yale UP, 1975.

Berger, Peter L. and Thomas Luckmann. *The Social Construction of Reality: A Treatise in the Sociology of Knowledge.* New York: Anchor, 1966.

Billig, Michael. *Arguing and Thinking: A Rhetorical Approach to Social Psychology.* Cambridge: Cambridge UP, 1989.

Blair, Hugh D. D. *Lectures on Rhetoric and Belles Letters.* Ed. Harold Harding. Carbondale: Southern Illinois UP, 1965.

Blassingame, John W. *The Slave Community: Plantation Life in the Antebellum South.* New York: Oxford UP, 1972.

Blassingame, John W., ed. *Slave Testimony: Two Centuries of Letters, Speeches, Interviews, and Autobiographies.* Baton Rouge: Louisiana UP, 1977.

Borchers, Gladys L. and Lillian R. Wagner. "Speech Education in Nineteenth-Century Schools." *History of Speech Education in America.* Ed. Karl R. Wallace. New York: Appleton-Century-Crofts, 1954. 277–300.

Bormann, Ernest. *Communication Theory.* New York: Holt, Rinehart, and Winston, 1980.

Bormann, Ernest. "Fantasy and Rhetorical Vision: The Rhetorical Criticism of Social Reality." *Quarterly Journal of Speech* 58 (1972): 396–407.

Bormann, Ernest. *The Forerunners of Black Power: The Rhetoric of Abolition.* Englewood Cliffs, NJ: Prentice-Hall, 1971.

Bosmajian, Haig A. "Nazi Persuasion and the Crowd Mentality." *Western Speech* 29 (1965): 68–78.

Braden, Waldo W., Jeffery Auer, and Bert E. Bradley, ed. *Oratory in the South, 1828–1860.* Baton Rouge: Louisiana State UP, 1970.

Brigance, William Norwood., ed. *A History and Criticism of American Public Address.* 2 Vols. New York: McGraw Hill, 1943.

Brogan, Hugh. *The Penguin History of the United States of America.* New York: Penguin Books, 1985.

Bruner, Jerome and Susan Weissner. "The Invention of Self: Autobiography and Its Forms." *Literacy and Orality.* Ed. David R. Olson and Nancy Torrance. New York: Cambridge UP, 1991. 129–148.

Burke, Kenneth. *A Grammar of Motives.* 1945. 3rd. ed. Berkeley: U of California P, 1969.

Burke, Kenneth. *Language as Symbolic Action.* Berkeley: U of California P, 1966.

Burke, Kenneth. *Permanence and Change: An Anatomy of Purpose.* 1935. 3rd ed. Berkeley: U of California P, 1984.

Burke, Kenneth. *The Philosophy of Literary Form: Studies in Symbolic Action.* 1941. 2nd ed. New York: Random House, 1957.

Burke, Kenneth. *A Rhetoric of Motives.* 1950. 3rd ed. Berkeley: U of California P, 1969.

Burke, Ronald K. *Frederick Douglass: Crusading Orator For Human Rights.* New York: Garland, 1996.

Butterfield, Stephen. *Black Autobiography in America.* Amherst: U of Massachusetts P, 1974.

Campbell, George. *The Philosophy of Rhetoric.* Ed. Lloyd Bitzer. Carbondale: Southern Illinois UP, 1963.

Carruthers, Mary. *The Book of Memory: a Study of Memory in Medieval Culture.* New York: Cambridge UP, 1990.

Chambers, Stephen and G. P. Mohrmann. "Rhetoric in Some American Periodicals, 1815–1850." *Speech Monographs* 37 (1970) 11–121.

Charland, Maurice. "Constitutive Rhetoric: The Case of the 'Peuple Quebecois.'" *Quarterly Journal of Speech* 73 (1987), 133-50.

Chesebrough, David B. *Frederick Douglass: Oratory from Slavery.* Westport, CT: Greenwood, 1998.

Clark, Gregory and S. Michael Halloran, eds. *Oratorical Culture in Nineteenth Century America: Transformations in the Theory and Practice of Rhetoric.* Carbondale: Southern Illinois UP, 1993.

Cmiel, Kenneth. *Democratic Eloquence: The Fight over Popular Speech in Nineteenth-Century America.* Berkeley: U of California P, 1990.

Commager, Henry Steele. *The Era of Reform, 1830–1860.* New York, Van Nostrand Reinhold, 1960.

Condit, Celeste Michelle, and John Louis Lucaites. *Crafting Equality: America's Anglo-African Word.* Chicago: U of Chicago P, 1993.

Corts, Thomas E. "The Derivation of Ethos." *Speech Monographs* 35 (1968): 201-2.

Cronkhite, Gary, and Jo Liska. "A Critique of Factor Analytic Approaches to the Study of Credibility." *Communication Monographs* 43 (1976): 91–107.

Crusius, Timothy. "A Case for Kenneth Burke's Dialectic and Rhetoric." *Philosophy and Rhetoric* 19 (1986): 23–37.

Crusius, Timothy. "Kenneth Burke's Auscultation: A 'Destruction' of Marxist Dialectics and Rhetoric." *Rhetorica* 4 (1988): 355–379.

Curti, Merle. *Human Nature in American Thought: A History.* Madison: U of Wisconsin P, 1980.

Darsey, James. *The Prophetic Tradition and Radical Rhetoric in America.* New York: New York UP, 1997.

de Tocqueville, Alexis. *Democracy in America.* Trans. George Lawrence. Ed. J. P. Mayer. Garden City, NY: Anchor Books, 1969.

Delia, Jesse G. "A Constructivist Analysis of the Concept of Credibility." *Quarterly Journal of Speech* 62 (1976): 361–375.

Delia, Jesse G. "Rhetoric in the Nazi Mind: Hitler's Theory of Persuasion." *Southern Speech Communication Journal* 37 (1965): 136–149.

Delia, Jesse G., Barbara.J. O'Keefe, and Daniel J. O'Keefe. "The Constructivist Approach to Communication." *Human Communication Theory: Comparative Essays.* Ed. F. E. X. Dance. New York: Harper, 1982. 147-91.

Dillon, Merton L. *The Abolitionists: The Growth of a Dissenting Minority.* De Kalb: Northern Illinois UP, 1975.

Douglass, Frederick. *The Frederick Douglass Papers.* ed. John W. Blassingame. Series 1. Speeches, Debates, and Interviews. 5 vols. New Haven, CT: Yale UP, 1979–1992.

Douglass, Frederick. *Life and Times of Frederick Douglass, Written by Himself.* Hartford, CT: Park Publishing Co., 1881.

Douglass, Frederick. *The Life and Writings of Frederick Douglass.* 5 vols. Ed. Philip S. Foner. New York: International Publishers, 1950–1975.

Douglass, Frederick. *My Bondage and My Freedom.* 1855. New York: Dover, 1969.

Douglass, Frederick. *Narrative of the Life of Frederick Douglass, an American Slave, Written by Himself.* 1845. New York: Signet, 1968.

Duffy, Bernard K., and Halford R. Ryan, eds. *American Orators Before 1900: Critical Studies and Sources.* New York: Greenwood Press, 1987.

Eakin, Paul John, ed. *American Autobiography: Retrospect and Prospect.* Madison: U of Wisconsin P, 1991.

Eakin, Paul John, ed. *Fictions in Autobiography: Studies in the Art of Self-Invention.* Princeton: Princeton UP, 1992.

Emerson, Ralph Waldo. *Complete Works,* 12 vols. Boston: Houghton Mifflin, 1903-4.

Enos, Richard and Jeanne L. McClaran. "Audience and Image in Ciceronian Rome: Creation and Constraints of the *Vir Bonus* Personality." *Central States Speech Journal* 29 (1978): 98–106.

Farrell, Thomas B. *Norms of Rhetorical Culture.* New Haven: Yale UP, 1993.

Faust, Drew Gilpin, ed. *The Ideology of Slavery: Proslavery Thought in the Antebellum South, 1830–1860.* Baton Rouge: Louisiana State UP, 1981.

Filler, Louis. *Crusade against Slavery.* Algonac, MI: Reference Publications, Inc., 1986.

Finkleman, Paul, ed. *Proslavery Thought, Ideology, and Politics.* Articles on American Slavery. 12. New York: Garland, 1987.

Fisher, Dexter and Robert B. Stepto, eds. *Afro-American Literature.* New York: MLA, 1979.

Fitzhugh, George. *Cannibals All! Or, Slaves Without Masters.* (1856) Ed. C. Vann Woodward. Cambridge, MA: Harvard UP, 1960.

Foss, Sonja, Karen A. Foss, and Robert Trapp. *Contemporary Perspectives on Rhetoric.* 2nd ed. Prospect Heights, IL: Waveland Press, 1985.

Foster, Frances Smith. *Witnessing Slavery: The Development of Ante-bellum Slave Narratives.* Westport, CT: Greenwood Press, 1979

Fox, Richard Wrightman and T. J. Jackson Lears, eds. *The Culture of Consumption: Critical Essays in American History, 1880–1980.* New York: Pantheon Books, 1983.

Fredrickson, George M. *The Arrogance of Race: Historical Perspectives on Slavery, Racism, and Social Inequality.* Middletown, CT: Wesleyan UP, 1988.

Friedman, Lawrence Jacob. *Gregarious Saints: Self and Community in American Abolitionism, 1830-1870.* New York: Cambridge UP, 1982.

Fulkerson, Gerald. "Exile as Emergence: Frederick Douglass in Great Britain, 1845–1847." *Quarterly Journal of Speech* 60 (1974): 69–82.

Fulkerson, Gerald. "Frederick Douglass and the Anti-Slavery Crusade: His Career and Speeches, 1817–1861." Ph.D. diss., U of Illinois at Urbana-Champaign, 1971.

Gara, Larry. "The Professional Fugitive in the Abolition Movement." *Wisconsin Magazine of History* 49 (1965): 196–204.

Garrison, William Lloyd. *Thoughts on African Colonization.* Boston: Garrison and Knapp, 1832.

Gates, Henry Louis, Jr. *Figures in Black: Words, Signs, and the "Racial" Self.* New York: Oxford UP, 1987.

Gates, Henry Louis, Jr. *The Signifying Monkey: A Theory of Afro-American Literary Criticism.* New York: Oxford UP, 1988.

Genovese, Eugene D. *Roll Jordan Roll: The World the Slaves Made.* New York: Random House, 1974.

Giddens, Anthony. *Central Problems in Social Theory: Action, Structure, and Contradiction in Social Analysis.* Berkeley: U of California P, 1979.

Giddens, Anthony. *The Consequences of Modernity.* Stanford: Stanford UP, 1990.

Giddens, Anthony. *Modernity and Self-Identity: Self and Society in the Late Modern Age.* Stanford: Stanford UP, 1991.

Giffin, Kim. "The Contribution of Studies of Source Credibility to a Theory of Interpersonal Trust in the Communication Process." *Psychological Bulletin* 68 (1967): 104–120.

Gill, Christopher. "The Character-Personality Distinction." *Characterization and Individuality in Greek Literature.* Ed. Christopher Pelling. Oxford: Clarendon, 1990. 1–31.

Gill, Christopher. "The Ethos/Pathos Distinction in Rhetorical and Literary Criticism." *Classical Quarterly* 34 (1984): 149–166.

Gill, Christopher. "The Question of Character and Personality in Greek Tragedy." *Poetics Today,* 7/2 (1986): 251–273.

Goffman, Erving. *The Presentation of Self in Everyday Life.* Harmondsworth: Penguin, 1971.

Goodell, William. *Slavery and Antislavery: A History of the Great Struggle in Both Hemispheres; with a View of the Slavery Question in the United States.* 1852. New York: Negro Universities Press, 1968.

Gouldner, Alvin. *The Dialectic of Ideology and Technology: The Origins, Grammar, and Future of Ideology.* New York: Oxford UP, 1976.

Gregg, Gary S. *Self-Representation: Life Narrative Studies in Identity and Ideology.* New York: Greenwood Press, 1991.

Gregory, James M. *Frederick Douglass, The Orator.* 1893. Chicago: Afro-Am Press, 1969.

Griffin, Charles J. G. "The Rhetoric of Form in Conversion Narratives." *Quarterly Journal of Speech* 77 (1990) 152–163.

Grimstead, David. "Uncle Tom from Page to Stage," *Quarterly Journal of Speech* 56 (1970): 235–244.

Gronbeck, Bruce E. "Negative Narratives in 1988 Presidential Campaign Ads." *Quarterly Journal of Speech* 78 (1992): 333–346.

Gunderson, Robert Gray. "The Magnanimous Mr. Clay." *Southern Speech Communication Journal.* 16 (1950): 133–40.

Guthrie, Warren. "The Development of Rhetorical Theory in America, 1635–1850, I." *Speech Monographs* 13 (1946): 14–22.

Guthrie, Warren. "The Development of Rhetorical Theory in America, 1635–1850, II." *Speech Monographs* 14 (1947): 38–54.

Hariman, Robert, Dilip Parameshwar Gaonkar, and Maurice Charland. "The Forum: Norms of Rhetorical Culture." *Quarterly Journal of Speech* 80 (1994): 329–342.

Harrold, Stanley. *The Abolitionists and the South, 1831–1861.* Lexington: U of Kentucky P, 1995.

Hatch, Nathan O. *The Democratization of American Christianity.* New Haven: Yale UP, 1989.

Hauser, Gerald. "Empiricism, Description, and the New Rhetoric." *Philosophy and Rhetoric* 5 (1972): 24–44.

Havelock, Eric A. *The Muse Learns to Write: Reflections on Orality and Literacy from Antiquity to the Present.* New Haven: Yale UP, 1986.

Havelock, Eric A. *Preface to Plato.* Cambridge, MA: Belknap Press of Harvard UP, 1963.

Hinshaw, George Asher. "A Rhetorical Analysis of the Speeches of Frederick Douglass during and after the Civil War." Diss., U of Nebraska at Lincoln, 1972.

Hovland, Carl I., Irving L. Janis, and Harold H. Kelly. *Communication and Persuasion.* New Haven: Yale UP, 1953.

Howell, Wilbur Samuel. *Eighteenth-Century British Logic and Rhetoric.* Princeton: Princeton UP, 1971.

Huggins, Nathan Irvin. *Slave and Citizen: The Life of Fredrick Douglass.* Boston: Little, Brown, and Co., 1980.

Hunt, H. A. K. *The Humanism of Cicero.* Victoria: Melbourne UP, 1954.

Jackson Lears, T. J. "From Salvation to Self-Realization: Advertising and the Therapeutic Roots of the Consumer Culture, 1880–1930." *The Culture of Consumption: Critical Essays in American History, 1880–1980.* Ed. Richard Wrightman Fox and T. J. Jackson Lears. New York: Pantheon Books, 1983.

Janson, C. W. *The Stranger in America, 1793–1806.* New York: Press of the Pioneers, 1935.

Jefferson, Thomas. *Notes on the State of Virginia.* New York: Norton, 1982.

Johnson, Nan. *Nineteenth-Century Rhetoric in North America.* Carbondale: Southern Illinois UP, 1991.

Johnstone, Henry W., Jr., "Bilaterality in Argument and Communication." *Advances in Argumentation Theory and Research* Ed. J. Robert Cox and Charles Arthur Willard. Carbondale: Southern Illinois UP, 1982.

Jordan, Winthrop D. *White over Black: American Attitudes Toward the Negro, 1550 – 1812.* Chapel Hill: U North Carolina P, 1968.

Katriel, Tamar, and Gerald Philipsen. "What We Need is Communication: Communication as a Cultural Category in Some American Speech." *Communication Monographs* 48, 301-17.

Kelly, George. *A Theory of Personality: The Psychology of Personal Constructs.* 2 vols. New York: Norton, 1955.

Kennedy, George. *The Art of Persuasion in Greece.* Princeton: Princeton UP, 1963.

Kimmel, Michael. *Manhood in America: A Cultural History.* New York: Free Press, 1996.

Laclau, Ernesto, ed. *The Making of Political Identities.* London: Verso, 1994.

Lasch, Christopher. *The Culture of Narcissism: American Life in An Age of Diminishing Expectations.* New York: Norton, 1979.

Lee, Lisa Yun. "The Politics of Language in Frederick Douglass's *Narrative of the Life of an American Slave.*" *MELUS* 17.2 (1991-92): 51–59.

Lejeune, Phillipe. *On Autobiography.* Ed. Paul John Eakin. Minneapolis: U of Minnesota P, 1989.

Lewis, Helen. "Studies in the Principles of Language and Judgments and Attitudes: IV. The Operation of 'Prestige Suggestion.'" *Journal of Social Psychology* 14 (1941): 229–256.

Leverenz, David. "Frederick Douglass's Self-Refashioning." *Criticism* 29 (1987): 341–370.

Leverenz, David. *Manhood and the American Renaissance.* Ithaca: Cornell UP, 1989.

Levine, Robert S. *Martin Delany, Frederick Douglass, and the Politics of Representative Identity.* Chapel Hill: U of North Carolina P, 1997.

Logue, Cal M., and Thurmon Garner. "Shift in Rhetorical Status of Blacks after Freedom." *Southern Communication Journal* 54 (FA, 1988): 1–39.

Logue, Cal M., and Eugene F. Miller. "Rhetorical Status: A Study of Its Origins, Functions, and Consequences." *Quarterly Journal of Speech* 81 (1995): 20–47.

MacIntyre, Alisdair. *After Virtue: A Study in Moral Theory.* Notre Dame, IN: Indiana UP, 1984.

MacLeod, Duncan J. *Slavery, Race and the American Revolution.* Cambridge: Cambridge UP 1974.

Mann, Kenneth Eugene. "Nineteenth Century Black Militant: Henry Highland Garnet's Address to the Slaves." *The Southern Speech Journal* 36 (1970): 11–21.

Martin, Waldo E. *The Mind of Frederick Douglass.* Chapel Hill, NC: U of North Carolina P, 1984.

Matlaw, Myron. *American Popular Entertainment.* Papers and Proceedings on theHistory of American Popular Entertainment. Westport, CT: Greenwood, 1979.

May, James M. *Trials of Character: The Eloquence of Ciceronian Ethos.* Chapel Hill, NC: U of North Carolina P, 1988.

McCroskey, James C. *An Introduction to Rhetorical Communication.* 3rd ed. Englewood Cliffs, NJ: Prentice Hall, 1978.

McFeely, William S. *Frederick Douglass.* New York: Norton, 1991.

McGee, Michael Calvin. "The Ideograph: A Link between Rhetoric and Ideology." *Quarterly Journal of Speech* 66 (1): 1–16.

McGee, Michael Calvin. "Text Context and the Fragmentation of Contemporary Culture." *Western Journal of Speech Communication* 54 (1990): 274– 289.

Meyers, Marvin. *The Jacksonian Persuasion: Politics & Belief.* Stanford: Stanford UP, 1957.

Miller, Arthur B. "Aristotle on Habit and Character: Implications for the Rhetoric." *Communication Monographs* 41 (1974): 309–316.

Miller, Marion M., ed. *Great Debates in American History.* 14 vols. New York: Current Literature Pub. Co., 1913.

Miller, Perry. *The Life of the Mind in America: From the Revolution to the Civil War.* New York: Harcourt, Brace & World, 1965.

Miller, William Lee. *Arguing about Slavery: The Great Battle in the United States Congress.* New York: Alfred A. Knopf, 1996.

Mills, Glen E. "Daniel Webster's Principles of Rhetoric." *Speech Monographs* 9 (1942): 124–140.

Moore, Wilbert E. *American Negro Slavery and Abolition: A Sociological Study.* New York: Third Press, 1971.

Moses, Wilson J. "Writing Freely? Frederick Douglass and the Constraints of Racialized Writing." *Frederick Douglass: New Literary and Historical Essays.* Ed. Eric J. Sundquist. Cambridge UP, 1990. 99–117.

Mott, Frank Luther. *A History of American Magazines 1741–1850.* New York: D. Appleton and Co., 1930.

Mott, Frank Luther. *A History of American Magazines 1850–1865.* Cambridge, MA: Harvard UP, 1938.

Newbury, Michael. "Eaten Alive: Slavery and Celebrity in Antebellum America." *ELH.* 61 (1994): 159–187.

Ober, Josiah. *Mass and Elite in Democratic Athens: Rhetoric, Ideology, and the Power of the People.* Princeton: Princeton UP, 1989.

Oliver, Robert T. *History of Public Speaking in America.* Boston: Allyn and Bacon, 1965.

Olney, James. *Metaphors of Self: The Meaning of Autobiography.* Princeton: Princeton UP, 1972.

Ong, Walter. *Orality and Literacy: The Technologizing of the Word.* New York: Methuen, 1982

Oravec, Christine. "The Democratic Critics: An Alternative American Rhetorical Tradition of the Nineteenth Century." *Rhetorica.* 4 (1996): 395–491.

Oravec, Christine. "Kenneth Burke's Concept of Association and the Complexity of Identity." *The Legacy of Kenneth Burke.* Ed. Herbert W. Simons and Trevor Melia. Madison: U Wisconsin P, 1989. 174-95.

Owens, Harry P., ed. *Perspectives and Irony in American Slavery.* Jackson: UP of Mississippi, 1976.

Parker, Edward G. *The Golden Age of American Oratory.* Boston: Whittemoore, Niles, and Hall, 1857.

Parry-Giles, Trevor. "Character, the Constitution, and the Ideological Embodiment of 'Civil Rights' in the 1967 Nomination of Thurgood Marshall to the Supreme Court," *Quarterly Journal of Speech* 82 (1996): 377, 376.

Pease, Jane H. and William H. Pease. *They Who Would Be Free: Blacks' Search for Freedom, 1830–1861.* Urbana: U of Illinois P, 1990.

Pelling, Christopher, ed. *Characterization and Individuality in Greek Literature.* Oxford: Clarendon Press, 1990.

Perry, Lewis. *Intellectual Life in America.* Chicago: U of Chicago P, 1989.

Pessen, Edward O., ed. *The Many Faceted Jacksonian Era: New Interpretations.* Contributions in American History 67. Westport, CT: Greenwood, 1977.

Phillips, Wendell. *Speeches, Lectures, and Letters.* Boston: Lothrop, 1891.

Phillips, William A. "A Note on the Generality of Source-Credibility Scales." *Speech Monographs* 36 (1967): 185–186

Plato. *Gorgias.* Trans. Walter Hamilton. London: Penguin, 1971.

Preston, Dickson, J. *Young Frederick Douglass: The Maryland Years.* Baltimore: Johns Hopkins UP, 1980.

Quarles, Benjamin. *Black Abolitionists.* New York: Oxford UP, 1969.

Quarles, Benjamin. *Frederick Douglass.* Washington, DC: Associated Publishers, 1948.

Quarles, Benjamin., ed. *Frederick Douglass.* Great Lives Observed. Englewood Cliffs, NJ: Prentice-Hall, 1968.

Richards, Leonard. *"Gentlemen of Property and Standing": Anti-Abolition Mobs in Jacksonian America.* New York: Oxford UP, 1970

Ried, Paul Eugene. *The Philosophy of American Rhetoric as It Developed in the Boylston Chair of Rhetoric and Oratory At Harvard University.* Diss. Ohio State U, 1959. Ann Arbor: UMI, 1960.

Rieff, Philip. *The Triumph of the Therapeutic: Uses of Faith after Freud.* New York: Harper and Row, 1966.

Ripley, C. Peter, et al. eds. *The Black Abolitionist Papers.* 5 vols. Chapel Hill: U of North Carolina P, 1985 – 1991.

Roberts, Jennifer. "The Creation of a Legacy: A Manufactured Crisis in Eighteenth-Century Thought." *Athenian Political Thought and the Reconstruction of American Democracy.* Ed. J. Peter Euben, John R. Wallach, and Josiah Ober. Ithaca: Cornell UP, 1994.

Royer, Daniel J. "The Process of Literacy as Communal Involvement in the Narratives of Frederick Douglass." *African American Review* 28 (1994): 363–374.

Russell, D.A. "Ethos in Oratory and Rhetoric." *Characterization and Individuality in Greek Literature.* Ed. Christopher Pelling. Oxford: Clarendon Press, 1990.

Sargent, Nathan. *Public Men and Events in the United States.* 1875. 3 Vols. New York: Da Capo Press, 1970.

Sattler, William M. "Conceptions of *Ethos* in Ancient Rhetoric." *Speech Monographs* 14 (1947): 55–65.

Scherer, Lester B. *Slavery and the Churches in Early America, 1619–1819.* Grand Rapids: Eerdman's, 1975.

Schudson, Michael. "Was There Ever a Public Sphere? If So, When? Reflections on the American Case." *Habermas and the Public Sphere.* Ed. Craig Calhoun. Cambridge, MA: MIT Press, 1994.

Sellers, Charles. *The Market Revolution: Jacksonian America, 1815–1846.* New York: Oxford UP, 1991.

Sennett, Richard. *The Fall of Public Man.* New York: Knopf, 1977.

Shaw, Warren Choate. *History of American Oratory.* Indianapolis: The Bobbs-Merrill Company, 1928.

Shea, Jr., Daniel B. *Spiritual Autobiography in Early America.* Princeton: Princeton UP, 1968.

Sheridan, Thomas. *A Course of Lectures on Elocution.* New York, NY: Benjamin Blom, Inc., 1968.

Simpson, Lewis, P., ed. *The Federalist Literary Mind.* Baltimore: J. H. Furst Co., 1962.

Sloan, John H. "'The Miraculous Uplifting': Emerson's Relationship with His Audience." *Quarterly Journal of Speech* 52 (1966): 10–15.

Smith, Adam. *Lectures on Rhetoric and Belles Lectures.* Edinburgh: Thomas Nelson and Sons LTD, 1963.

Smith, Ralph R. and Russell R. Windes. "Symbolic Convergence and Abolitionism: A Terministic Reinterpretation," *Southern Communication Journal* 59 (1993).

Stepto, Robert B. *From Behind the Veil: A Study of Afro-American Narrative.* Urbana: U of Illinois P., 1979.

Storey, John. *An Introductory Guide to Cultural Theory and Popular Culture.* Athens, GA: U of Georgia P, 1993.

Sundquist, Eric J., Ed. "Introduction." *Frederick Douglass: New Literary and Historical Essays.* New York: Cambridge UP, 1990.

Susman, Warren I. *Culture as History: The Transformation of American Society in the Twentieth Century.* New York: Pantheon, 1984.

Tanner, Laura E. "Self-Conscious Representation in the Slave Narrative," *Black American Literature Forum* 21 (1987): 415–424.

Taylor, Charles. *Sources of the Self: The Making of Modern Identity.* Cambridge, MA: Harvard UP, 1989.

Trilling, Lionel. *Sincerity and Authenticity.* Cambridge, MA: Harvard UP, 1972.

Tuppen, Christopher J. S. "Dimensions of Communicator Credibility: Oblique Solution," *Speech Monographs* 41 (1974): 253–260.

Wallace, Karl R., ed. *History of Speech Education in America.* New York: Appleton-Century-Crofts, Inc., 1954.

Wallace, Maurice O. *Constructing the Black Masculine: Identity and Ideality in African American Men's Literature and Culture, 1775–1995.* Durham NC: Duke UP, 2002.

Walter, Otis. "Toward an Analysis of Ethos." *Pennsylvania Speech Annual* 21 (September 1964): 37–45.

Walters, Ronald G. *American Reformers 1815–1860.* New York: Hill and Wang, 1978.

Walters, Ronald G. *The Antislavery Appeal: American Abolitionism After 1830.* Baltimore: Johns Hopkins UP, 1976.

Ward, John. *Systems of Oratory.* (London, 1759).

Washington, Booker T. *Frederick Douglass.* 1907. New York: Haskell House, 1968.

Weld, Theodore Dwight. *American Slavery as It Is; Testimony of a Thousand Witnesses.* 1839. New York: Arno Press, 1968.

Welter, Rush. *The Mind of American 1820–1860.* New York: Columbia UP, 1975.

Whately, Richard. *The Elements of Rhetoric.* 1855. Carbondale: Southern Illinois UP, 1963.

Whitehead, Jack L., Jr. "Factors of Source Credibility." *Quarterly Journal of Speech* 54 (1968): 59–63.

Willey, Austin. *The History of the Antislavery Cause in State and Nation.* 1860. New York: Negro UP, 1969.

Wisse, Jakob. *Ethos and Pathos from Aristotle to Cicero.* Amsterdam: Adolf M. Hakkert, 1989.

Woodson, Carter G. *Negro Orators and Their Orators.* New York: Russell & Russell, 1925.

Yoos, George E. "A Revision of the Concept of Ethical Appeal." *Philosophy and Rhetoric* 12 (1979): 41–58.

Yunis, Harvey. *Taming Democracy: Models of Political Rhetoric in Classical Athens.* Ithaca, NY: Cornell UP, 1996.

Zafar, Rafia. "Franklinian Douglass: The Afro-American as Representative Man." *Frederick Douglass: New Literary and Historical Essays.* Ed. Eric J. Sundquist. Cambridge UP, 1990. 99–117.

Zulick, Margaret. "The Agon of Jeremiah: On the Dialogic Invention of Prophetic Ethos." *Quarterly Journal of Speech* 78 (1992): 125–148

Index